Oracle RMAN for Absolute Beginners

Darl Kuhn

Apress®

Oracle RMAN for Absolute Beginners

ISBN-13 (pbk): 978-1-4842-0764-2

ISBN-13 (electronic): 978-1-4842-0763-5

Managing Director: Welmoed Spahr
Lead Editor: Jonathan Gennick
Editorial Board: Steve Anglin, Mark Beckner, Ewan Buckingham, Gary Cornell, Louise Corrigan, Jim DeWolf, Jonathan Gennick, Robert Hutchinson, Michelle Lowman, James Markham, Matthew Moodie, Jeff Olson, Jeffrey Pepper, Douglas Pundick, Ben Renow-Clarke, Dominic Shakeshaft, Gwenan Spearing, Matt Wade, Steve Weiss
Coordinating Editor: Jill Balzano
Compositor: SPi Global
Indexer: SPi Global
Artist: SPi Global
Cover Designer: Anna Ishchenko

Distributed to the book trade worldwide by Springer Science+Business Media New York, 233 Spring Street, 6th Floor, New York, NY 10013. Phone 1-800-SPRINGER, fax (201) 348-4505, e-mail orders-ny@springer-sbm.com, or visit www.springeronline.com. Apress Media, LLC is a California LLC and the sole member (owner) is Springer Science + Business Media Finance Inc (SSBM Finance Inc). SSBM Finance Inc is a Delaware corporation.

For information on translations, please e-mail rights@apress.com, or visit www.apress.com.

Apress and friends of ED books may be purchased in bulk for academic, corporate, or promotional use. eBook versions and licenses are also available for most titles. For more information, reference our Special Bulk Sales–eBook Licensing web page at www.apress.com/bulk-sales.

Any source code or other supplementary material referenced by the author in this text is available to readers at www.apress.com. For detailed information about how to locate your book's source code, go to www.apress.com/source-code/.

To Mom, who has had two strokes now, and to her kids, who contributed to them.

Contents at a Glance

Contents

About the Author

Darl Kuhn is a DBA/developer working for Oracle. He also teaches Oracle classes at Regis University in Denver, Colorado, and is an active member of the Rocky Mountain Oracle Users Group. Darl enjoys sharing knowledge, which has led to several book projects over the years.

Acknowledgments

This book is the brainchild of Jonathan Gennick. It is a focused book introducing the reader to backup and recovery concepts, including topics on user-managed backups, RMAN, and Data Pump. Thanks to Jill Balzano and the Apress staff; it takes a good (coordinated) team to produce a quality book.

Also thanks to the many developers and DBAs that I've learned from over the years: Bob Suehrstedt, Dave Jennings, Scott Schulze, Venkatesh Ranganathan, Valerie Eipper, Mike Tanaka, Simon Ip, Nitin Mittal, Mohan Shanmugavelu, Ric Ambridge, Kamal Chamakura, Dallas Powell, Krishna (KP) Tallapaneni, Laurie Bourgeois, Todd Sherman, Radha Ponnapalli, Mohan Koneru, Kevin O'Grady, Peter Schow, Sujit Pattnaik, Roger Murphy, Barb Sannwald, Pete Mullineaux, Janet Bacon, Shawn Heisdorffer, Mehran Sowdaey, Patrick David, Carson Vowles, Aaron Isom, Tim Gorman, Tom Kyte, and Jim Stark.

Introduction

Backup and recovery abilities are arguably the most critical skills required of a database administrator. Recovery Manager (RMAN) is Oracle's standard backup and recovery tool; every Oracle DBA should be familiar with utilizing RMAN. This book introduces you to RMAN; it starts with the very basics of how to set up and configure RMAN, and works through to more advanced topics, such as various restore and recovery scenarios.

What This Book Covers

Chapter 1 covers the essentials of your environment setup and how to connect to RMAN. Chapter 2 details the files that are part of backup and recovery operations (control files, online redo logs, archive redo logs, and data files).

User-managed backups are the focus of Chapter 3. User-managed backups are rarely used nowadays, but an understanding of them builds the foundation for appreciating the mechanics of backup and recovery. With this information you'll be able to more fully utilize RMAN and think your way through any backup and recovery situation.

Chapters 4, 5, and 6 concentrate on RMAN. Chapter 4 introduces you to typical RMAN configuration and setup tasks. Here you'll be given examples of how to implement the most commonly used RMAN configurations. Chapter 5 walks you through using RMAN to back up your database. Chapter 6 is dedicated to the critical tasks of restore and recovery.

Chapter 7 provides in-depth details on handling online redo log failures. If there's a failure with the online redo logs, you must be able to step in and take corrective actions. The topic of Chapter 8 is Data Pump. This tool is highly flexible and feature rich. Many DBAs use this tool to augment their backup and recovery strategy.

These eight chapters will provide you with a solid foundation for Oracle backup and recovery skills. With this knowledge, you'll be able to protect your company's data and keep it available; these skills are needed by all DBAs.

Conventions

The following typographical conventions are used in this book:

- $ is used to denote Linux/Unix commands that can be run by the operating system owner of the Oracle binaries (usually named oracle).

- # is used to denote Linux/Unix commands that should be run as the root operating system user.

- SQL> is used to denote one-line SQL*Plus statements.

- Monospaced font is used for code examples, utility names, file names, URLs, and directory paths.

- Italic is used to highlight a new concept or word.

- UPPERCASE indicates names of database objects like views, tables, and corresponding column names.

- < > is used where you need to provide input, such as a file name or password.

Source Code

The code for the examples shown in this book is available on the Apress web site (`www.apress.com`). A link can be found on the book's information page under the Source Code/Downloads tab. This tab is located underneath the Related Titles section of the page.

Errata

Apress makes every effort to make sure that there are no errors in the text or the code. However, to err is human, and as such we recognize the need to keep you informed of any mistakes as they're discovered and corrected. Errata sheets are available for all our books at `www.apress.com`. If you find an error that hasn't already been reported, please let us know. The Apress web site acts as a focus for other information and support, including the code from all Apress books, sample chapters, previews of forthcoming titles, and articles on related topics.

Contacting the Author

If you have any questions regarding this book, feel free to contact me directly at the following e-mail address: `darl.kuhn@gmail.com`.

CHAPTER 1

■ ■ ■

Getting Started

Backup and recovery skills are at the top of the list for desired DBA abilities. Protecting and keeping data available form the foundation of database administration. Your DBA job depends on your ability to regularly perform backups, and when necessary, restore and recover a database. Recovery Manager (RMAN) is Oracle's flagship backup and recovery tool. This tool is an efficient and effective way to protect your data. Every DBA must know how to implement and use RMAN.

RMAN is a flexible tool that contains a wide variety of backup and recovery features. The purpose of this book is to give you a solid understanding of the most common ways in which you can use RMAN to back up, restore, and recover your database. I'll show numerous real-word examples along with the code required to implement various features. With this foundation you'll be able to implement RMAN in any environment.

I'll also cover user-managed backup techniques (hot and cold backups). I find that DBAs who understand the mechanics of user-managed backups are much better equipped to troubleshoot and resolve any type of database problem (including (but not limited to) backup and recovery issues). I'll also cover the use of Data Pump. DBAs often implement Data Pump features to augment backup and recovery needs (e.g., a quick backup of a single table). In short, every DBA should be familiar with all Oracle tools used to protect data.

To get started, there are a few basic tasks that you should be familiar with when working with Oracle backup and recovery, namely:

- Connecting to your database

- Starting/stopping your database

An understanding of these topics is prerequisite to using RMAN (and other Oracle tools as well). The purpose of this chapter is to familiarize you with these initial tasks. First up is connecting to your database.

■ **Note** This chapter assumes you have Oracle installed and have a database created and available.

Connecting to Your Database

Prior to connecting to your database, you must establish the required operating system variables. Additionally, if you're going to run backup and recovery commands, you need access to either a privileged operating system (OS) account or a database user who has been granted the appropriate privileges (via a password file). These topics are discussed in the following subsections.

Establishing OS Variables

Before connecting to your database via SQL*Plus, RMAN, Data Pump (or any other Oracle utility), you must first set several OS variables:

- `ORACLE_HOME`

- `ORACLE_SID`

- `LD_LIBRARY_PATH`

- `PATH`

The `ORACLE_HOME` variable is important because it defines the starting point directory for locating the Oracle binary files (such as `sqlplus`, `dbca`, `netca`, `rman`, and so on) that are located in `ORACLE_HOME/bin`.

The `ORACLE_SID` (site identifier) variable defines the default name of the database you'll connect to. `ORACLE_SID` is also used to establish the default name for the parameter file, which is `init<ORACLE_SID>.ora` or `spfile<ORACLE_SID>.ora`. By default, Oracle will look in `ORACLE_HOME/dbs` for these initialization files on Linux/Unix systems and `ORACLE_HOME\database` on Windows systems. The initialization file contains parameters that govern aspects of your database, such as how much memory to allocate to your database, the maximum number of connections, and so on.

The `LD_LIBRARY_PATH` variable is important because it specifies where to search for libraries on Linux/Unix boxes. The value of this variable is typically set to include `ORACLE_HOME/lib`.

The `PATH` variable specifies which directories are looked in by default when you type a command from the OS prompt. In almost all situations, `ORACLE_HOME/bin` (the location of the Oracle binaries) must be included in your `PATH` variable.

You can either manually set these variables or use a standard script provided by Oracle to set these variables.

Manually Setting Variables

In Linux/Unix, when you're using the Bourne, Bash, or Korn shell, you can set OS variables manually from the OS command line with the following `export` command:

```
$ export ORACLE_HOME=/orahome/app/oracle/product/12.1.0.1/db_1
$ export ORACLE_SID=O12C
$ export LD_LIBRARY_PATH=/usr/lib:$ORACLE_HOME/lib
$ export PATH=$ORACLE_HOME/bin:$PATH
```

Note that the prior commands are for my particular development environment; you'll need to adjust those to match the Oracle home and database name used in your environment.

For the C or `tcsh` shell, use the `setenv` command to set variables:

```
$ setenv ORACLE_HOME <path>
$ setenv ORACLE_SID <sid>
$ setenv LD_LIBRARY_PATH <path>
$ setenv PATH <path>
```

Another way that DBAs set these variables is by placing the previous export or `setenv` commands into a Linux/Unix startup file, such as `.bash_profile`, `.bashrc`, or `.profile`. That way, the variables are automatically set upon login.

However, manually setting OS variables (either from the command line or by hard-coding values into a startup file) isn't the optimal way to instantiate these variables. For example, if you have multiple databases with multiple Oracle homes on a box, manually setting these variables quickly becomes unwieldy and not very maintainable.

Using Oracle's Script

A much better method for setting OS variables is use of a script that uses a file that contains the names of all Oracle databases on a server and their associated Oracle homes. This approach is flexible and maintainable. For instance, if a database's Oracle home changes (e.g., after an upgrade), you only have to modify one file on the server and not hunt down where the Oracle home variables may be hard-coded into scripts.

Oracle provides a mechanism for automatically setting the required OS variables. This approach relies on two files: oratab and oraenv.

Understanding oratab

You can think of the entries in the oratab file as a registry of what databases are installed on a box and their corresponding Oracle home directories. The oratab file is automatically created for you when you install the Oracle software. On Linux boxes, oratab is usually placed in the /etc directory. On Solaris servers, the oratab file is placed in the /var/opt/oracle directory. If, for some reason, the oratab file isn't automatically created, you can manually create it (with a text editor).

The oratab file is used in Linux/Unix environments for the following purposes:

- Automating the sourcing of required OS variables
- Automating the start and stop of Oracle databases on the server

The oratab file has three columns with this format:

```
<database_sid>:<oracle_home_dir>:Y|N
```

The Y or N indicates whether you want Oracle to restart automatically on reboot of the box; Y indicates yes, and N indicates no (the automatic restart feature requires additional tasks not covered in this book).

Comments in the oratab file start with a pound sign (#). Here is a typical oratab file entry:

```
O12C:/orahome/app/oracle/product/12.1.0.1/db_1:N
ORA12CR1:/orahome/app/oracle/product/12.1.0.1/db_1:N
```

The names of the databases on the previous lines are O12C and ORA12CR1. The path of each database's Oracle home directory is next on the line (separated from the database name by a colon [:]).

Several Oracle-supplied utilities use the oratab file:

- oraenv uses oratab to set the OS variables.
- dbstart uses it to start the database automatically on server reboots (if the third field in oratab is Y).
- dbshut uses it to stop the database automatically on server reboots (if the third field in oratab is Y).

The oraenv tool is discussed in the following section.

Using oraenv

If you don't properly set the required OS variables for an Oracle environment, then utilities such as SQL*Plus, RMAN, Data Pump, and so on won't work correctly. The oraenv utility automates the setting of required OS variables (such as ORACLE_HOME, ORACLE_SID, and PATH) on an Oracle database server. This utility is used in Bash, Korn, and Bourne shell environments (if you're in a C shell environment, there is a corresponding coraenv utility).

The oraenv utility is located in the ORACLE_HOME/bin directory. You'll have to navigate to your ORACLE_HOME/bin directory first (you'll have to modify the following path to match your environment):

```
$ cd /orahome/app/oracle/product/12.1.0.1/db_1/bin
```

And then you can run oraenv manually, like this:

```
$ . ./oraenv
```

You'll be prompted for ORACLE_SID (and if the ORACLE_SID isn't in the oratab file, you'll additionally be prompted for an ORACLE_HOME value):

```
ORACLE_SID = [oracle] ?
ORACLE_HOME = [/home/oracle] ?
```

You can also run the oraenv utility non-interactively by setting OS variables before you run it. This is useful for scripting when you don't want to be prompted for input:

```
$ export ORACLE_SID=O12C
$ export ORACLE_HOME=/orahome/app/oracle/product/12.1.0.1/db_1
$ export ORAENV_ASK=NO
$ cd /orahome/app/oracle/product/12.1.0.1/db_1/bin
$ . ./oraenv
```

■ **Note** In Windows the operating system, variables are set in the registry.

You can verify that the OS variable settings with the echo command, for example:

```
$ echo $ORACLE_SID
O12C

$ echo $ORACLE_HOME
/orahome/app/oracle/product/12.1.0.1/db_1
```

After you've established your operating system variables, you need to connect to the database with the proper privileges. You can do this in one of two ways: using OS authentication or using a password file.

Using OS Authentication

Before you can connect to the Oracle database, you need to have the proper OS variables set (covered in the prior section). Additionally, if you want to connect to Oracle as a privileged user, then you must also have access to either a privileged OS account or a privileged database user. Connecting as a privileged user allows you to perform administrative tasks, such as starting and stopping a database. You can use either OS authentication or a password file to connect to your database as a privileged user.

The concept of a privileged user is also important to RMAN backup and recovery. RMAN uses OS authentication and password files to allow privileged users to establish a privileged database session (via the rman utility). Only a privileged account is allowed to back up, restore, and recover a database.

If your Linux/Unix account is a member of the dba group (your shop might use a different group name, but dba is the most common), you can connect to your database with the required privileges via SQL*Plus by virtue of being logged in to your Linux/Unix account.

On Windows, the OS user must be part of either the ora_dba group or the ora_oper group. In Windows environments, you can verify which OS users belong to the ora_dba group as follows: select Control Panel ➤ Administrative Tools ➤ Computer Management ➤ Local Users and Groups ➤ Groups. You should see a group named something like ora_dba. You can click that group and view which OS users are assigned to it. Additionally, for OS authentication to work in Windows environments, you must have the following entry in your sqlnet.ora file: SQLNET. AUTHENTICATION_SERVICES=(NTS).

On Linux/Unix, you can quickly verify the operating system groups that your account belongs to using the id command without any parameters:

```
$ id
uid=500(oracle) gid=500(oinstall) groups=500(oinstall),501(dba),502(oper),503(asmdba),
504(asmoper),505(asmadmin),506(backupdba)
```

The prior output indicates that the oracle user is included in several groups, one of which is dba. Any user who belongs to the dba group can connect to the database with SYSDBA privileges. A user with SYSDBA privileges can start and stop the database. This example uses OS authentication to connect to your database as the user SYS:

```
$ sqlplus / as sysdba
```

No username or password is required when using OS authentication (hence just the slash without a user/password) because Oracle first checks to see if the OS user is a member of a privileged OS group, and if so, connects without checking the username/password. You can verify that you have connected as SYS by issuing the following:

```
SQL> show user
USER is "SYS"
```

The privileged OS groups are established when installing the Oracle software. There are a few OS groups that pertain to backup and recovery:

- dba
- oper
- backupdba (available starting with Oracle 12c)

Each OS group corresponds to certain database privileges. Table 1-1 shows the mapping of OS groups to database system privileges and operations.

Table 1-1. Mapping of OS Groups to Privileges Related to Backup and Recovery

Operating System Group	Database System Privilege	Authorized Operations
dba	sysdba	Start up, shut down, alter database, create and drop database, toggle archivelog mode, back up, and recover database.
oinstall	none	Install and upgrade Oracle binaries.
oper	sysoper	Start up, shut down, alter database, toggle archivelog mode, back up, and recover database.
backupdba	sysbackup	Available starting with Oracle 12c, this privilege allows you to start up, shut down, and perform all backup and recovery operations.

Using a Password File

If you aren't using OS authentication, then you can use a password file to connect to the database as a privileged user. A password file allows you to do the following from SQL*Plus or RMAN:

- Connect to your database with sys* privileges as a non-SYS database user
- Connect to remote database (over the network) with sys* privileges

The password file must be manually created with the orapwd utility and is populated via the SQL grant command. To implement a password file, perform the following steps:

1. Create the password file with the orapwd utility.

2. Set the initialization parameter remote_login_passwordfile to exclusive.

In a Linux/Unix environment, use the orapwd utility to create a password file as follows:

```
$ cd $ORACLE_HOME/dbs
$ orapwd file=orapw$ORACLE_SID password=<sys password>
```

In a Linux/Unix environment, the password file is usually stored in the ORACLE_HOME/dbs directory, and in Windows, it's typically placed in the ORACLE_HOME\database directory. The format of the file name that you specify in the previous command may vary by OS. For example, on Windows the format is PWD<ORACLE_SID>.ora. The following shows the syntax in a Windows environment:

```
c:\> cd %ORACLE_HOME%\database
c:\> orapwd file=PWD<ORACLE_SID>.ora password=<sys password>
```

To enable the use of the password file, set the initialization parameter remote_login_passwordfile to exclusive (this is the default value). You can verify its value as shown next:

```
SQL> show parameter remote_login_password
```

NAME	TYPE	VALUE
remote_login_passwordfile	string	EXCLUSIVE

If need be, you can manually set the remote_login_passwordfile parameter as shown:

```
$ sqlplus / as sysdba
SQL> alter system set remote_login_passwordfile=exclusive scope=spfile;
```

You will then need to stop and start your database for this parameter to take effect (more details on stopping/ starting your database later in this chapter). The prior example assumes you are using a server parameter file (spfile). If you are not using a spfile, you will have to manually edit the init.ora file by adding this entry with a text editor:

```
remote_login_passwordfile=exclusive
```

Then stop and start your database to instantiate the parameter. Once the password file is enabled, you can then create database users and assign them the sys* privileges as required. For example, suppose you had a database user named DBA_MAINT that you wanted to grant SYSBACKUP privileges:

```
$ sqlplus / as sysdba
SQL> grant sysbackup to dba_maint;
```

The syntax for using a password file to connect to a database is as follows:

```
$ sqlplus <username>/<password>[@<db conn string>] as sys[dba|oper|backup]
```

For example, using the DBA_MAINT database user, you can connect to the database with SYSBACKUP privileges as follows:

```
$ sqlplus dba_maint/foo as sysbackup
```

Because you are providing a username/password and attempting to connect with a sys* level privilege (as a non-SYS user), Oracle will verify that a password file is in place (for the local database) and that the supplied username/password is in the password file. You can verify which users have sys* privileges by querying the V$PWFILE_USERS view:

```
SQL> select * from v$pwfile_users;
```

Here is some sample output:

```
USERNAME               SYSDB SYSOP SYSAS SYSBA SYSDG SYSKM  CON_ID
-----------------      ----- ----- ----- ----- ----- ----- ----------
SYS                    TRUE  TRUE  FALSE FALSE FALSE FALSE           0
DBA_MAINT              FALSE FALSE FALSE TRUE  FALSE FALSE           0
```

OS AUTHENTICATION VS. PASSWORD FILE

For local connections (made while physically logged on to the database server), operating system authentication takes precedence over password file authentication. In other words, if you're logged on to an OS account that is a member of an authenticated group, such as dba, it doesn't matter what you type in for the username and password when connecting to a local database with sys* privileges. For example, you can connect as sysdba with a nonexistent username/password:

```
$ sqlplus bogus/wrong as sysdba
SQL> show user;
USER is "SYS"
```

The prior connection works because Oracle ignores the username/password provided, as the user was first verified via OS authentication. However, a password file is used when you're not using OS authentication to establish a privileged local connection or when you're trying to make a privileged connection to a remote database via the network.

One key aspect about using a password file is that this is the mechanism that allows you to use SQL*Plus or RMAN to connect to a remote database over the network with sys* privileges. For example, if you want to connect to a user named chaya with a password of heera to a remote database named HATHI with sysdba privileges, you would do as follows:

```
$ sqlplus chaya/heera@HATHI as sysdba
```

Oracle will verify that the username password combination exists in a password file on the remote server that is associated with the database defined by the HATHI net service name. In this example, Oracle uses the information in a local tnsnames.ora file to determine the location of the database on the network (host, port, and database).

■ **Tip**　Using a local tnsnames.ora file is known as the *local naming* connection method. There are other remote database name resolution methods, such as easy connect, directory naming, and external naming. See the *Oracle Database Net Services Administrator's Guide* for details on how to implement these.

EASY CONNECT

The easy connect method allows you to connect to a remote database without the need of a tnsnames.ora file (or other methods of resolving the location of the database). If you know the name of the host, server, port, and service name, you can directly enter those on the command line. The syntax is as follows:

```
sqlplus username@[//]host[:port][/service_name][:server][/instance_name]
```

For example, assuming the host name is hesta, the port is 1521, and the service name is O12C, then you can connect as follows:

```
$ sqlplus user/pass@hesta:1521/O12C
```

The easy connect method is handy for situations in which you're troubleshooting connectivity issues or when you don't have a tnsnames.ora file available (or other ways to resolve the remote connection).

Starting the Database

Starting and stopping your database is a task that you'll perform frequently. To start/stop your database, connect with a SYSDBA or SYSOPER privileged user account, and issue the STARTUP and SHUTDOWN statements. The following example uses OS authentication to connect to the database:

```
$ sqlplus / as sysdba
```

After you're connected as a privileged account, you can start your database, as follows:

```
SQL> startup;
```

■ **Note**   For the prior command to work, you need either an `spfile` or `init.ora` file in the `ORACLE_HOME/dbs` directory.

When your instance starts successfully, you should see messages from Oracle indicating that the system global area (SGA) has been allocated. The database is mounted and then opened:

```
ORACLE instance started.

Total System Global Area 2137886720 bytes
Fixed Size                   2290416 bytes
Variable Size             1207962896 bytes
Database Buffers           922746880 bytes
Redo Buffers                 4886528 bytes
Database mounted.
Database opened.
```

From the prior output the database startup operation goes through three distinct phases in opening an Oracle database:

1. Starting the instance

2. Mounting the database

3. Opening the database

You can step through these one at a time when you start your database. First, start the Oracle instance (background processes and memory structures):

```
SQL> startup nomount;
```

Next, mount the database. At this point, Oracle reads the control files:

```
SQL> alter database mount;
```

Finally, open the data files and online redo log files:

```
SQL> alter database open;
```

■ **Tip**   As you'll see later in this book, it's especially important to understand these startup phases when performing RMAN backup and recovery tasks. For example, in some scenarios you may need your database to be in mount mode. In that mode, it's important to understand that the control file is open but the data files and online redo logs have not been opened yet.

This startup process is depicted graphically in Figure 1-1.

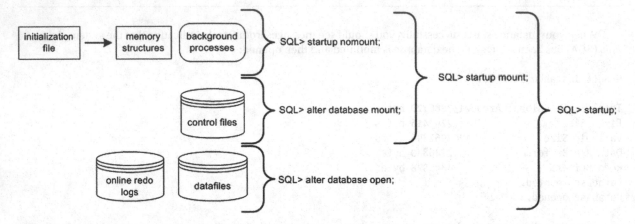

Figure 1-1. *Phases of Oracle startup*

When you issue a STARTUP statement without any parameters, Oracle automatically steps through the three startup phases (nomount, mount, open). In most cases, you will issue a STARTUP statement with no parameters to start your database. In many RMAN backup and recovery scenarios, you'll issue a STARTUP MOUNT to place your database in mount mode (instance started and control files opened). Table 1-2 describes the meanings of parameters that you can use with the database STARTUP statement.

Table 1-2. *Parameters Available with the STARTUP Command*

Parameter	Meaning
FORCE	Shuts down the instance with ABORT before restarting it; useful for troubleshooting startup issues
RESTRICT	Only allows users with the RESTRICTED SESSION privilege to connect to the database
PFILE	Specifies the client parameter file to be used when starting the instance
QUIET	Suppresses the display of SGA information when starting the instance
NOMOUNT	Starts background processes and allocates memory; doesn't read control files
MOUNT	Starts background processes, allocates memory, and reads control files
OPEN	Starts background processes, allocates memory, reads control files, and opens online redo logs and data files
OPEN RECOVER	Attempts media recovery before opening the database
OPEN READ ONLY	Opens the database in read-only mode
UPGRADE	Used when upgrading a database
DOWNGRADE	Used when downgrading a database

Stopping the Database

Normally, you use the SHUTDOWN IMMEDIATE statement to stop a database. The IMMEDIATE parameter instructs Oracle to halt database activity and roll back any open transactions, for example:

```
SQL> shutdown immediate;
Database closed.
Database dismounted.
ORACLE instance shut down.
```

Table 1-3 provides a detailed definition of the parameters available with the SHUTDOWN statement. In most cases, SHUTDOWN IMMEDIATE is an acceptable method of shutting down your database. If you issue the SHUTDOWN command with no parameters, it's equivalent to issuing SHUTDOWN NORMAL.

Table 1-3. Parameters Available with the SHUTDOWN Command

Parameter	Meaning
NORMAL	Wait for users to log out of active sessions before shutting down.
TRANSACTIONAL	Wait for transactions to finish, and then terminate the session.
TRANSACTIONAL LOCAL	Perform a transactional shutdown for local instance only.
IMMEDIATE	Terminate active sessions immediately. Open transactions are rolled back.
ABORT	Terminate the instance immediately. Transactions are terminated and aren't rolled back.

You should rarely need to use the SHUTDOWN ABORT statement. Usually, SHUTDOWN IMMEDIATE is sufficient. Having said that, there is nothing wrong with using SHUTDOWN ABORT. If SHUTDOWN IMMEDIATE isn't working for any reason, then use SHUTDOWN ABORT.

■ **Note** Stopping and restarting your database in quick succession is known colloquially as "bouncing the database."

Starting and stopping your database is a fairly simple process. If the environment is set up correctly, you should be able to connect to your database as a privileged user, and issue the appropriate startup and shutdown statements.

STARTUP FORCE

Sometimes in development environments, I'll quickly want to stop and start my database. For example, I might want to do this because I've modified an initialization parameter that requires a database restart. You can stop/start your database with one command:

```
SQL> startup force;
```

If your instance is currently running, the STARTUP FORCE command will shut down the instance (abort mode) and restart it. This behavior may not be what you want in a production environment, but for test/development databases, this is usually fine.

Summary

This chapter covered tasks such as establishing OS variables, connecting to your database, and starting/stopping your database. These operations are prerequisites for many DBA tasks, especially backup and recovery. When starting your database, it's important to understand the phases that Oracle goes through and at what point the control file is accessed and the data files and online redo logs are opened. Now that you have an understanding of these basics, we're ready to move on to describe the Oracle files used when working with backup and recovery.

CHAPTER 2

■ ■ ■

Files in Support of Backup and Recovery Operations

An Oracle database consists of three types of mandatory files: control files, online redo logs, and data files. This chapter looks at the basics of managing these critical files. This chapter also discusses how to implement archiving (which generates archive redo log files) and enabling a fast recovery area (FRA). Understanding how to enable archiving and how to manage archive redo logs is a crucial part of database administration and backup and recovery. It's also important to understand basic FRA concepts as RMAN (unless otherwise directed) will by default write backup files to the FRA.

When working with RMAN, it's essential to understand the files that comprise the database. Being familiar with the physical characteristics of your database lay the foundation for understanding how RMAN performs backup and recovery operations. This knowledge will enable you to better understand the underlying mechanics and also provide the base information required for troubleshooting when problems arise. First up is managing control files.

Managing Control Files

A control file is a small binary file that stores information such as the database name, names and locations of data files, names and locations of online redo log files, current online redo log sequence number, checkpoint information, and names and locations of RMAN backup files (if using). You can query much of the information stored in the control file from data dictionary views. This example displays the types of information stored in the control file by querying V$CONTROLFILE_RECORD_SECTION:

```
SQL> select distinct type from v$controlfile_record_section;

TYPE
----------------------------
FILENAME
TABLESPACE
RMAN CONFIGURATION
BACKUP CORRUPTION
PROXY COPY
FLASHBACK LOG
...
```

You can view database-related information stored in the control file via the V$DATABASE view:

```
SQL> select name, open_mode, created, current_scn from v$database;

NAME      OPEN_MODE            CREATED   CURRENT_SCN
--------- -------------------- --------- -----------
O12C      READ WRITE           27-SEP-14      319781
```

Every Oracle database must have at least one control file. When you start your database in nomount mode, the instance is aware of the location of the control files from the CONTROL_FILES initialization parameter in the spfile or init.ora file. When you issue a STARTUP NOMOUNT command, Oracle reads the parameter file and starts the background processes and allocates memory structures:

```
-- locations of control files are known to the instance
SQL> startup nomount;
```

At this point, the control files haven't been touched by any processes. When you alter your database into mount mode, the control files are read and opened for use:

```
-- control files opened
SQL> alter database mount;
```

If any of the control files listed in the CONTROL_FILES initialization parameter aren't available, then you can't mount your database.

When you successfully mount your database, the instance is aware of the locations of the data files and online redo logs but hasn't yet opened them. After you alter your database into open mode, the data files and online redo logs are opened:

```
-- datafiles and online redo logs opened
SQL> alter database open;
```

■ **Note** Keep in mind that when you issue the STARTUP command (with no options), the previously described three phases are automatically performed in this order: nomount, mount, open. When you issue a SHUTDOWN command, the phases are reversed: close the database, unmount the control file, and stop the instance.

The control file is created when the database is created. If possible you should have multiple control files stored on separate storage devices controlled by separate controllers.

After the database has been opened, Oracle will frequently write information to the control files, such as when you make any physical modifications (e.g., creating a tablespace, adding/removing/resizing a data file). Oracle writes to all control files specified by the CONTROL_FILES initialization parameter. If Oracle can't write to one of the control files, an error is thrown:

```
ORA-00210: cannot open the specified control file
```

If one of your control files becomes unavailable, shut down your database, and resolve the issue before restarting (see Chapter 6 for using RMAN to restore a control file). Fixing the problem may mean resolving a storage-device failure or modifying the CONTROL_FILES initialization parameter to remove the control file entry for the control file that isn't available.

```
┌─────────────────────────────────────────────────────────────────┐
│          DISPLAYING THE CONTENTS OF A CONTROL FILE                │
└─────────────────────────────────────────────────────────────────┘
```

You can use the ALTER SESSION statement to display the physical contents of the control file; for example,

```
SQL> oradebug setmypid
SQL> oradebug unlimit
SQL> alter session set events 'immediate trace name controlf level 9';
SQL> oradebug tracefile_name
```

The prior line of code displays the following name of the trace file:

```
/orahome/app/oracle/diag/rdbms/o12c/O12C/trace/O12C_ora_15545.trc
```

In Oracle 11g and above, the trace file is written to the $ADR_HOME/trace directory. You can also view the trace directory name via this query:

```
SQL> select value from v$diag_info where name='Diag Trace';
```

In Oracle 10g and below, the trace directory is defined by the USER_DUMP_DEST initialization parameter. You can inspect the contents of the control file when troubleshooting or when you're trying to gain a better understanding of Oracle internals.

Viewing Control File Names and Locations

If your database is in a nomount state, a mounted state, or an open state, you can view the names and locations of the control files, as follows:

```
SQL> show parameter control_files
```

You can also view control file location and name information by querying the V$CONTROLFILE view. This query works while your database is mounted or open:

```
SQL> select name from v$controlfile;
```

If, for some reason, you can't start your database at all, and you need to know the names and locations of the control files, you can inspect the contents of the initialization (parameter) file to see where they're located. If you're using an spfile, even though it's a binary file, you can still open it with a text editor. The safest approach is to make a copy of the spfile and then inspect its contents with an OS editor:

```
$ cp $ORACLE_HOME/dbs/spfileO12C.ora $ORACLE_HOME/dbs/spfileO12C.copy
$ vi $ORACLE_HOME/dbs/spfileO12C.copy
```

You can also use the strings command to search for values in a binary file:

```
$ strings $ORACLE_HOME/dbs/spfileO12C.ora | grep -i control_files
```

If you're using a text-based initialization file, you can view the file directly, with an OS editor, or use the grep command:

```
$ grep -i control_files $ORACLE_HOME/dbs/initO12C.ora
```

Adding a Control File

Adding a control file means copying an existing control file and making your database aware of the copy by modifying your CONTROL_FILES parameter. This task must be done while your database is shut down. This procedure only works when you have a good existing control file that can be copied. Adding a control file isn't the same thing as creating or restoring a control file.

If your database uses only one control file, and that control file becomes damaged, you need to either restore a control file from a backup (if available) and perform a recovery or re-create the control file. If you're using two or more control files, and one becomes damaged, you can use the remaining good control file(s) to quickly get your database into an operating state.

If a database is using only one control file, the basic procedure for adding a control file is as follows:

1. Alter the initialization file CONTROL_FILES parameter to include the new location and name of the control file.

2. Shut down your database.

3. Use an OS command to copy an existing control file to the new location and name.

4. Restart your database.

Depending on whether you use an spfile or an init.ora file, the previous steps vary slightly. The next two sections detail these different scenarios.

Spfile Scenario

If your database is open, you can quickly determine whether you're using an spfile with the following SQL statement:

```
SQL> show parameter spfile
```

Here is some sample output:

```
NAME      TYPE        VALUE
--------- ----------- -------------------------------
spfile    string      /orahome/app/oracle/product/12
                      .1.0.1/db_1/dbs/spfileO12C.ora
```

When you've determined that you're using an spfile, use the following steps to add a control file:

1. Determine the CONTROL_FILES parameter's current value:

   ```
   SQL> show parameter control_files
   ```

The output shows that this database is using only one control file:

```
NAME              TYPE         VALUE
----------------- ------------ -------------------------------
control_files     string       /u01/dbfile/O12C/control01.ctl
```

2. Alter your CONTROL_FILES parameter to include the new control file that you want to add, but limit the scope of the operation to the spfile (you can't modify this parameter in memory). Make sure you also include any control files listed in step 1:

```
SQL> alter system set control_files='/u01/dbfile/O12C/control01.ctl',
'/u01/dbfile/O12C/control02.ctl' scope=spfile;
```

3. Shut down your database:

```
SQL> shutdown immediate;
```

4. Copy an existing control file to the new location and name. In this example a new control file named control02.ctl is created via the OS cp command:

```
$ cp /u01/dbfile/O12C/control01.ctl /u01/dbfile/O12C/control02.ctl
```

5. Start up your database:

```
SQL> startup;
```

You can verify that the new control file is being used by displaying the CONTROL_FILES parameter:

```
SQL> show parameter control_files
```

Here is the output for this example:

```
NAME              TYPE         VALUE
----------------- ------------ -------------------------------
control_files     string       /u01/dbfile/O12C/control01.ctl
                               ,/u01/dbfile/O12C/control02.ctl
```

Init.ora Scenario

Run the following statement to verify that you're using an init.ora file. If you're not using an spfile, the VALUE column is blank:

```
SQL> show parameter spfile
NAME       TYPE         VALUE
---------- ------------ ------------------------------
spfile     string
```

To add a control file when using a text `init.ora` file, perform the following steps:

1. Shut down your database:

   ```
   SQL> shutdown immediate;
   ```

2. Edit your `init.ora` file with an OS utility (such as `vi`), and add the new control file location and name to the `CONTROL_FILES` parameter. This example opens the `init.ora` file, using `vi`, and adds `control02.ctl` to the `CONTROL_FILES` parameter:

   ```
   $ vi $ORACLE_HOME/dbs/init012C.ora
   ```

   Listed next is the `CONTROL_FILES` parameter after `control02.ctl` is added:

   ```
   control_files='/u01/dbfile/012C/control01.ctl',
                 '/u01/dbfile/012C/control02.ctl'
   ```

3. From the OS, copy the existing control file to the location, and name of the control file being added:

   ```
   $ cp /u01/dbfile/012C/control01.ctl /u01/dbfile/012C/control02.ctl
   ```

4. Start up your database:

   ```
   SQL> startup;
   ```

You can view the control files in use by displaying the `CONTROL_FILES` parameter:

```
SQL> show parameter control_files
```

For this example, here is the output:

```
NAME              TYPE         VALUE
---------------   -----------  -------------------------------
control_files     string       /u01/dbfile/012C/control01.ctl
                               ,/u01/dbfile/012C/control02.ctl
```

Moving a Control File

You may occasionally need to move a control file from one location to another. For example, if new storage is added to the database server, you may want to move an existing control file to the newly available location.

The procedure for moving a control file is very similar to adding a control file. The only difference is that you rename the control file instead of copying it. This example shows how to move a control file when you're using an spfile:

1. Determine the CONTROL_FILES parameter's current value:

   ```
   SQL> show parameter control_files

   NAME              TYPE         VALUE
   ----------------  -----------  ------------------------------------
   control_files     string       /u01/dbfile/012C/control01.ctl
   ```

2. Alter your CONTROL_FILES parameter to reflect that you're moving a control file. In this example the control file is currently in this location:

   ```
   /u01/dbfile/012C/control01.ctl
   ```

   You're moving the control file to this location:

   ```
   /u02/dbfile/012C/control01.ctl
   ```

   Alter the spfile to reflect the new location for the control file. You have to specify SCOPE=SPFILE because the CONTROL_FILES parameter can't be modified in memory:

   ```
   SQL> alter system set
        control_files='/u02/dbfile/012C/control01.ctl' scope=spfile;
   ```

3. Shut down your database:

   ```
   SQL> shutdown immediate;
   ```

4. At the OS prompt, move the control file to the new location. This example uses the OS mv command:

   ```
   $ mv /u01/dbfile/012C/control01.ctl /u02/dbfile/012C/control01.ctl
   ```

5. Start up your database:

   ```
   SQL> startup;
   ```

You can verify that the new control file is being used by displaying the CONTROL_FILES parameter:

```
SQL> show parameter control_files
```

Here is the output for this example:

```
NAME              TYPE         VALUE
----------------  -----------  --------------------------------
control_files     string       /u02/dbfile/012C/control01.ctl
```

Removing a Control File

You may run into a situation in which you experience a media failure with a storage device that contains one of your multiplexed control files:

```
ORA-00205: error in identifying control file, check alert log for more info
```

In this scenario, you still have at least one good control file. To remove a control file, follow these steps:

1. Identify which control file has experienced media failure by inspecting the `alert.log` for information:

    ```
    ORA-00210: cannot open the specified control file
    ORA-00202: control file: '/u01/dbfile/O12C/control02.ctl'
    ```

2. Remove the unavailable control file name from the `CONTROL_FILES` parameter. If you're using an `init.ora` file, modify the file directly with an OS editor (such as `vi`). If you're using an `spfile`, modify the `CONTROL_FILES` parameter with the `ALTER SYSTEM` statement. In this `spfile` example the `control02.ctl` control file is removed from the `CONTROL_FILES` parameter:

    ```
    SQL> alter system set control_files='/u01/dbfile/O12C/control01.ctl'
         scope=spfile;
    ```

    This database now has only one control file associated with it. You should never run a production database with just one control file. See the section "Adding a Control File," earlier in this chapter, for details on how to add more control files to your database.

3. Stop and start your database:

    ```
    SQL> shutdown immediate;
    SQL> startup;
    ```

Managing Online Redo Logs

Online redo logs store a record of transactions that have occurred in your database. These logs serve the following purposes:

-   Provide a mechanism for recording changes to the database so that in the event of a media failure, you have a method of recovering transactions.

-   Ensure that in the event of total instance failure, committed transactions can be recovered (crash recovery) even if committed data changes have not yet been written to the data files.

-   Allow administrators to inspect historical database transactions through the Oracle LogMiner utility.

-   They are read by Oracle tools such as GoldenGate or Streams to replicate data.

You're required to have at least two online redo log groups in your database. Each online redo log group must contain at least one online redo log member. The member is the physical file that exists on disk. You can create multiple members in each redo log group, which is known as multiplexing your online redo log group.

■ **Tip**   I highly recommend that you multiplex your online redo log groups and, if possible, have each member on a separate physical device governed by a separate controller.

The log writer is the background process responsible for writing transaction information from the redo log buffer (in the SGA) to the online redo log files (on disk). Log writer flushes the contents of the redo log buffer when any of the following are true:

- A COMMIT or ROLLBACK issued.

- A log switch occurs.

- Three seconds go by.

- The redo log buffer is one-third full.

- The redo log buffer fills to one megabyte.

The online redo log group that the log writer is actively writing to is the *current online redo log group*. The log writer writes simultaneously to all members of a redo log group. The log writer needs to successfully write to only one member in order for the database to continue operating. The database ceases operating if the log writer can't write successfully to at least one member of the current group.

When the current online redo log group fills up, a log switch occurs, and the log writer starts writing to the next online redo log group. The log writer writes to the online redo log groups in a round-robin fashion. Because you have a finite number of online redo log groups, eventually the contents of each online redo log group are overwritten. If you want to save a history of the transaction information, you must place your database in archivelog mode (see the section "Implementing Archivelog Mode," later in this chapter).

When your database is in archivelog mode, after every log switch the archiver background process copies the contents of the online redo log file to an archived redo log file. In the event of a failure the archived redo log files allow you to restore the complete history of transactions that have occurred since your last database backup.

Figure 2-1 displays a typical setup for the online redo log files. This figure shows three online redo log groups, each containing two members. The database is in archivelog mode. In the figure, group 2 has recently been filled with transactions, a log switch has occurred, and the log writer is now writing to group 3. The archiver process is copying the contents of group 2 to an archived redo log file. When group 3 fills up, another log switch will occur, and the log writer will begin writing to group 1. At the same time, the archiver process will copy the contents of group 3 to archive log sequence 3 (and so forth).

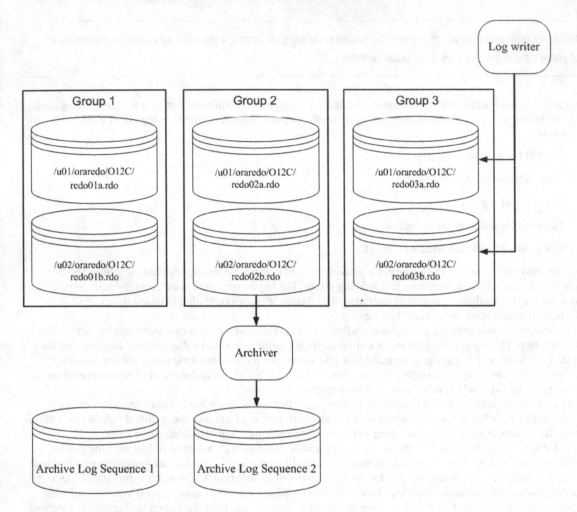

Figure 2-1. *Online redo log configuration*

The online redo log files aren't intended to be backed up. These files contain only the most recent redo transaction information generated by the database. When you enable archiving, the archived redo log files are the mechanism for protecting your database transaction history.

■ **Note**   In an Oracle Real Application Cluster (RAC) database, each instance has its own set of online redo logs. This is known as a *thread* of redo. Each RAC instance writes to its own online redo logs and generates its own thread of archive redo log files. Additionally, each instance must be able to read any other instance's online redo logs. This is important because if one instance crashes, then the other surviving instances can initiate instance recovery via reading the crashed instance's online redo logs.

The contents of the current online redo log files aren't archived until a log switch occurs. This means that if you lose all members of the current online redo log file, you lose transactions. Listed next are several mechanisms you can implement to minimize the chance of failure with the online redo log files:

- Multiplex the groups.

- If possible, never allow two members of the same group to share the same controller.

- If possible, never put two members of the same group on the same physical disk.

- Ensure that OS file permissions are set appropriately (restrictive, that only the owner of the Oracle binaries has permissions to write and read).

- Use physical storage devices that are redundant (i.e., RAID [redundant array of inexpensive disks]).

- Appropriately size the log files, so that they switch and are archived at regular intervals.

- Consider setting the ARCHIVE_LAG_TARGET initialization parameter to ensure that the online redo logs are switched at regular intervals.

■ **Note** The only tool provided by Oracle that can protect you and preserve all committed transactions in the event you lose all members of the current online redo log group is Oracle Data Guard, implemented in maximum protection mode. See MOS note 239100.1 for more details regarding Oracle Data Guard protection modes.

The online redo log files are never backed up by an RMAN backup or by a user-managed hot backup. If you did back up the online redo log files, it would be meaningless to restore them. The online redo log files contain the latest redo generated by the database. You wouldn't want to overwrite them from a backup with old redo information. For a database in archivelog mode the online redo log files contain the most recently generated transactions that are required to perform a complete recovery.

Displaying Online Redo Log Information

Use the V$LOG and V$LOGFILE views to display information about online redo log groups and corresponding members:

```
COL group#      FORM 99999
COL thread#     FORM 99999
COL grp_status FORM a10
COL member      FORM a30
COL mem_status FORM a10
COL mbytes      FORM 999999
--
SELECT
 a.group#
,a.thread#
,a.status grp_status
,b.member member
,b.status mem_status
,a.bytes/1024/1024 mbytes
```

```
FROM v$log       a,
     v$logfile b
WHERE a.group# = b.group#
ORDER BY a.group#, b.member;

GROUP# THREAD# GRP_STATUS MEMBER                               MEM_STATUS  MBYTES
------ ------- ---------- ----------------------------------- ----------  -------
     1       1 CURRENT    /u01/oraredo/012C/redo01a.rdo                       50
     1       1 CURRENT    /u02/oraredo/012C/redo01b.rdo                       50
     2       1 INACTIVE   /u01/oraredo/012C/redo02a.rdo                       50
     2       1 INACTIVE   /u02/oraredo/012C/redo02b.rdo                       50
     3       1 INACTIVE   /u01/oraredo/012C/redo03a.rdo                       50
     3       1 INACTIVE   /u02/oraredo/012C/redo03b.rdo                       50
```

When you're diagnosing online redo log issues, the V$LOG and V$LOGFILE views are particularly helpful. You can query these views while the database is mounted or open.

Determining the Optimal Size of Online Redo Log Groups

Try to size the online redo logs so that they switch anywhere from two to six times per hour. The V$LOG_HISTORY contains a history of how frequently the online redo logs have switched. Execute this query to view the number of log switches per hour:

```
select count(*)
,to_char(first_time,'YYYY:MM:DD:HH24')
from v$log_history
group by to_char(first_time,'YYYY:MM:DD:HH24')
order by 2;

  COUNT(*) TO_CHAR(FIRST
---------- -------------
         2 2014:09:24:04
        80 2014:09:24:05
        44 2014:09:24:06
        10 2014:09:24:12
```

From the previous output, you can see that a great deal of log switch activity occurred from approximately 4:00 AM to 6:00 AM This could be due to a nightly batch job or users' in different time zones updating data. For this database the size of the online redo logs should be increased. You should try to size the online redo logs to accommodate peak transaction loads on the database.

The V$LOG_HISTORY derives its data from the control file. Each time there is a log switch, an entry is recorded in this view that details information such as the time of the switch and the system change number (SCN). As stated, a general rule of thumb is that you should size your online redo log files so that they switch approximately two to six times per hour. You don't want them switching too often because there is overhead with the log switch. Oracle initiates a checkpoint as part of a log switch. During a checkpoint the database writer background process writes modified (also called dirty) blocks to disk, which is resource intensive.

Then again, you don't want online redo log files never to switch, because the current online redo log contains transactions that you may need in the event of a recovery. If a disaster causes a media failure in your current online redo log, you can lose those transactions that haven't been archived.

■ **Tip** Use the ARCHIVE_LAG_TARGET initialization parameter to set a maximum amount of time (in seconds) between log switches. A typical setting for this parameter is 1,800 seconds (30 minutes). A value of 0 (default) disables this feature. This parameter is commonly used in Oracle Data Guard environments to force log switches after the specified amount of time elapses.

You can also query the OPTIMAL_LOGFILE_SIZE column from the V$INSTANCE_RECOVERY view to determine if your online redo log files have been sized correctly:

```
SQL> select optimal_logfile_size from v$instance_recovery;
```

This column reports the redo log file size (in megabytes) that is considered optimal, based on the initialization parameter setting of FAST_START_MTTR_TARGET. Oracle recommends that you configure all online redo logs to be at least the value of OPTIMAL_LOGFILE_SIZE. However, when sizing your online redo logs, you must take into consideration information about your environment (such as the frequency of the switches).

Determining the Optimal Number of Redo Log Groups

Oracle requires at least two redo log groups in order to function. But, having just two groups sometimes isn't enough. To understand why this is so, remember that every time a log switch occurs, it initiates a checkpoint. As part of a checkpoint the database writer writes all modified (dirty) blocks from the SGA to the data files on disk. Also recall that the online redo logs are written to in a round-robin fashion and that eventually the information in a given log is overwritten. Before the log writer can begin to overwrite information in an online redo log, all modified blocks in the SGA associated with the redo log must first be written to a data file. If not all modified blocks have been written to the data files, you see this message in the alert.log file:

```
Thread 1 cannot allocate new log, sequence <sequence number>
Checkpoint not complete
```

Another way to explain this issue is that Oracle needs to store in the online redo logs any information that would be required to perform a crash recovery. To help you visualize this, see Figure 2-2.

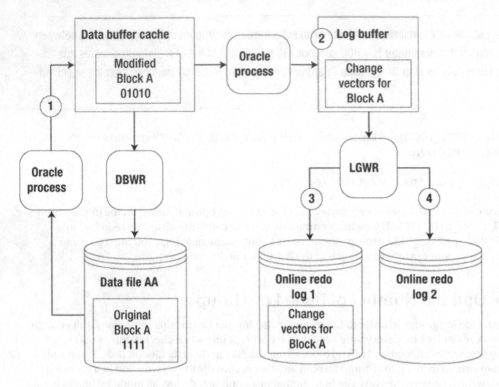

Figure 2-2. *Redo protected until the modified (dirty) buffer is written to disk*

At time 1, Block A is read from Data File AA into the buffer cache and modified. At time 2 the redo-change vector information (how the block changed) is written to the log buffer. At time 3 the log-writer process writes the Block A change-vector information to online redo log 1. At time 4 a log switch occurs, and online redo log 2 becomes the current online redo log.

Now, suppose that online redo log 2 fills up quickly and another log switch occurs, at which point the log writer attempts to write to online redo log 1. The log writer isn't allowed to overwrite information in online redo log 1 until the database block writer writes Block A to Data File AA. Until Block A is written to Data File AA, Oracle needs information in the online redo logs to recover this block in the event of a power failure or shutdown abort. Before Oracle overwrites information in the online redo logs, it ensures that blocks protected by redo have been written to disk. If these modified blocks haven't been written to disk, Oracle temporarily suspends processing until this occurs. There are a few ways to resolve this issue:

- Add more redo log groups.

- Lower the value of FAST_START_MTTR_TARGET. Doing so causes the database writer process to write older modified blocks to disk in a shorter time frame.

- Tune the database-writer process (modify DB_WRITER_PROCESSES).

If you notice that the Checkpoint not complete message is occurring often (say, several times a day), I recommend that you add one or more log groups to resolve the issue. Adding an extra redo log gives the database writer more time to write modified blocks in the database buffer cache to the data files before the associated redo with a block is overwritten. There is little downside to adding more redo log groups. The main concern is that you could bump up against the MAXLOGFILES value that was used when you created the database. If you need to add more groups and have exceeded the value of MAXLOGFILES, then you must re-create your control file and specify a high value for this parameter.

If adding more redo log groups doesn't resolve the issue, you should carefully consider lowering the value of FAST_START_MTTR_TARGET. When you lower this value, you can potentially see more I/O because the database writer process is more actively writing modified blocks to data files. Ideally, it would be nice to verify the impact of modifying FAST_START_MTTR_TARGET in a test environment before making the change in production. You can modify this parameter while your instance is up; this means you can quickly modify it back to its original setting if there are unforeseen side effects.

Finally, consider increasing the value of the DB_WRITER_PROCESSES parameter. Carefully analyze the impact of modifying this parameter in a test environment before you apply it to production. This value requires that you stop and start your database; therefore, if there are adverse effects, downtime is required to change this value back to the original setting.

Adding Online Redo Log Groups

If you determine that you need to add an online redo log group, use the ADD LOGFILE GROUP statement. In this example the database already contains two online redo log groups that are sized at 50M each. An additional log group is added that has two members and is sized at 50MB:

```
alter database add logfile group 3
('/u01/oraredo/012C/redo03a.rdo',
 '/u02/oraredo/012C/redo03b.rdo') SIZE 50M;
```

In this scenario I highly recommend that the log group you add be the same size and have the same number of members as the existing online redo logs. If the newly added group doesn't have the same physical characteristics as the existing groups, it's harder to accurately determine performance issues.

For example, if you have two log groups sized at 50MB, and you add a new log group sized at 500MB, this is very likely to produce the Checkpoint not complete issue described in the previous section. This is because flushing all modified blocks from the SGA that are protected by the redo in a 500MB log file can potentially take much longer than flushing modified blocks from the SGA that are protected by a 50MB log file.

Resizing and Dropping Online Redo Log Groups

You may need to change the size of your online redo logs (see the section "Determining the Optimal Size of Online Redo Log Groups," earlier in this chapter). You can't directly modify the size of an existing online redo log. To resize an online redo log, you have to first add online redo log groups that are the size you want, and then drop the online redo logs that are the old size.

Say you want to resize the online redo logs to be 200MB each. First, you add new groups that are 200MB, using the ADD LOGFILE GROUP statement. The following example adds log group 4, with two members sized at 200MB:

```
alter database add logfile group 4
('/u01/oraredo/012C/redo04a.rdo',
 '/u02/oraredo/012C/redo04b.rdo') SIZE 200M;
```

▪ **Note**   You can specify the size of the log file in bytes, kilobytes, megabytes, or gigabytes.

After you've added the log files with the new size, you can drop the old online redo logs. A log group must have an INACTIVE status before you can drop it. You can check the status of the log group, as shown here:

```
SQL> select group#, status, archived, thread#, sequence# from v$log;
```

You can drop an inactive log group with the ALTER DATABASE DROP LOGFILE GROUP statement:

```
SQL> alter database drop logfile group <group #>;
```

If you attempt to drop the current online log group, Oracle returns an ORA-01623 error, stating that you can't drop the current group. Use the ALTER SYSTEM SWITCH LOGFILE statement to switch the logs and make the next group the current group:

```
SQL> alter system switch logfile;
```

After a log switch the log group that was previously the current group retains an active status as long as it contains redo that Oracle requires to perform crash recovery. If you attempt to drop a log group with an active status, Oracle throws an ORA-01624 error, indicating that the log group is required for crash recovery. Issue an ALTER SYSTEM CHECKPOINT command to make the log group inactive:

```
SQL> alter system checkpoint;
```

Additionally, you can't drop an online redo log group if doing so leaves your database with only one log group. If you attempt to do this, Oracle throws an ORA-01567 error and informs you that dropping the log group isn't permitted because it would leave you with fewer than two log groups for your database (as mentioned earlier, Oracle requires at least two redo log groups in order to function).

Dropping an online redo log group doesn't remove the log files from the OS. You have to use an OS command to do this (such as the rm Linux/Unix command). Before you remove a file from the OS, ensure that it isn't in use and that you don't remove a live online redo log file. For every database on the server, issue this query to view which online redo log files are in use:

```
SQL> select member from v$logfile;
```

Before you physically remove a log file, first switch the online redo logs enough times that all online redo log groups have recently been switched; doing so causes the OS to write to the file and thus give it a new timestamp. For example, if you have three groups, make sure you perform at least three log switches:

```
SQL> alter system switch logfile;
SQL> /
SQL> /
```

Now, verify at the OS prompt that the log file you intend to remove doesn't have a new timestamp. First, go to the directory containing the online redo log files:

```
$ cd /u01/oraredo/O12C
```

Then, list the files to view the latest modification date:

```
$ ls -altr
```

When you're absolutely sure the file isn't in use, you can remove it. The danger in removing a file is that if it happens to be an in-use online redo log, and the only member of a group, you can cause serious damage to your database. Ensure that you have a good backup of your database and that the file you're removing isn't used by any databases on the server.

Adding Online Redo Log Files to a Group

You may occasionally need to add a log file to an existing group. For example, if you have an online redo log group that contains only one member, you should consider adding a log file (to provide a higher level of protection against a single-log file member failure). Use the ALTER DATABASE ADD LOGFILE MEMBER statement to add a member file to an existing online redo log group. You need to specify the new member file location, name, and group to which you want to add the file:

```
SQL> alter database add logfile member '/u02/oraredo/O12C/redo01b.rdo' to group 1;
```

Make certain you follow standards with regard to the location and names of any newly added redo log files.

Removing Online Redo Log Files from a Group

Occasionally, you may need to remove an online redo log file from a group. For example, your database may have experienced a failure with one member of a multiplexed group, and you want to remove the apostate member. First, make sure the log file you want to drop isn't in the current group:

```
SELECT a.group#, a.member, b.status, b.archived, SUM(b.bytes)/1024/1024 mbytes
FROM v$logfile a, v$log b
WHERE a.group# = b.group#
GROUP BY a.group#, a.member, b.status, b.archived
ORDER BY 1, 2;
```

If you attempt to drop a log file that is in the group with the CURRENT status, you receive the following error:

```
ORA-01623: log 2 is current log for instance O12C (thread 1) - cannot drop
```

If you're attempting to drop a member from the current online redo log group, then force a switch, as follows:

```
SQL> alter system switch logfile;
```

Use the ALTER DATABASE DROP LOGFILE MEMBER statement to remove a member file from an existing online redo log group. You don't need to specify the group number because you're removing a specific file:

```
SQL> alter database drop logfile member '/u01/oraredo/O12C/redo04a.rdo';
```

You also can't drop the last remaining log file of a group. A group must contain at least one log file. If you attempt to drop the last remaining log file of a group, you receive the following error:

```
ORA-00361: cannot remove last log member ...
```

Moving or Renaming Redo Log Files

Sometimes, you need to move or rename online redo log files. For example, you may have added some new mount points to the system, and you want to move the online redo logs to the new storage. You can use two methods to accomplish this task:

- Add the new log files in the new location, and drop the old log files.
- Physically rename the files from the OS.

If you can't afford any downtime, consider adding new log files in the new location and then dropping the old log files. See the section "Adding Online Redo Log Groups," earlier in this chapter, for details on how to add a log group. See also the section "Resizing and Dropping Online Redo Log Groups," earlier in this chapter, for details on how to drop a log group.

Alternatively, you can physically move the files from the OS. You can do this with the database open or closed. If your database is open, ensure that the files you move aren't part of the current online redo log group (because those are actively written to by the log writer background process). It's dangerous to try to do this task while your database is open because on an active system, the online redo logs may be switching at a rapid rate, which creates the possibility of attempting to move a file while it's being switched to be the current online redo log. Therefore, I strongly recommend that you only try to do this while your database is closed.

The next example shows how to move the online redo log files with the database shut down. Here are the steps:

1. Shut down your database:

    ```
    SQL> shutdown immediate;
    ```

2. From the OS prompt, move the files. This example uses the mv command to accomplish this task:

    ```
    $ mv /u02/oraredo/012C/redo02b.rdo /u01/oraredo/012C/redo02b.rdo
    ```

3. Start up your database in mount mode:

    ```
    SQL> startup mount;
    ```

4. Update the control file with the new file locations and names:

    ```
    SQL> alter database rename file '/u02/oraredo/012C/redo02b.rdo'
        to '/u01/oraredo/012C/redo02b.rdo';
    ```

5. Open your database:

    ```
    SQL> alter database open;
    ```

You can verify that your online redo logs are in the new locations by querying the V$LOGFILE view. I recommend as well that you switch your online redo logs several times and then verify from the OS that the files have recent timestamps. Also check the alert.log file for any pertinent errors.

Implementing Archivelog Mode

Recall from the discussion earlier in this chapter that archive redo logs are created only if your database is in archivelog mode. If you want to preserve your database transaction history to facilitate point-in-time and other types of recovery, you need to enable that mode.

In normal operation, changes to your data generate entries in the database redo log files. As each online redo log group fills up, a log switch is initiated. When a log switch occurs, the log writer process stops writing to the most recently filled online redo log group and starts writing to a new online redo log group. The online redo log groups are written to in a round-robin fashion—meaning the contents of any given online redo log group will eventually be overwritten. Archivelog mode preserves redo data for the long term by employing an archiver background process to copy the contents of a filled online redo log to what is termed an *archive redo log file*. The trail of archive redo log files is crucial to your ability to recover the database with all changes intact, right up to the precise point of failure.

Making Architectural Decisions

When you implement archivelog mode, you also need a strategy for managing the archived log files. The archive redo logs consume disk space. If left unattended, these files will eventually use up all the space allocated for them. If this happens, the archiver can't write a new archive redo log file to disk, and your database will stop processing transactions. At that point, you have a hung database. You then need to intervene manually by creating space for the archiver to resume work. For these reasons, there are several architectural decisions you must carefully consider before you enable archiving:

- Where to place the archive redo logs and whether to use the FRA to store them

- How to name the archive redo logs

- How much space to allocate to the archive redo log location

- How often to back up the archive redo logs

- When it's okay to permanently remove archive redo logs from disk

- How to remove archive redo logs (e.g., have RMAN remove the logs, based on a retention policy)

- Whether multiple archive redo log locations should be enabled

- (When to schedule the small amount of downtime that's required (if a production database)

As a general rule of thumb, you should have enough space in your primary archive redo location to hold at least a day's worth of archive redo logs. This lets you back them up on a daily basis and then remove them from disk after they've been backed up.

If you decide to use a FRA for your archive redo log location, you must ensure that it contains sufficient space to hold the number of archive redo logs generated between backups. Keep in mind that the FRA typically contains other types of files, such as RMAN backup files, flashback logs, and so on. If you use a FRA, be aware that the generation of other types of files can potentially impact the space required by the archive redo log files.

You need a strategy for automating the backup and removal of archive redo log files. For user-managed backups, this can be implemented with a shell script that periodically copies the archive redo logs to a backup location and then removes them from the primary location. As you will see in later chapters, RMAN automates the backup and removal of archive redo log files.

If your business requirements are such that you must have a certain degree of high availability and redundancy, then you should consider writing your archive redo logs to more than one location. Some shops set up jobs to copy the archive redo logs periodically to a different location on disk or even to a different server.

Setting the Archive Redo File Location

Before you set your database mode to archiving, you should specifically instruct Oracle where you want the archive redo logs to be placed. You can set the archive redo log file destination with the following techniques:

- Set the LOG_ARCHIVE_DEST_N database initialization parameter.

- Implement a FRA.

These two approaches are discussed in detail in the following sections.

■ **Tip** If you don't specifically set the archive redo log location via an initialization parameter or by enabling the FRA, then the archive redo logs are written to a default location. For Linux/Unix the default location is ORACLE_HOME/dbs. For Windows the default location is ORACLE_HOME\database. For active production database systems, the default archive redo log location is rarely appropriate.

Setting the Archive Location to a User-Defined Disk Location (non-FRA)

If you're using an init<SID>.ora file, modify the file with an OS utility (such as vi). In this example the archive redo log location is set to /u01/oraarch/O12C:

```
log_archive_dest_1='location=/u01/oraarch/O12C'
log_archive_format='O12C_%t_%s_%r.arc'
```

In the prior line of code, my standard for naming archive redo log files includes the ORACLE_SID (in this example, O12C to start the string); the mandatory parameters %t, %s, and %r; and the string .arc, to end. I like to embed the name of the ORACLE_SID in the string to avoid confusion when multiple databases are housed on one server. I like to use the extension .arc to differentiate the files from other types of database files.

■ **Tip** If you don't specify a value for LOG_ARCHIVE_FORMAT, Oracle uses a default, such as %t_%s_%r.dbf. One aspect of the default format that I don't like is that it ends with the extension .dbf, which is widely used for data files. This can cause confusion about whether a particular file can be safely removed because it's an old archive redo log file or shouldn't be touched because it's a live data file. Most DBAs are reluctant to issue commands such as rm *.dbf for fear of accidentally removing live data files.

If you're using an spfile, use ALTER SYSTEM to modify the appropriate initialization variables:

```
SQL> alter system set log_archive_dest_1='location=/u01/oraarch/O12C' scope=both;
SQL> alter system set log_archive_format='O12C_%t_%s_%r.arc' scope=spfile;
```

You can dynamically change the LOG_ARCHIVE_DEST_n parameters while your database is open. However, you have to stop and start your database for the LOG_ARCHIVE_FORMAT parameter to take effect.

RECOVERING FROM SETTING A BAD SPFILE PARAMETER

Take care not to set the LOG_ARCHIVE_FORMAT to an invalid value; for example,

```
SQL> alter system set log_archive_format='%r_%y_%dk.arc' scope=spfile;
```

If you do so, when you attempt to stop and start your database, you won't even get to the nomount phase (because the spfile contains an invalid parameter):

```
SQL> startup nomount;
ORA-19905: log_archive_format must contain %s, %t and %r
```

In this situation, if you're using an spfile, you can't start your instance. The easiest thing to do at this point is to create a text based init.ora file from the contents of the spfile. You can use the Linux/Unix strings command to accomplish this:

```
$ cd $ORACLE_HOME/dbs
$ strings spfile$ORACLE_SID.ora
```

The prior command will extract the text out of the binary spfile and display it on your screen. You can then cut and paste that text into an init.ora file and use that to start your database. If you're using Windows, you can use a utility such as write.exe to display the text in a binary file.

When you specify LOG_ARCHIVE_FORMAT, you must include %t (or %T), %s (or %S), and d% in the format string. Table 2-1 lists the valid variables you can use with the LOG_ARCHIVE_FORMAT initialization parameter.

Table 2-1. *Valid Variables for the Log Archive Format String*

Format String	Meaning
%s	Log sequence number
%S	Log sequence number padded to the left with zeros
%t	Thread number
%T	Thread number padded to the left with zeros
%a	Activation ID
%d	Database ID
%r	Resetlogs ID required to ensure uniqueness across multiple incarnations of the database

You can view the value of the LOG_ARCHIVE_DEST_N parameter by running the following:

```
SQL> show parameter log_archive_dest
```

Here is a partial listing of the output:

```
NAME                    TYPE        VALUE
--------------------    ----------  ----------------------------
log_archive_dest        string
log_archive_dest_1      string      location=/u01/oraarch/O12C
log_archive_dest_10     string
```

For Oracle 11g and higher you can enable up to 31 different locations for the archive redo log file destination. For most production systems one archive redo log destination location is usually sufficient. If you need a higher degree of protection, you can enable multiple destinations. Keep in mind that when you use multiple destinations, the archiver must be able to write to at least one location successfully. If you enable multiple mandatory locations and set LOG_ARCHIVE_MIN_SUCCEED_DEST to be higher than 1, then your database may hang if the archiver can't write to all mandatory locations.

You can check the details regarding the status of archive redo log locations via this query:

```
SQL> select dest_name, destination, status, binding from v$archive_dest;

DEST_NAME           DESTINATION           STATUS    BINDING
-----------------   -------------------   --------  ---------
LOG_ARCHIVE_DEST_1  /u01/archive/O12C     VALID     OPTIONAL
LOG_ARCHIVE_DEST_2                        INACTIVE  OPTIONAL
...
```

Using the FRA for Archive Log Files

The FRA is an area on disk—specified via database initialization parameters—that can be used to store files, such as archive redo logs, RMAN backup files, flashback logs, and multiplexed control files and online redo logs. To enable the use of a FRA, you must set two initialization parameters (in this order):

- DB_RECOVERY_FILE_DEST_SIZE specifies the maximum space to be used for all files that are stored in the FRA for a database.

- DB_RECOVERY_FILE_DEST specifies the base directory for the FRA.

When you create a FRA, you're not really creating anything—you're telling Oracle which directory to use when storing files that go in the FRA. For example, say 200GB of space are reserved on a mount point, and you want the base directory for the FRA to be /u01/fra. To enable the FRA, first set DB_RECOVERY_FILE_DEST_SIZE:

```
SQL> alter system set db_recovery_file_dest_size=200g scope=both;
```

Next, set the DB_RECOVERY_FILE_DEST parameter:

```
SQL> alter system set db_recovery_file_dest='/u01/fra' scope=both;
```

If you're using an init.ora file, modify it with an OS utility (such as vi) with the appropriate entries.
After you enable a FRA, by default, Oracle writes archive redo logs to subdirectories in the FRA.

■ **Note** If you've set the LOG_ARCHIVE_DEST_N parameter to be a location on disk, archive redo logs aren't written to the FRA.

You can verify that the archive location is using a FRA:

```
SQL> archive log list;
```

If archive files are being written to the FRA, you should see output like this:

```
Database log mode              Archive Mode
Automatic archival             Enabled
Archive destination            USE_DB_RECOVERY_FILE_DEST
```

You can display the directory associated with the FRA like this:

```
SQL> show parameter db_recovery_file_dest
```

When you first implement a FRA, there are no subdirectories beneath the base FRA directory (specified with DB_RECOVERY_FILE_DEST). The first time Oracle needs to write a file to the FRA, it creates any required directories beneath the base directory. For example, after you implement a FRA, if archiving for your database is enabled, then the first time a log switch occurs, Oracle creates the following directories beneath the base FRA directory:

```
<SID>/archivelog/<YYYY_MM_DD>
```

Each day that archive redo logs are generated results in a new directory's being created in the FRA, using the directory name format YYYY_MM_DD. Archive redo logs written to the FRA use the OMF format naming convention (regardless of whether you've set the LOG_ARCHIVE_FORMAT parameter).

If you want archive redo logs written to both a FRA and a non-FRA location, you can enable that, as follows:

```
SQL> alter system set log_archive_dest_1='location=/u01/oraarch/O12C';
SQL> alter system set log_archive_dest_2='location=USE_DB_RECOVERY_FILE_DEST';
```

The archive destination of USE_DB_RECOVERY_FILE_DEST indicates a FRA is in use. If you want to disable the use of a FRA, simply set the db_recovery_file_dest parameter to a null string:

```
SQL> alter system set db_recovery_file_dest='';
```

I'm not going to discuss all aspects of enabling and managing a FRA. Just be aware that once enabled, you'll need to take care when issuing RMAN backup commands and ensure that you have a strategy in place for regularly removing old backups. Chapter 4 contains more details on the use of a FRA and RMAN backups.

Enabling Archivelog Mode

After you've set the location for your archive redo log files, you can enable archiving. To enable archiving, you need to connect to the database as SYS (or a user with the SYSDBA privilege) and do the following:

```
SQL> shutdown immediate;
SQL> startup mount;
SQL> alter database archivelog;
SQL> alter database open;
```

You can confirm archivelog mode with this query:

```
SQL> archive log list;
```

You can also confirm it as follows:

```
SQL> select log_mode from v$database;

LOG_MODE
------------
ARCHIVELOG
```

Disabling Archivelog Mode

Usually, you don't disable archivelog mode for a production database. However, you may be doing a big data load and want to reduce any overhead associated with the archiving process, and so you want to turn off archivelog mode before the load begins and then reenable it after the load. If you do this, be sure you make a backup as soon as possible after reenabling archiving.

To disable archiving, do the following as SYS (or a user with the SYSDBA privilege):

```
SQL> shutdown immediate;
SQL> startup mount;
SQL> alter database noarchivelog;
SQL> alter database open;
```

Reacting to a Lack of Disk Space in Your Archive Log Destination

The archiver background process writes archive redo logs to a location that you specify. If, for any reason, the archiver process can't write to the archive location, your database hangs. Any users attempting to connect receive this error:

```
ORA-00257: archiver error. Connect internal only, until freed.
```

As a production-support DBA, you never want to let your database get into that state. Sometimes, unpredictable events happen, and you have to deal with unforeseen issues.

■ **Note**   DBAs who support production databases have a mindset completely different from that of architect DBAs, who get new ideas from flashy presentations or regurgitated documentation.

In this situation your database is as good as down and completely unavailable. To fix the issue, you have to act quickly:

- Move files to a different location.

- Compress old files in the archive redo log location.

- Permanently remove old files.

- Switch the archive redo log destination to a different location (this can be changed dynamically, while the database is up and running).

Moving files is usually the quickest and safest way to resolve the archiver error. You can use an OS utility such as mv to move old archive redo logs to a different location. If they're needed for a subsequent restore and recovery, you can let the recovery process know about the new location. Be careful not to move an archive redo log that is currently being written to. If an archived redo log file appears in V$ARCHIVED_LOG, that means it has been completely archived.

You can use an OS utility such as gzip to compress archive redo log files in the current archive destination. If you do this, you have to remember to uncompress any files that may be later needed for a restore and recovery. Be careful not to compress an archive redo log that is currently being written to.

Another option is to use an OS utility such as rm to remove archive redo logs from disk permanently. This approach is dangerous because you may need those archive redo logs for a subsequent recovery. If you do remove archive redo log files, and you don't have a backup of them, you should make a full backup of your database as soon as possible. Again, this approach is risky and should only be done as a last resort; if you delete archive redo logs that haven't been backed up, then you chance not being able to perform a complete recovery.

If another location on your server has plenty of space, you can consider changing the location to which the archive redo logs are being written. You can perform this operation while the database is up and running; for example,

```
SQL> alter system set log_archive_dest_1='location=/u02/oraarch/O12C';
```

After you've resolved the issue with the primary location, you can switch back the original location.

For most databases, writing the archive redo logs to one location is sufficient. However, if you have any type of disaster recovery or high-availability requirement, then you should write to multiple locations. Sometimes, DBAs set up a job to back up the archive redo logs every hour and copy them to an alternate location or even to an alternate server.

Backing Up Archive Redo Log Files

Depending on your business requirements, you may need a strategy for backing up archive redo log files. Minimally, you should back up any archive redo logs generated during a backup of a database in archivelog mode. Additional strategies may include

- periodically copying archive redo logs to an alternate location and then removing them from the primary destination
- copying the archive redo logs to tape and then deleting them from disk
- using two archive redo log locations
- using Data Guard for a robust disaster recovery solution

Keep in mind that you need all archive redo logs generated since the begin time of the last good backup to ensure that you can completely recover your database. Only after you're sure you have a good backup of your database should you consider removing archive redo logs that were generated prior to the backup.

If you're using RMAN as a backup and recovery strategy, then you should use RMAN to backup the archive redo logs. Additionally, you should specify an RMAN retention policy for these files and have RMAN remove the archive redo logs only after the retention policy requirements are met (e.g., back up files at least once before removing from disk) (see Chapter 5 for details on using RMAN).

Managing Tablespaces and Data files

The term *tablespace* is something of a misnomer, in that it's not just a space for tables. Rather, a tablespace is a logical container that allows you to manage groups of data files, the physical files on disk that consume space. Once a tablespace is created, you can then create database objects (tables and indexes) within tablespaces, which results in space allocated on disk in the associated data files.

A tablespace is logical in the sense that it is only visible through data dictionary views (such as DBA_TABLESPACES); you manage tablespaces through SQL*Plus or graphical tools (such as Enterprise Manager), or both. Tablespaces only exist while the database is up and running.

Data files can also be viewed through data dictionary views (such as DBA_DATA_FILES) but additionally have a physical presence, as they can be viewed outside the database through OS utilities (such as ls). Data files persist whether the database is open or closed.

Oracle databases typically contain several tablespaces. A tablespace can have one or more data files associated with it, but a data file can be associated with only one tablespace. In other words, a data file can't be shared between two (or more) tablespaces.

Objects (such as tables and indexes) are owned by users and created within tablespaces. An object is logically instantiated as a segment. A segment consists of extents of space within the tablespace. An extent consists of a set of database blocks. Figure 2-3 shows the relationships between these logical and physical constructs used to manage space within an Oracle database.

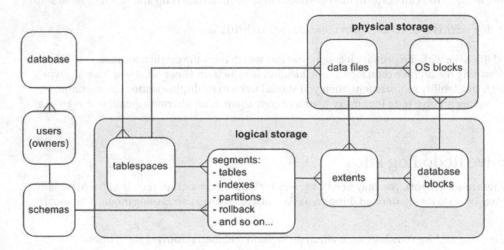

Figure 2-3. *Relationships of logical storage objects and physical storage*

When you create a database, typically five tablespaces are created when you execute the CREATE DATABASE statement: SYSTEM, SYSAUX, UNDO, TEMP, and USERS.

These five tablespaces are the minimal set of storage containers you need to operate a database (one could argue, however, you don't need the USERS tablespace; more on that in the next section). As you open a database for use, you should quickly create additional tablespaces for storing application data. This chapter discusses the purpose of the standard set of tablespaces, the need for additional tablespaces, and how to manage these critical database storage containers. The chapter focuses on the most common and critical tasks associated with creating and maintaining tablespaces and data files, progressing to more advanced topics, such as moving and renaming data files.

Understanding the First Five

The SYSTEM tablespace provides storage for the Oracle data dictionary objects. This tablespace is where all objects owned by the SYS user are stored. The SYS user should be the only user that owns objects created in the SYSTEM tablespace.

Starting with Oracle 10g, the SYSAUX (system auxiliary) tablespace is created when you create the database. This is an auxiliary tablespace used as a data repository for Oracle database tools, such as Enterprise Manager, Statspack, LogMiner, Logical Standby, and so on.

The UNDO tablespace stores the information required to undo the effects of a transaction (insert, update, delete, or merge). This information is required in the event a transaction is purposely rolled back (via a ROLLBACK statement). The undo information is also used by Oracle to recover from unexpected instance crashes and to provide read consistency for SQL statements. Additionally, some database features, such as Flashback Query, use the undo information.

Some Oracle SQL statements require a sort area, either in memory or on disk. For example, the results of a query may need to be sorted before being returned to the user. Oracle first uses memory to sort the query results, and when there is no longer sufficient memory, the TEMP tablespace is used as a sorting area on disk. Extra temporary storage may also be required when creating or rebuilding indexes. When you create a database, typically you create the TEMP tablespace and specify it to be the default temporary tablespace for any users you create.

The USERS tablespace is not absolutely required but is often used as a default permanent tablespace for table and index data for users. This means that when a user attempts to create a table or index, if no tablespace is specified during object creation, by default the object is created in the default permanent tablespace.

Understanding the Need for More

Although you could put every database user's data in the USERS tablespace, this usually isn't scalable or maintainable for any type of serious database application. Instead, it's more efficient to create additional tablespaces for application users. You typically create at least two tablespaces specific to each application using the database: one for the application table data and one for the application index data. For example, for the APP user, you can create tablespaces named APP_DATA and APP_INDEX for table and index data, respectively.

DBAs used to separate table and index data for performance reasons. The thinking was that separating table data from index data would reduce input/output (I/O) contention. This is because the data files (for each tablespace) could be placed on different disks, with separate controllers.

With modern storage configurations, which have multiple layers of abstraction between the application and the underlying physical storage devices, it's debatable whether you can realize any performance gains by creating multiple separate tablespaces. But, there still are valid reasons for creating multiple tablespaces for table and index data:

- Backup and recovery requirements may be different for the tables and indexes.

- The indexes may have storage requirements different from those of the table data.

- You may be using BLOB and CLOB data types, which typically have considerably different sizing requirements than non-LOB data. Therefore DBAs tend to separate LOB data in its own tablespace(s).

Depending on your requirements, you should consider creating separate tablespaces for each application using the database. For example, for an inventory application, create INV_DATA and INV_INDEX; for a human resources application, create HR_DATA and HR_INDEX. Here are some reasons to consider creating separate tablespaces for each application using the database:

- Applications may have different availability requirements. Separate tablespaces lets you take tablespaces offline for one application without affecting another application.

- Applications may have different backup and recovery requirements. Separate tablespaces lets tablespaces be backed up and recovered independently.

- Applications may have different storage requirements. Separate tablespaces allows for different settings for space quotas, extent sizes, and segment management.

- You may have some data that is purely read-only. Separate tablespaces lets you put a tablespace that contains only read-only data into read-only mode.

The next section discusses creating tablespaces.

Creating Tablespaces

You use the CREATE TABLESPACE statement to create tablespaces. The *Oracle SQL Reference Manual* contains more than a dozen pages of syntax and examples for creating tablespaces. In most scenarios, you need to use only a few of the features available, namely, locally managed extent allocation, and automatic segment space management. The following code snippet demonstrates how to create a tablespace that employs the most common features:

```
create tablespace tools datafile '/u01/dbfile/O12C/tools01.dbf'
  size 100m
  segment space management auto;
```

You need to modify this script for your environment. By default, tablespaces will be created as locally managed. A locally managed tablespace uses a bitmap in the data file to efficiently determine whether an extent is in use. The storage parameters NEXT, PCTINCREASE, MINEXTENTS, MAXEXTENTS, and DEFAULT aren't valid for extent options in locally managed tablespaces.

The SEGMENT SPACE MANAGEMENT AUTO clause instructs Oracle to manage the space within the block. When you use this clause, there is no need to specify parameters, such as PCTUSED, FREELISTS, and FREELIST GROUPS. The alternative to AUTO space management is MANUAL. When you use MANUAL, you can adjust the parameters to the requirements of your application. I recommend that you use AUTO and not MANUAL. Using AUTO vastly reduces the number of parameters you need to configure and manage.

As you create tables and indexes within a tablespace, Oracle will automatically allocate space to segments within a tablespace's datafile as required. The default type of allocation is to automatically allocate space. You can explicitly instruct Oracle to use automatic allocation via the AUTOALLOCATE clause. Oracle allocates extent sizes of 64KB, 1MB, 8MB, or 64MB. Using AUTOALLOCATE is appropriate when you think objects in one tablespace will be of varying sizes (which is often the case). I usually use the default of allowing Oracle to automatically determine the extent sizes.

The alternative to AUTOALLOCATE is uniform extent sizes. You can instruct Oracle to allocate a uniform size for each extent via the UNIFORM SIZE [size] clause. If you don't specify a size, then the default uniform extent size is 1MB. The uniform extent size that you use varies, depending on the storage requirements of your tables and indexes. In some scenarios, I create several tablespaces for a given application. For instance, you can create a tablespace for small objects that has a uniform extent size of 512KB, a tablespace for medium-sized objects that has a uniform extent size of 4MB, a tablespace for large objects with a uniform extent size of 16MB, and so on.

When a data file fills up, you can instruct Oracle to increase the size of the data file automatically, with the AUTOEXTEND feature. I recommend that you don't use this feature. Instead, you should monitor tablespace growth and add space as necessary. Manually adding space is preferable to having a runaway SQL process that accidentally grows a tablespace until it has consumed all the space on a mount point. If you inadvertently fill up a mount point that contains a control file or the Oracle binaries, you can hang your database.

If you do use the AUTOEXTEND feature, I suggest that you always specify a corresponding MAXSIZE so that a runaway SQL process doesn't accidentally fill up a tablespace that in turn fills up a mount point. Here is an example of creating an autoextending tablespace with a cap on its maximum size:

```
create tablespace tools datafile '/u01/dbfile/O12C/tools01.dbf'
  size 100m
  autoextend on maxsize 1000m
  segment space management auto;
```

When you're using CREATE TABLESPACE scripts in different environments, it's useful to be able to parameterize portions of the script. For instance, in development you may size the data files at 100MB, whereas in production the data files may be 100GB. Use ampersand (&) variables to make CREATE TABLESPACE scripts more portable among environments.

The next listing defines ampersand variables at the top of the script, and those variables determine the sizes of data files created for the tablespaces:

```
define tbsp_large=5G
define tbsp_med=500M
--
create tablespace reg_data datafile '/u01/dbfile/O12C/reg_data01.dbf'
  size &&tbsp_large segment space management auto;
--
create tablespace reg_index datafile '/u01/dbfile/O12C/reg_index01.dbf'
  size &&tbsp_med segment space management auto;
```

Using ampersand variables allows you to modify the script once and have the variables reused throughout the script. You can parameterize all aspects of the script, including data file mount points and extent sizes.

You can also pass the values of the ampersand variables in to the CREATE TABLESPACE script from the SQL*Plus command line. This lets you avoid hard-coding a specific size in the script and instead provide the sizes at runtime. To accomplish this, first define at the top of the script the ampersand variables to accept the values being passed in:

```
define tbsp_large=&1
define tbsp_med=&2
--
create tablespace reg_data datafile '/u01/dbfile/O12C/reg_data01.dbf'
  size &&tbsp_large segment space management auto;
--
create tablespace reg_index datafile '/u01/dbfile/O12C/reg_index01.dbf'
  size &&tbsp_med segment space management auto;
```

Now, you can pass variables in to the script from the SQL*Plus command line. The following example executes a script named cretbsp.sql and passes in two values that set the ampersand variables to 5G and 500M, respectively:

```
SQL> @cretbsp 5G 500M
```

Table 2-2 summarizes the best practices for creating and managing tablespaces.

Table 2-2. *Best Practices for Creating and Managing Tablespaces*

Best Practice	Reasoning
Create separate tablespaces for different applications using the same database.	If a tablespace needs to be taken offline, it affects only one application.
For an application, separate table data from index data in different tablespaces.	Table and index data may have different storage requirements.
Don't use the AUTOEXTEND feature for data files. If you do use AUTOEXTEND, specify a maximum size.	Specifying a maximum size prevents a runaway SQL statement from filling up a storage device.
Create tablespaces as locally managed. You shouldn't create a tablespace as dictionary managed.	This provides better performance and manageability.
For a tablespace's data file naming convention, use a name that contains the tablespace name followed by a two-digit number that's unique within data files for that tablespace.	Doing this makes it easy to identify which data files are associated with which tablespaces.
Try to minimize the number of data files associated with a tablespace.	You have fewer data files to manage.
In tablespace CREATE scripts, use ampersand variables to define aspects such as storage characteristics.	This makes scripts more reusable among various environments.

If you ever need to verify the SQL required to re-create an existing tablespace, you can do so with the DBMS_METADATA package. First, set the LONG variable to a large value:

```
SQL> set long 1000000
```

Next, use the DBMS_METADATA package to display the CREATE TABLESPACE data definition language (DDL) for all tablespaces within the database:

```
SQL> select dbms_metadata.get_ddl('TABLESPACE',tablespace_name) from dba_tablespaces;
```

■ **Tip** You can also use Data Pump to extract the DDL of database objects. See Chapter 8 for details.

Renaming a Tablespace

Sometimes, you need to rename a tablespace. You may want to do this because a tablespace was initially erroneously named, or you may want the tablespace name to better conform to your database naming standards. Use the ALTER TABLESPACE statement to rename a tablespace. This example renames a tablespace from TOOLS to TOOLS_DEV:

```
SQL> alter tablespace tools rename to tools_dev;
```

When you rename a tablespace, Oracle updates the name of the tablespace in the data dictionary, control files, and data file headers. Keep in mind that renaming a tablespace doesn't rename any associated data files. See the section "Renaming or Relocating a Data File," later in this chapter, for information on renaming data files.

■ **Note**   You can't rename the SYSTEM tablespace or the SYSAUX tablespace.

Controlling the Generation of Redo

For some types of applications, you may know beforehand that you can easily re-create the data. An example might be a data warehouse environment in which you perform direct path inserts or use SQL*Loader to load data. In these scenarios you can turn off the generation of redo for direct path loading. You use the NOLOGGING clause to do this:

```
create tablespace inv_mgmt_data
  datafile '/u01/dbfile/O12C/inv_mgmt_data01.dbf' size 100m
  segment space management auto
  nologging;
```

If you have an existing tablespace and want to alter its logging mode, use the ALTER TABLESPACE statement:

```
SQL> alter tablespace inv_mgmt_data nologging;
```

You can confirm the tablespace logging mode by querying the DBA_TABLESPACES view:

```
SQL> select tablespace_name, logging from dba_tablespaces;
```

The generation of redo logging can't be suppressed for regular INSERT, UPDATE, and DELETE statements. For regular data manipulation language (DML) statements, the NOLOGGING clause is ignored. The NOLOGGING clause does apply, however, to the following types of DML:

- Direct path INSERT statements

- Direct path SQL*Loader

The NOLOGGING clause also applies to the following types of DDL statements:

- CREATE TABLE ... AS SELECT (NOLOGGING only affects the initial create, not subsequent regular DML, statements against the table)

- ALTER TABLE ... MOVE

- ALTER TABLE ... ADD/MERGE/SPLIT/MOVE/MODIFY PARTITION

- CREATE INDEX

- ALTER INDEX ... REBUILD

- CREATE MATERIALIZED VIEW

- ALTER MATERIALIZED VIEW ... MOVE

- CREATE MATERIALIZED VIEW LOG

- ALTER MATERIALIZED VIEW LOG ... MOVE

Be aware that if redo isn't logged for a table or index, and you have a media failure before the object is backed up, then you can't recover the data; you receive an ORA-01578 error, indicating that there is logical corruption of the data.

■ **Note**   You can also override the tablespace level of logging at the object level. For example, even if a tablespace is specified as NOLOGGING, you can create a table with the LOGGING clause.

Changing a Tablespace's Write Mode

In environments such as data warehouses, you may need to load data into tables and then never modify the data again. To enforce that no objects in a tablespace can be modified, you can alter the tablespace to be read-only. To do this, use the ALTER TABLESPACE statement:

```
SQL> alter tablespace inv_mgmt_rep read only;
```

One advantage of a read-only tablespace is that you only have to back it up once. You should be able to restore the data files from a read-only tablespace no matter how long ago the backup was made.

If you need to modify the tablespace out of read-only mode, you do so as follows:

```
SQL> alter tablespace inv_mgmt_rep read write;
```

Make sure you reenable backups of a tablespace after you place it in read/write mode.

■ **Note**   You can't make a tablespace that contains active rollback segments read-only. For this reason, the SYSTEM tablespace can't be made read-only, because it contains the SYSTEM rollback segment.

Be aware that in Oracle 11g and above, you can modify individual tables to be read-only. This allows you to control the read-only at a much more granular level (than at the tablespace level); for example,

```
SQL> alter table my_tab read only;
```

While in read-only mode, you can't issue any insert, update, or delete statements against the table. Making individual tables read/write can be advantageous when you're doing maintenance (such as a data migration) and you want to ensure that users don't update the data.

This example modifies a table back to read/write mode:

```
SQL> alter table my_tab read write;
```

Dropping a Tablespace

If you have a tablespace that is unused, it's best to drop it so it doesn't clutter your database, consume unnecessary resources, and potentially confuse DBAs who aren't familiar with the database. Before dropping a tablespace, it's a good practice to first take it offline:

```
SQL> alter tablespace inv_data offline;
```

You may want to wait to see if anybody screams that an application is broken because it can't write to a table or index in the tablespace to be dropped. When you're sure the tablespace isn't required, drop it, and delete its data files:

```
SQL> drop tablespace inv_data including contents and datafiles;
```

■ **Tip** You can drop a tablespace whether it's online or offline. The exception to this is the SYSTEM tablespace, which can't be dropped. It's always a good idea to take a tablespace offline before you drop it. By doing so, you can better determine if an application is using any objects in the tablespace. If you attempt to query a table in an offline tablespace, you receive this error: ORA-00376: file can't be read at this time.

Dropping a tablespace using INCLUDING CONTENTS AND DATAFILES permanently removes the tablespace and any of its data files. Make certain the tablespace doesn't contain any data you want to keep before you drop it.

If you attempt to drop a tablespace that contains a primary key that is referenced by a foreign key associated with a table in a tablespace different from the one you're trying to drop, you receive this error:

```
ORA-02449: unique/primary keys in table referenced by foreign keys
```

Run this query first to determine whether any foreign key constraints will be affected:

```
select  p.owner,
        p.table_name,
        p.constraint_name,
        f.table_name refcrencing_table,
        f.constraint_name foreign_key_name,
        f.status fk_status
from    dba_constraints p,
        dba_constraints f,
        dba_tables      t
where   p.constraint_name = f.r_constraint_name
and     f.constraint_type = 'R'
and     p.table_name = t.table_name
and     t.tablespace_name = UPPER('&tablespace_name')
order by 1,2,3,4,5;
```

If there are referenced constraints, you need to first drop the constraints or use the CASCADE CONSTRAINTS clause of the DROP TABLESPACE statement. This statement uses CASCADE CONSTRAINTS to drop any affected constraints automatically:

```
SQL> drop tablespace inv_data including contents and data files cascade constraints;
```

This statement drops any referential integrity constraints from tables outside the tablespace being dropped that reference tables within the dropped tablespace.

If you drop a tablespace that has required objects in a production system, the results can be catastrophic. You must perform some sort of recovery to get the tablespace and its objects back. Needless to say, be very careful when dropping a tablespace. Table 2-3 lists recommendations to consider when you do this.

Table 2-3. Best Practices for Dropping Tablespaces

Best Practice	Reasoning

Before dropping a tablespace, run a script such as this to determine if any objects exist in the tablespace:
 	
`select owner, segment_name, segment_type`
`from dba_segments`
`where tablespace_name=upper('&&tbsp_name');`
	Doing this ensures that no tables or indexes exist in the tablespace before you drop it.

Consider renaming tables in a tablespace before you drop it.	If any applications are using tables within the tablespace to be dropped, the application throws an error when a required table is renamed.
If there are no objects in the tablespace, resize the associated data files to a very small number, such as 10MB.	Reducing the size of the data files to a miniscule amount of space quickly shows whether any applications are trying to access objects that require space in a tablespace.
Make a backup of your database before dropping a tablespace.	This ensures that you have a way to recover objects that are discovered to be in use after you drop the tablespace.
Take the tablespace and data files offline before you drop the tablespace. Use the `ALTER TABLESPACE` statement to take the tablespace offline.	This helps determine if any applications or users are using objects in the tablespace. They can't access the objects if the tablespace and data files are offline.
When you're sure a tablespace isn't in use, use the `DROP TABLESPACE ... INCLUDING CONTENTS AND DATAFILES` statement.	This removes the tablespace and physically removes any data files associated with it. Some DBAs don't like this approach, but you should be fine if you've taken the necessary precautions.

Using Oracle Managed Files

The Oracle Managed File (OMF) feature automates many aspects of tablespace management, such as file placement, naming, and sizing. You control OMF by setting the following initialization parameters:

- `DB_CREATE_FILE_DEST`
- `DB_CREATE_ONLINE_LOG_DEST_N`
- `DB_RECOVERY_FILE_DEST`

If you set these parameters before you create the database, Oracle uses them for the placement of the data files, control files, and online redo logs. You can also enable OMF after your database has been created. Oracle uses the values of the initialization parameters for the locations of any newly added files. Oracle also determines the name of the newly added file.

The advantage of using OMF is that creating tablespaces is simplified. For example, the `CREATE TABLESPACE` statement doesn't need to specify anything other than the tablespace name. First, enable the OMF feature by setting the `DB_CREATE_FILE_DEST` parameter:

```
SQL> alter system set db_create_file_dest='/u01';
```

Now, issue the CREATE TABLESPACE statement:

```
SQL> create tablespace inv1;
```

This statement creates a tablespace named INV1, with a default data file size of 100MB. Keep in mind that you can override the default size of 100MB by specifying a size:

```
SQL> create tablespace inv2 datafile size 20m;
```

To view the details of the associated data files, query the V$DATAFILE view, and note that Oracle has created subdirectories beneath the /u01 directory and named the file with the OMF format:

```
SQL> select name from v$datafile where name like '%inv%';
NAME
--------------------------------------------------
/u01/O12C/datafile/o1_mf_inv1_8b5l63q6_.dbf
/u01/O12C/datafile/o1_mf_inv2_8b5lflfc_.dbf
```

One limitation of OMF is that you're limited to one directory for the placement of data files. If you want to add data files to a different directory, you can alter the location dynamically:

```
SQL> alter system set db_create_file_dest='/u02';
```

Although this procedure isn't a huge deal, I find it easier not to use OMF. Most of the environments I've worked in have many mount points assigned for database use. You don't want to have to modify an initialization parameter every time you need a data file added to a directory that isn't in the current definition of DB_CREATE_FILE_DEST. It's easier to issue a CREATE TABLESPACE statement or ALTER TABLESPACE statement that has the file location and storage parameters in the script. It isn't cumbersome to provide directory names and file names to the tablespace-management statements.

Creating a Bigfile Tablespace

The bigfile feature allows you to create a tablespace with a very large data file assigned to it. The advantage of using the bigfile feature is this potential to create very large files. With an 8KB block size, you can create a data file as large as 32TB. With a 32KB block size, you can create a data file up to 128TB.

Use the BIGFILE clause to create a bigfile tablespace:

```
create bigfile tablespace inv_big_data
datafile '/u01/dbfile/O12C/inv_big_data01.dbf'
  size 10g
  segment space management auto;
```

As long as you have plenty of space associated with the filesystem supporting the bigfile tablespace data file, you can store massive amounts of data in a tablespace.

One potential disadvantage of using a bigfile tablespace is that if, for any reason, you run out of space on a filesystem that supports the data file associated with the bigfile, you can't expand the size of the tablespace (unless you can add space to the filesystem). You can't add more data files to a bigfile tablespace if they're placed on separate mount points. A bigfile tablespace allows only one data file to be associated with it.

You can make the bigfile tablespace the default type of tablespace for a database, using the ALTER DATABASE SET DEFAULT BIGFILE TABLESPACE statement. However, I don't recommend doing that. You could potentially create a tablespace, not knowing it was a bigfile tablespace (because you forgot it was the default or because you're a new DBA on the project and didn't realize it), and create a tablespace on a mount point. Then, when you discovered that you needed more space, you wouldn't know that you couldn't add another data file on a different mount point for this tablespace.

Enabling Default Table Compression within a Tablespace

When working with large databases, you may want to consider compressing the data. Compressed data results in less disk space, less memory, and fewer I/O operations. Queries reading compressed data potentially execute faster because fewer blocks are required to satisfy the result of the query. But, compression does have a cost; it requires more CPU resources, as the data are compressed and uncompressed while reading and writing.

When creating a tablespace, you can enable data compression features. Doing so doesn't compress the tablespace. Rather, any tables you create within the tablespace inherit the compression characteristics of the tablespace. This example creates a tablespace with ROW STORE COMPRESS ADVANCED:

```
CREATE TABLESPACE tools_comp
  DATAFILE '/u01/dbfile/O12C/tools_comp01.dbf'
  SIZE 100m
  SEGMENT SPACE MANAGEMENT AUTO
  DEFAULT ROW STORE COMPRESS ADVANCED;
```

■ **Note** If you're using Oracle 11g, then use the COMPRESS FOR OLTP clause instead of ROW STORE COMPRESS ADVANCED.

Now when a table is created within this tablespace, it will automatically be created with the ROW STORE COMPRESS ADVANCED feature. You can verify the compression characteristics of a tablespace via this query:

```
SQL> select tablespace_name, def_tab_compression, compress_for from dba_tablespaces;
```

If a tablespace is already created, you can alter its compression characters, as follows:

```
SQL> alter tablespace tools_comp default row store compress advanced;
```

Here's an example that alters a tablespace's default compress to BASIC:

```
SQL> alter tablespace tools_comp default compress basic;
```

You can disable tablespace compression via the NOCOMPRESS clause:

```
SQL> alter tablespace tools_comp default nocompress;
```

■ **Note** Most compression features require the Enterprise Edition and the Advanced Compression option.

Displaying Tablespace Size

DBAs often use monitoring scripts to alert them when they need to increase the space allocated to a tablespace. Depending on whether or not you're in a pluggable database environment, your SQL for determining space usage will vary. For a regular database (nonpluggable), you can use the regular DBA-level views to determine space usage. The following script displays the percentage of free space left in a tablespace and data file:

```
SET PAGESIZE 100 LINES 132 ECHO OFF VERIFY OFF FEEDB OFF SPACE 1 TRIMSP ON
COMPUTE SUM OF a_byt t_byt f_byt ON REPORT
BREAK ON REPORT ON tablespace_name ON pf
COL tablespace_name FOR A17    TRU HEAD 'Tablespace|Name'
COL file_name       FOR A40    TRU HEAD 'Filename'
COL a_byt           FOR 9,990.999 HEAD 'Allocated|GB'
COL t_byt           FOR 9,990.999 HEAD 'Current|Used GB'
COL f_byt           FOR 9,990.999 HEAD 'Current|Free GB'
COL pct_free        FOR 990.0     HEAD 'File %|Free'
COL pf              FOR 990.0     HEAD 'Tbsp %|Free'
COL seq NOPRINT
DEFINE b_div=1073741824
--
SELECT 1 seq, b.tablespace_name, nvl(x.fs,0)/y.ap*100 pf, b.file_name file_name,
  b.bytes/&&b_div a_byt, NVL((b.bytes-SUM(f.bytes))/&&b_div,b.bytes/&&b_div) t_byt,
  NVL(SUM(f.bytes)/&&b_div,0) f_byt, NVL(SUM(f.bytes)/b.bytes*100,0) pct_free
FROM dba_free_space f, dba_data_files b
 ,(SELECT y.tablespace_name, SUM(y.bytes) fs
   FROM dba_free_space y GROUP BY y.tablespace_name) x
 ,(SELECT x.tablespace_name, SUM(x.bytes) ap
   FROM dba_data_files x GROUP BY x.tablespace_name) y
WHERE f.file_id(+) = b.file_id
AND   x.tablespace_name(+) = y.tablespace_name
and   y.tablespace_name =  b.tablespace_name
AND   f.tablespace_name(+) = b.tablespace_name
GROUP BY b.tablespace_name, nvl(x.fs,0)/y.ap*100, b.file_name, b.bytes
UNION
SELECT 2 seq, tablespace_name,
  j.bf/k.bb*100 pf, b.name file_name, b.bytes/&&b_div a_byt,
  a.bytes_used/&&b_div t_byt, a.bytes_free/&&b_div f_byt,
  a.bytes_free/b.bytes*100 pct_free
FROM v$temp_space_header a, v$tempfile b
 ,(SELECT SUM(bytes_free) bf FROM v$temp_space_header) j
 ,(SELECT SUM(bytes) bb FROM v$tempfile) k
WHERE a.file_id = b.file#
ORDER BY 1,2,4,3;
```

If you don't have any monitoring in place, you're alerted via the SQL statement that is attempting to perform an insert or update operation that the tablespace requires more space but isn't able to allocate more. At that point, an ORA-01653 error is thrown, indicating the object can't extend.

After you determine that a tablespace needs more space, you need to either increase the size of a data file or add a data file to the tablespace. See the section "Altering Tablespace Size," later in this chapter, for a discussion of these topics.

DISPLAYING ORACLE ERROR MESSAGES AND ACTIONS

You can use the `oerr` utility to quickly display the cause of an error and simple instructions on what actions to take; for example,

```
$ oerr ora 01653
```

Here is the output for this example:

```
01653, 00000, "unable to extend table %s.%s by %s in tablespace %s"
// *Cause:  Failed to allocate an extent of the required number of blocks for
//          a table segment in the tablespace indicated.
// *Action: Use ALTER TABLESPACE ADD DATAFILE statement to add one or more
//          files to the tablespace indicated.
```

The `oerr` utility's output gives you a fast and easy way to triage problems. If the information provided isn't enough, then Google is a good second option.

Altering Tablespace Size

When you've determined which data file you want to resize, first make sure you have enough disk space to increase the size of the data file on the mount point on which the data file exists:

```
$ df -h | sort
```

Use the `ALTER DATABASE DATAFILE ... RESIZE` command to increase the data file's size. This example resizes the data file to 1GB:

```
SQL> alter database datafile '/u01/dbfile/O12C/users01.dbf' resize 1g;
```

If you don't have space on an existing mount point to increase the size of a data file, then you must add a data file. To add a data file to an existing tablespace, use the `ALTER TABLESPACE ... ADD DATAFILE` statement:

```
SQL> alter tablespace users add datafile '/u02/dbfile/O12C/users02.dbf' size 100m;
```

With bigfile tablespaces, you have the option of using the `ALTER TABLESPACE` statement to resize the data file. This works because only one data file can be associated with a bigfile tablespace:

```
SQL> alter tablespace inv_big_data resize 1P;
```

Resizing data files can be a daily task when you're managing databases with heavy transaction loads. Increasing the size of an existing data file allows you to add space to a tablespace without adding more data files. If there isn't enough disk space left on the storage device that contains an existing data file, you can add a data file in a different location to an existing tablespace.

To add space to a temporary tablespace, first query the `V$TEMPFILE` view to verify the current size and location of temporary data files:

```
SQL> select name, bytes from v$tempfile;
```

Then, use the TEMPFILE option of the ALTER DATABASE statement:

```
SQL> alter database tempfile '/u01/dbfile/O12C/temp01.dbf' resize 500m;
```

You can also add a file to a temporary tablespace via the ALTER TABLESPACE statement:

```
SQL> alter tablespace temp add tempfile '/u01/dbfile/O12C/temp02.dbf' size 5000m;
```

Toggling Data Files Offline and Online

Sometimes, when you're performing maintenance operations (such as renaming data files), you may need to first take a data file offline. You can use either the ALTER TABLESPACE or the ALTER DATABASE DATAFILE statement to toggle data files offline and online.

■ **Tip** As of Oracle 12c, you can move and rename data files while they are online and open for use. See "Renaming or Relocating a Data File," later in this chapter, for a discussion of this.

Use the ALTER TABLESPACE ... OFFLINE NORMAL statement to take a tablespace and its associated data files offline. You don't need to specify NORMAL, because it's the default:

```
SQL> alter tablespace users offline;
```

When you place a tablespace offline in normal mode, Oracle performs a checkpoint on the data files associated with the tablespace. This ensures that all modified blocks in memory that are associated with the tablespace are flushed and written to the data files. You don't need to perform media recovery when you bring the tablespace and its associated data files back online.

You can't use the ALTER TABLESPACE statement to place tablespaces offline when the database is in mount mode. If you attempt to take a tablespace offline while the database is mounted (but not open), you receive the following error:

```
ORA-01109: database not open
```

■ **Note** When in mount mode, you must use the ALTER DATABASE DATAFILE statement to take a data file offline.

When taking a tablespace offline, you can also specify ALTER TABLESPACE ... OFFLINE TEMPORARY. In this scenario, Oracle initiates a checkpoint on all data files associated with the tablespace that are online. Oracle doesn't initiate a checkpoint on offline data files associated with the tablespace.

You can specify ALTER TABLESPACE ... OFFLINE IMMEDIATE when taking a tablespace offline. Your database must be in archivelog mode in this situation, or the following error is thrown:

```
ORA-01145: offline immediate disallowed unless media recovery enabled
```

When using OFFLINE IMMEDIATE, Oracle doesn't issue a checkpoint on the data files. You must perform media recovery on the tablespace before bringing it back online.

■ **Note** You can't take the SYSTEM or UNDO tablespace offline while the database is open.

You can also use the ALTER DATABASE DATAFILE statement to take a data file offline. If your database is open for use, then it must be in archivelog mode in order for you to take a data file offline with the ALTER DATABASE DATAFILE statement. If you attempt to take a data file offline using the ALTER DATABASE DATAFILE statement, and your database isn't in archivelog mode, the ORA-01145 error is thrown.

If your database isn't in archivelog mode, you must specify ALTER DATABASE DATAFILE ... OFFLINE FOR DROP when taking a data file offline. You can specify the entire file name or provide the file number. In this example, data file 4 is taken offline:

```
SQL> alter database datafile 4 offline for drop;
```

Now, if you attempt to bring online the offline data file, you receive the following error:

```
SQL> alter database datafile 4 online;
ORA-01113: file 4 needs media recovery
```

When you use the OFFLINE FOR DROP clause, no checkpoint is taken on the data file. This means you need to perform media recovery on the data file before bringing it online. Performing media recovery applies any changes to the data file that are recorded in the online redo logs that aren't in the data files themselves. Before you can bring online a data file that was taken offline with the OFFLINE FOR DROP clause, you must perform media recovery on it. You can specify either the entire file name or the file number:

```
SQL> recover datafile 4;
```

If the redo information that Oracle needs is contained in the online redo logs, you should see this message:

```
Media recovery complete.
```

If your database isn't in archivelog mode, and if Oracle needs redo information not contained in the online redo logs to recover the data file, then you can't recover the data file and place it back online.

If your database is in archivelog mode, you can take it offline without the FOR DROP clause. In this scenario, Oracle overlooks the FOR DROP clause. Even when your database is in archivelog mode, you need to perform media recovery on a data file that has been taken offline with the ALTER DATABASE DATAFILE statement. Table 2-4 summarizes the options you must consider when taking a tablespace/data files offline.

Table 2-4. *Options for Taking Tablespaces/Data Files Offline*

Statement	Archivelog Mode Required?	Media Recovery Required When Toggling Online?	Works in Mount Mode?
ALTER TABLESPACE ... OFFLINE NORMAL	No	No	No
ALTER TABLESPACE ... OFFLINE TEMPORARY	No	Maybe: Depends on whether any data files already have offline status	No
ALTER TABLESPACE ... OFFLINE IMMEDIATE	No	Yes	No
ALTER DATABASE DATAFILE ... OFFLINE	Yes	Yes	Yes
ALTER DATABASE DATAFILE ... OFFLINE FOR DROP	No	Yes	Yes

■ **Note** While the database is in mount mode (and not open), you can use the ALTER DATABASE DATAFILE command to take any data file offline, including SYSTEM and UNDO.

Renaming or Relocating a Data File

You may occasionally need to move or rename a data file. For example, you may need to move data files because of changes in the storage devices or because the files were created in the wrong location or with a nonstandard name. As of Oracle 12c, you have the option of renaming or moving data files, or both, while they are online. Otherwise, you will have to take data files offline for maintenance operations.

Performing Online Data File Operations

Starting with Oracle 12c is the ALTER DATABASE MOVE DATAFILE command. This command allows you to rename or move data files without any downtime. This vastly simplifies the task of moving or renaming a data file, as there is no need to manually place data files offline/online and use OS commands to physically move the files. This once manually intensive (and error-prone) operation has now been simplified to a single SQL command.

A data file must be online for the online move or rename to work. Here is an example of renaming an online data file:

```
SQL> alter database move datafile '/u01/dbfile/O12C/users01.dbf' to
     '/u01/dbfile/O12C/users_dev01.dbf';
```

Here is an example of moving a data file to a new mount point:

```
SQL> alter database move datafile '/u01/dbfile/O12C/system01.dbf' to
     '/u02/dbfile/O12C/system01.dbf';
```

You can also specify the data file number when renaming or moving a data file; for example,

```
SQL> alter database move datafile 2 to '/u02/dbfile/O12C/sysuax01.dbf';
```

In the previous example, you are specifying that data file 2 be moved.

If you're moving a data file and, for any reason, want to keep a copy of the original file, you can use the KEEP option:

```
SQL> alter database move datafile 4 to '/u02/dbfile/O12C/users01.dbf' keep;
```

You can specify the REUSE clause to overwrite an existing file:

```
SQL> alter database move datafile 4 to '/u01/dbfile/O12C/users01.dbf' reuse;
```

Oracle will not allow you to overwrite (reuse) a data file that is currently being used by the database. That's a good thing.

Performing Offline Data File Operations

If you are using Oracle 11g or lower, before you rename or move a data file, you must take the data file offline. There are two somewhat different approaches to moving and renaming offline data files:

- Use a combination of SQL commands and OS commands.

- Use a combination of re-creating the control file and OS commands.

These two techniques are discussed in the next two sections.

Using SQL and OS Commands

Here are the steps for renaming a data file using SQL commands and OS commands:

1. Use the following query to determine the names of existing data files:

   ```
   SQL> select name from v$datafile;
   ```

2. Take the data file offline, using either the ALTER TABLESPACE or ALTER DATABASE DATAFILE statement (see the previous section, "Performing Offline Data File Operations," for details on how to do this). You can also shut down your database and then start it in mount mode; the data files can be moved while in this mode because they aren't open for use.

3. Physically move the data file to the new location, using either an OS command (like mv or cp) or the COPY_FILE procedure of the DBMS_FILE_TRANSFER built-in PL/SQL package.

4. Use either the ALTER TABLESPACE ... RENAME DATAFILE ... TO statement or the ALTER DATABASE RENAME FILE ... TO statement to update the control file with the new data file name.

5. Alter the data file online.

■ **Note** If you need to rename data files associated with the SYSTEM or UNDO tablespace, you must shut down your database and start it in mount mode. When your database is in mount mode, you can rename these data files via the ALTER DATABASE RENAME FILE statement.

The following example demonstrates how to move the data files associated with a single tablespace. First, take the data files offline with the ALTER TABLESPACE statement:

```
SQL> alter tablespace users offline;
```

Now, from the OS prompt, move the data files to a new location, using the Linux/Unix mv command:

```
$ mv /u01/dbfile/O12C/users01.dbf /u02/dbfile/O12C/users01.dbf
```

Update the control file with the ALTER TABLESPACE statement:

```
alter tablespace users
rename datafile
'/u01/dbfile/O12C/users01.dbf'
to
'/u02/dbfile/O12C/users01.dbf';
```

Finally, bring the data files within the tablespace back online:

```
SQL> alter tablespace users online;
```

If you want to rename data files from multiple tablespaces in one operation, you can use the ALTER DATABASE RENAME FILE statement (instead of the ALTER TABLESPACE...RENAME DATAFILE statement). The following example renames several data files in the database. Because the SYSTEM and UNDO tablespaces' data files are being moved, you must shut down the database first and then place it in mount mode:

```
SQL> conn / as sysdba
SQL> shutdown immediate;
SQL> startup mount;
```

Because the database is in mount mode, the data files aren't open for use, and thus there is no need to take the data files offline. Next, physically move the files via the Linux/Unix mv command:

```
$ mv /u01/dbfile/O12C/system01.dbf /u02/dbfile/O12C/system01.dbf
$ mv /u01/dbfile/O12C/sysaux01.dbf /u02/dbfile/O12C/sysaux01.dbf
$ mv /u01/dbfile/O12C/undotbs01.dbf /u02/dbfile/O12C/undotbs01.dbf
```

■ **Note** You must move the files before you update the control file. The ALTER DATABASE RENAME FILE command expects the file to be in the renamed location. If the file isn't there, an error is thrown: ORA-27037: unable to obtain file status.

Now, you can update the control file to be aware of the new file name:

```
alter database rename file
'/u01/dbfile/O12C/system01.dbf',
'/u01/dbfile/O12C/sysaux01.dbf',
'/u01/dbfile/O12C/undotbs01.dbf'
to
'/u02/dbfile/O12C/system01.dbf',
'/u02/dbfile/O12C/sysaux01.dbf',
'/u02/dbfile/O12C/undotbs01.dbf';
```

You should be able to open your database:

```
SQL> alter database open;
```

Re-Creating the Control File and OS Commands

Another way you can relocate all data files in a database is to use a combination of a re-created control file and OS commands. The steps for this operation are as follows:

1. Create a trace file that contains a CREATE CONTROLFILE statement.

2. Modify the trace file to display the new location of the data files.

3. Shut down the database.

4. Physically move the data files, using an OS command.

5. Start the database in nomount mode.

6. Run the CREATE CONTROLFILE command.

■ **Note**   When you re-create a control file, be aware that any RMAN information that was contained in the file will be lost. If you're not using a recovery catalog, you can repopulate the control file with RMAN backup information, using the RMAN CATALOG command.

The following example walks through the previous steps. First, you write a CREATE CONTROLFILE statement to a trace file via an ALTER DATABASE BACKUP CONTROLFILE TO TRACE statement:

```
SQL> alter database backup controlfile to trace as '/tmp/mv.sql' noresetlogs;
```

There are a couple of items to note about the prior statement. First, a file named mv.sql is created in the /tmp directory; this file contains a CREATE CONTROLFILE statement. Second, the prior statement uses the NORESETLOGS clause; this instructs Oracle to write only one SQL statement to the trace file. If you don't specify NORESETLOGS, Oracle writes two SQL statements to the trace file: one to re-create the control file with the NORESETLOGS option and one to re-create the control file with RESETLOGS. Normally, you know whether you want to reset the online redo logs as part of re-creating the control file. In this case, you know that you don't need to reset the online redo logs when you re-create the control file (because the online redo logs haven't been damaged and are still in the normal location for the database).

Next, edit the /tmp/mv.sql file, and change the names of the directory paths to the new locations. Here is a CREATE CONTROLFILE statement for this example:

```
CREATE CONTROLFILE REUSE DATABASE "O12C" NORESETLOGS  NOARCHIVELOG
    MAXLOGFILES 16
    MAXLOGMEMBERS 4
    MAXDATAFILES 1024
    MAXINSTANCES 1
    MAXLOGHISTORY 876
LOGFILE
  GROUP 1 (
    '/u01/oraredo/O12C/redo01a.rdo',
    '/u02/oraredo/O12C/redo01b.rdo'
  ) SIZE 50M BLOCKSIZE 512,
  GROUP 2 (
    '/u01/oraredo/O12C/redo02a.rdo',
    '/u02/oraredo/O12C/redo02b.rdo'
  ) SIZE 50M BLOCKSIZE 512,
  GROUP 3 (
    '/u01/oraredo/O12C/redo03a.rdo',
    '/u02/oraredo/O12C/redo03b.rdo'
  ) SIZE 50M BLOCKSIZE 512
DATAFILE
    '/u01/dbfile/O12C/system01.dbf',
    '/u01/dbfile/O12C/sysaux01.dbf',
    '/u01/dbfile/O12C/undotbs01.dbf',
    '/u01/dbfile/O12C/users01.dbf'
CHARACTER SET AL32UTF8;
```

Now, shut down the database:

```
SQL> shutdown immediate;
```

Physically move the files from the OS prompt. This example uses the Linux/Unix mv command to move the files:

```
$ mv /u02/dbfile/O12C/system01.dbf /u01/dbfile/O12C/system01.dbf
$ mv /u02/dbfile/O12C/sysaux01.dbf /u01/dbfile/O12C/sysaux01.dbf
$ mv /u02/dbfile/O12C/undotbs01.dbf /u01/dbfile/O12C/undotbs01.dbf
$ mv /u02/dbfile/O12C/users01.dbf /u01/dbfile/O12C/users01.dbf
```

Start up the database in nomount mode:

```
SQL> startup nomount;
```

Then, execute the file that contains the CREATE CONTROLFILE statement (in this example, mv.sql):

```
SQL> @/tmp/mv.sql
```

If the statement is successful, you see the following message:

```
Control file created.
```

Finally, alter your database open:

```
SQL> alter database open;
```

Summary

This chapter described how to configure and manage control files, online redo log files, enable archiving, and managing tablespaces and data files. Control files, online redo logs, and data files are critical database files; a normally operating database can't function without them.

Control files are small binary files that contain information about the structure of the database. Any control files specified in the parameter file must be available in order for you to mount the database. If a control file becomes unavailable, then your database will cease operating until you resolve the issue. I highly recommend that you configure your database with at least three control files. If one control file becomes unavailable, you can replace it with a copy of a good existing control file. It's critical that you know how to configure, add, and remove these files.

Online redo logs are crucial files that record the database's transaction history. If you have multiple instances connected to one database, then each instance generates its own redo thread. Each database must be created with two or more online redo log groups. You can operate a database with each group's having just one online redo log member. However, I highly recommend that you create your online redo log groups with two members in each group. If an online redo log has at least one member that can be written to, your database will continue to function. If all members of an online redo log group are unavailable, then your database will cease to operate. As a DBA you must be extremely proficient in creating, adding, moving, and dropping these critical database files.

Archiving is the mechanism for ensuring you have all the transactions required to recover the database. Once enabled, the archiver needs to successfully copy the online redo log after a log switch occurs. If the archiver can't write to the primary archive destination, then your database will hang. Therefore, you need to map out carefully the amount of disk space required and how often to back up and subsequently remove these files.

Tablespaces and data files are where your data is stored. These typically make up the bulk of any backup and recovery operation. Therefore it's critical that you understand how to work with and manage data files.

The chapters up to this point in the book have covered tasks connecting to Oracle, performing routine DBA tasks, and managing critical files. The next several chapters concentrate backup and recovery operations.

CHAPTER 3

■ ■ ■

User-Managed Backup and Recovery

All DBAs should know how to back up a database. Even more critical, a DBA must be able to restore and recover a database. When media failures occur, everybody looks to the DBA to get the database up and running. There are two common, yet very different, Oracle approaches for backup and recovery:

- User-managed approach

- RMAN approach

User-managed backups are aptly named because you manually perform all steps associated with the backup or recovery, or both. There are two types of user-managed backups: cold backups and hot backups. Cold backups are sometimes called offline backups because the database is shut down during the backup process. Hot backups are also referred to as online backups because the database is available during the backup procedure.

RMAN is Oracle's flagship backup and recovery tool. It automates and manages most aspects of backup and recovery. For Oracle backup and recovery, you should use RMAN. So, why have a chapter about user-managed backups when this approach has been gathering dust for more than a decade? Consider the following reasons for understanding user-managed backup and recovery:

- You still find shops using user-managed backup and recovery techniques. Therefore, you're required to be knowledgeable about this technology.

- Manually executing a user-managed backup, restore, and recovery solidifies your understanding of the Oracle backup and recovery architecture. This helps immensely when you're troubleshooting issues with any backup and recovery tool and lays the foundation of core knowledge for key Oracle tools, such as RMAN and Data Guard.

- You'll more fully appreciate RMAN and the value of its features.

- Nightmarish database recovery stories recounted by the old DBAs will now make sense.

For these reasons, you should be familiar with user-managed backup and recovery techniques. Manually working through the scenarios in this chapter will greatly increase your understanding of which files are backed up and how they're used in a recovery. You'll be much better prepared to use RMAN. RMAN makes much of backup and recovery automated and push-button. However, knowledge of how to back up and recover a database manually helps you think through and troubleshoot issues with any type of backup technology.

This chapter begins with cold backups. These types of backups are viewed as the simplest form of user-managed backup because even a system administrator can implement them. Next, the chapter discusses hot backups. You also investigate several common restore-and-recovery scenarios. These examples build your base knowledge of Oracle backup and recovery internals.

■ **Tip** In Oracle 12c, you can perform user-managed hot backups and cold backups on pluggable databases; the user-managed backup and recovery technology works fine. However, I would strongly recommend that you use RMAN to manage backup and recovery in a pluggable environment. When connected to either the root container or a pluggable container, RMAN automatically determines which data files need to be backed up, their locations, and how to restore and recover. This task quickly becomes unwieldy for user-managed backups, in which the DBA has to manage this information for the root container and, potentially, numerous pluggable databases.

Implementing a Cold-Backup Strategy for a Noarchivelog Mode Database

You perform a user-managed cold backup by copying files after the database has been shut down. This type of backup is also known as an offline backup. Your database can be in either noarchivelog mode or archivelog mode when you make a cold backup.

DBAs tend to think of a cold backup as being synonymous with a backup of a database in noarchivelog mode. That isn't correct. You can make a cold backup of a database in archivelog mode, and that's a backup strategy that many shops employ. The differences between a cold backup with the database in noarchivelog mode and in archivelog mode are detailed in the following sections.

Making a Cold Backup of a Noarchivelog Mode Database

One main reason for making a cold backup of a database in noarchivelog mode is to give you a way to restore a database back to a point in time in the past. You should use this type of backup only if you don't need to recover transactions that occurred after the backup. This type of backup and recovery strategy is acceptable only if your business requirements allow for the loss of data and downtime. Rarely would you ever implement this type of backup and recovery solution for a production business database.

Having said that, there are some good reasons to implement this type of backup. One common use is to make a cold backup of a development/test/training database and periodically reset the database back to the baseline. This gives you a way to restart a performance test or a training session with the same point-in-time snapshot of the database.

■ **Tip** Consider using the Flashback Database feature to set your database back to a point in time in the past (see Chapter 6 for more details).

The example in this section shows you how to make a backup of every critical file in your database: all control files, data files, temporary data files, and online redo log files. With this type of backup, you can easily restore your database back to the point in time when the backup was made. The main advantages of this approach are that it's conceptually simple and easy to implement. Here are the steps required for a cold backup of a database in noarchivelog mode:

1. Determine where to copy the backup files and how much space is required.

2. Identify the locations and names of the database files to copy.

3. Shut down the database with the IMMEDIATE, TRANSACTIONAL, or NORMAL clause.

4. Copy the files (identified in step 2) to the backup location (determined in step 1).

5. Restart your database.

The following sections elaborate on these steps.

Step 1. Determine Where to Copy the Backup Files and How Much Space Is Required

Ideally, the backup location should be on a set of disks separate from your live data files location. However, in many shops, you may not have a choice and may be told which mount points are to be used by the database. For this example the backup location is the directory /u01/cbackup/012C. To get a rough idea of how much space you need to store one copy of the backups, you can run this query:

```
select sum(sum_bytes)/1024/1024 m_bytes
from(
select sum(bytes) sum_bytes from v$datafile
union
select sum(bytes) sum_bytes from v$tempfile
union
select (sum(bytes) * members) sum_bytes from v$log
group by members);
```

You can verify how much operating disk space is available with the Linux/Unix df (disk free) command. Make sure that the amount of disk space available at the OS is greater than the sum returned from the prior query:

```
$ df -h
```

Step 2. Identify the Locations and Names of the Database Files to Copy

Run this query to list the names (and paths) of the files that are included in a cold backup of a noarchivelog mode database:

```
select name from v$datafile
union
select name from v$controlfile
union
select name from v$tempfile
union
select member from v$logfile;
```

BACKING UP ONLINE REDO LOGS (OR NOT)

Do you need to back up the online redo logs? No; you never need to back up the online redo logs as part of any type of backup. Then, why do DBAs back up the online redo logs as part of a cold backup? One reason is that it makes the restore process for the noarchivelog mode scenario slightly easier. The online redo logs are required to open the database in a normal manner.

If you back up all files (including the online redo logs), then to get your database back to the state it was in at the time of the backup, you restore all files (including the online redo logs) and start up your database.

Step 3. Shut Down the Database

Connect to your database as the SYS (or as a SYSDBA-privileged user), and shut down your database, using IMMEDIATE, TRANSACTIONAL, or NORMAL. In almost every situation, using IMMEDIATE is the preferred method. This mode disconnects users, rolls back incomplete transactions, and shuts down the database:

```
$ sqlplus / as sysdba
SQL> shutdown immediate;
```

Step 4. Create Backup Copies of the Files

For every file identified in step 2, use an OS utility to copy the files to a backup directory (identified in step 1). In this simple example all the data files, control files, temporary database files, and online redo logs are in the same directory. In production environments, you'll most likely have files spread out in several different directories. This example uses the Linux/Unix cp command to copy the database files from /u01/dbfile/012C to the /u01/cbackup/012C directory:

```
$ cp /u01/dbfile/012C/*.*  /u01/cbackup/012C
```

Step 5. Restart Your Database

After all the files are copied, you can start up your database:

```
$ sqlplus / as sysdba
SQL> startup;
```

Restoring a Cold Backup in Noarchivelog Mode with Online Redo Logs

The next example explains how to restore from a cold backup of a database in noarchivelog mode. If you included the online redo logs as part of the cold backup, you can include them when you restore the files. Here are the steps involved in this procedure:

1. Shut down the instance.

2. Copy the data files, online redo logs, temporary files, and control files back from the backup to the live database data file locations.

3. Start up your database.

These steps are detailed in the following sections.

Step 1. Shut Down the Instance

Shut down the instance, if it's running. In this scenario it doesn't matter how you shut down the database, because you're restoring back to a point in time (with no recovery of transactions). Any files in the live database directory locations are overwritten when the backup files are copied back. If your instance is running, you can abruptly abort it. As a SYSDBA-privileged user, do the following:

```
$ sqlplus / as sysdba
SQL> shutdown abort;
```

Step 2. Copy the Files Back from the Backup

This step does the reverse of the backup: you're copying files from the backup location to the live database file locations. In this example all the backup files are located in the /u01/cbackup/O12C directory, and all files are being copied to the /u01/dbfile/O12C directory:

```
$ cp /u01/cbackup/O12C/*.*  /u01/dbfile/O12C
```

Step 3. Start Up the Database

Connect to your database as SYS (or a user that has SYSDBA privileges), and start up your database:

```
$ sqlplus / as sysdba
SQL> startup;
```

After you finish these steps, you should have an exact copy of your database as it was when you made the cold backup. It's as if you set your database back to the point in time when you made the backup.

Restoring a Cold Backup in Noarchivelog Mode Without Online Redo Logs

As mentioned earlier, you don't ever need the online redo logs when restoring from a cold backup. If you made a cold backup of your database in noarchivelog mode and didn't include the online redo logs as part of the backup, the steps to restore are nearly identical to the steps in the previous section. The main difference is that the last step requires you to open your database, using the OPEN RESETLOGS clause. Here are the steps:

1. Shut down the instance.
2. Copy the control files and data files back from the backup.
3. Start up the database in mount mode.
4. Open the database with the OPEN RESETLOGS clause.

Step 1. Shut Down the Instance

Shut down the instance, if it's running. In this scenario it doesn't matter how you shut down the database, because you're restoring back to a point in time. Any files in the live database directory locations are overwritten when the backups are copied. If your instance is running, you can abruptly abort it. As a SYSDBA-privileged user, do the following:

```
$ sqlplus / as sysdba
SQL> shutdown abort;
```

Step 2. Copy the Files Back from the Backup

Copy the control files and data files from the backup location to the live data file locations:

```
$ cp <backup directory>/*.*  <live database file directory>
```

Step 3. Start Up the Database in Mount Mode

Connect to your database as SYS or a user with SYSDBA privileges, and start the database in mount mode:

```
$ sqlplus / as sysdba
SQL> startup mount
```

Step 4. Open the Database with the OPEN RESETLOGS Clause

Open your database for use with the OPEN RESETLOGS clause:

```
SQL> alter database open resetlogs;
```

If you see the Database altered message, the command was successful. However, you may see this error:

```
ORA-01139: RESETLOGS option only valid after an incomplete database recovery
```

In this case, issue the following command:

```
SQL> recover database until cancel;
```

You should see this message:

```
Media recovery complete.
```

Now, attempt to open your database with the OPEN RESETLOGS clause:

```
SQL> alter database open resetlogs;
```

This statement instructs Oracle to recreate the online redo logs. Oracle uses information in the control file for the placement, name, and size of the redo logs. If there are old online redo log files in those locations, they're overwritten.

If you're monitoring your alert.log throughout this process, you may see ORA-00312 and ORA-00313. This means that Oracle can't find the online redo log files; this is okay, because these files aren't physically available until they're recreated by the OPEN RESETLOGS command.

Scripting a Cold Backup and Restore

It's instructional to view how to script a cold backup. The basic idea is to dynamically query the data dictionary to determine the locations and names of the files to be backed up. This is preferable to hard-coding the directory locations and file names in a script. The dynamic generation of a script is less prone to errors and surprises (e.g., the addition of new data files to a database but not to an old, hard-coded backup script).

■ **Note**   The scripts in this section aren't meant to be production-strength backup and recovery scripts. Rather, they illustrate the basic concepts of scripting a cold backup and subsequent restore.

The first script in this section makes a cold backup of a database. Before you use the cold backup script, you need to modify these variables in the script to match your database environment:

- ORACLE_SID

- ORACLE_HOME

- cbdir

The cbdir variable specifies the name of the backup-directory location. The script creates a file named coldback.sql, which is executed from SQL*Plus to initiate a cold backup of the database:

```
#!/bin/bash
ORACLE_SID=O12C
ORACLE_HOME=/u01/app/oracle/product/12.1.0.1/db_1
PATH=$PATH:$ORACLE_HOME/bin
#
sqlplus -s <<EOF
/ as sysdba
set head off pages0 lines 132 verify off feed off trimsp on
define cbdir=/u01/cbackup/O12C
spo coldback.sql
select 'shutdown immediate;' from dual;
select '!cp ' || name    || ' ' || '&&cbdir'   from v\$datafile;
select '!cp ' || name    || ' ' || '&&cbdir'   from v\$tempfile;
select '!cp ' || member  || ' ' || '&&cbdir' from v\$logfile;
select '!cp ' || name    || ' ' || '&&cbdir'   from v\$controlfile;
select 'startup;' from dual;
spo off;
@@coldback.sql
EOF
exit 0
```

This file generates commands that are to be executed from an SQL*Plus script to make a cold backup of a database. You place an exclamation mark (!) in front of the Unix cp command to instruct SQL*Plus to host out to the OS to run the cp command. You also place a backward slash (\) in front of each dollar sign ($) when referencing v$ data dictionary views; this is required in a Linux/Unix shell script. The \ escapes the $ and tells the shell script not to treat the $ as a special character (the $ normally signifies a shell variable).

After you run this script, here is a sample of the copy commands written to the `coldback.sql` script:

```
shutdown immediate;
!cp /u01/dbfile/012C/system01.dbf /u01/cbackup/012C
!cp /u01/dbfile/012C/sysaux01.dbf /u01/cbackup/012C
!cp /u01/dbfile/012C/undotbs01.dbf /u01/cbackup/012C
!cp /u01/dbfile/012C/users01.dbf /u01/cbackup/012C
!cp /u01/dbfile/012C/tools01.dbf /u01/cbackup/012C
!cp /u01/dbfile/012C/temp01.dbf /u01/cbackup/012C
!cp /u01/oraredo/012C/redo02a.rdo /u01/cbackup/012C
!cp /u02/oraredo/012C/redo02b.rdo /u01/cbackup/012C
!cp /u01/oraredo/012C/redo01a.rdo /u01/cbackup/012C
!cp /u02/oraredo/012C/redo01b.rdo /u01/cbackup/012C
!cp /u01/oraredo/012C/redo03a.rdo /u01/cbackup/012C
!cp /u02/oraredo/012C/redo03b.rdo /u01/cbackup/012C
!cp /u01/dbfile/012C/control01.ctl /u01/cbackup/012C
!cp /u01/dbfile/012C/control02.ctl /u01/cbackup/012C
startup;
```

While you make a cold backup, you should also generate a script that provides the commands to copy data files, temp files, log files, and control files back to their original locations. You can use this script to restore from the cold backup. The next script in this section dynamically creates a `coldrest.sql` script that copies files from the backup location to the original data file locations. You need to modify this script in the same manner that you modified the cold backup script (i.e., change the `ORACLE_SID`, `ORACLE_HOME`, and `cbdir` variables to match your environment):

```
#!/bin/bash
ORACLE_SID=012C
ORACLE_HOME=/u01/app/oracle/product/12.1.0.1/db_1
PATH=$PATH:$ORACLE_HOME/bin
#
sqlplus -s <<EOF
/ as sysdba
set head off pages0 lines 132 verify off feed off trimsp on
define cbdir=/u01/cbackup/012C
define dbname=$ORACLE_SID
spo coldrest.sql
select 'shutdown abort;' from dual;
select '!cp ' || '&&cbdir/' || substr(name, instr(name,'/',-1,1)+1) ||
       ' ' || name    from v\$datafile;
select '!cp ' || '&&cbdir/' || substr(name, instr(name,'/',-1,1)+1) ||
       ' ' || name    from v\$tempfile;
select '!cp ' || '&&cbdir/' || substr(member, instr(member,'/',-1,1)+1) ||
       ' ' || member from v\$logfile;
select '!cp ' || '&&cbdir/' || substr(name, instr(name,'/',-1,1)+1) ||
       ' ' || name    from v\$controlfile;
select 'startup;' from dual;
spo off;
EOF
exit 0
```

This script creates a script, named `coldrest.sql`, that generates the copy commands to restore your data files, temp files, log files, and control files back to their original locations. After you run this shell script, here is a snippet of the code in the `coldrest.sql` file:

```
shutdown abort;
!cp /u01/cbackup/012C/system01.dbf /u01/dbfile/012C/system01.dbf
!cp /u01/cbackup/012C/sysaux01.dbf /u01/dbfile/012C/sysaux01.dbf
!cp /u01/cbackup/012C/undotbs01.dbf /u01/dbfile/012C/undotbs01.dbf
!cp /u01/cbackup/012C/users01.dbf /u01/dbfile/012C/users01.dbf
!cp /u01/cbackup/012C/tools01.dbf /u01/dbfile/012C/tools01.dbf
...
!cp /u01/cbackup/012C/redo03b.rdo /u02/oraredo/012C/redo03b.rdo
!cp /u01/cbackup/012C/control01.ctl /u01/dbfile/012C/control01.ctl
!cp /u01/cbackup/012C/control02.ctl /u01/dbfile/012C/control02.ctl
startup;
```

If you need to restore from a cold backup using this script, log in to SQL*Plus as SYS, and execute the script:

```
$ sqlplus / as sysdba
SQL> @coldrest.sql
```

Making a Cold Backup of an Archivelog Mode Database

You can use a backup of a database in archivelog mode to restore and recover up to the last committed transaction prior to a failure. Therefore, unlike a backup of a noarchivelog mode database, this type of backup is not necessarily intended to be used to reset the database back to a point in time in the past from which no recovery can be applied. The purpose of a backup of an archivelog mode database is usually to restore the database and roll forward and apply transactions to fully recover the database.

This has significant implications for the backups. Recall that for a noarchivelog mode database, DBAs sometimes include the online redo logs as part of the backup. For a backup of an archivelog mode database, you should never include the online redo logs in the backup. The online redo logs contain the most currently generated redo transaction information for the database. Any transactions in the current online redo logs that haven't been archived are required for a complete recovery. In the event of a failure, you don't want to overwrite the online redo logs with backups of online redo logs taken from a point in time in the past; this would result in the inability to perform a complete recovery.

The high-level steps for a cold backup of a database in archivelog mode are identical to those for a noarchivelog mode database:

1. Determine where to copy the backup files and how much space is required.

2. Identify the locations and names of the database files to copy.

3. Shut down the database with the IMMEDIATE, TRANSACTIONAL, or NORMAL clause.

4. Copy the files (identified in step 2) to the backup location (determined in step 1).

5. Restart your database.

The main difference between the cold archivelog mode backup and noarchivelog mode backup is that in step 2, you run this query to identify the files to be backed up:

```
select name from v$datafile
union
select name from v$controlfile;
```

Also, you don't need to back up the data files associated with the TEMP tablespace. As of Oracle 10g, Oracle automatically attempts to create missing data files associated with the TEMP tablespace (for locally managed temp tablespaces) when the database is started.

Restoring and recovering with a cold backup of a database in archivelog mode is nearly identical to the restore and recovery from a hot backup. See the sections "Performing a Complete Recovery of an Archivelog Mode Database" and "Performing an Incomplete Recovery of an Archivelog Mode Database," later in this chapter, for discussion of how to restore and recover from a database in archivelog mode.

UNDERSTANDING THE MECHANICS DOES MATTER

Knowing how a hot backup works also helps in untangling and surviving difficult RMAN scenarios. RMAN is a sophisticated and highly automated tool. With just a few commands, you can back up, restore, and recover your database. However, if there is a failure with any RMAN command or step, an understanding of Oracle's underlying internal restore-and-recovery architecture pays huge dividends. A detailed knowledge of how to restore and recover from a hot backup helps you logically think your way through any RMAN scenario.

When you ride a bike, understanding how the derailleurs and gears and shifting work helps a great deal. You can usually tell when a rider knows only to push one button to go slower and another button to go faster. Riders who understand in more detail how the chain moves between gears will always be smoother at shifting gears. My editor, Jonathan Gennick, recounted the following anecdote while reading an early draft of this chapter:

"I loaned my bike to a guy the other week and went on a ride with him. You should have heard the horrible noises he conjured out of my derailleurs and drivetrain. I thought he was going to damage the bike. After a few minutes, he rode up to me and told me that my front derailleur wasn't working right.

"The derailleur was fine. He was just one of those guys who knows only how to push the button, without any understanding of what goes on underneath that action."

Similarly, effort you put into understanding how backup and recovery is implemented pays off in the long run. You actually have less to remember—because your understanding of the underlying operation enables you to think through problems and solve them in ways that checklists don't.

Implementing a Hot Backup Strategy

As discussed previously, RMAN should be your tool of choice for any type of Oracle database backup (either online or offline). RMAN is more efficient than user-managed backups and automates most tasks. Having said that, one of the best ways to gain an understanding of Oracle backup and recovery internals is to make a hot backup and then use that backup to restore and recover your database. Manually issuing the commands involved in a hot backup, followed by a restore and recovery, helps you understand the role of each type of file (control files, data files, archive redo logs, online redo logs) in a restore-and-recovery scenario.

The following sections begin by showing you how to implement a hot backup. They also provide basic scripts that you can use to automate the hot backup process. Later sections explain some of the internal mechanics of a hot backup and clarify why you must put tablespaces in backup mode before the hot backup takes place.

Making a Hot Backup

Here are the steps required for a hot backup:

1. Ensure that the database is in archivelog mode.

2. Determine where to copy the backup files.

3. Identify which files need to be backed up.

4. Note the maximum sequence number of the online redo logs.

5. Alter the database/tablespace into backup mode.

6. Copy the data files with an OS utility to the location determined in step 2.

7. Alter the database/tablespace out of backup mode.

8. Archive the current online redo log, and note the maximum sequence number of the online redo logs.

9. Back up the control file.

10. Back up any archive redo logs generated during the backup.

These steps are covered in detail in the following sections.

Step 1. Ensure That the Database Is in Archivelog Mode

Run the following command to check the archivelog mode status of your database:

```
SQL> archive log list;
```

The output shows that this database is in archivelog mode:

```
Database log mode          Archive Mode
Automatic archival         Enabled
Archive destination        /u01/oraarch/O12C
```

If you're not sure how to enable archiving, see Chapter 2 for details.

Step 2. Determine Where to Copy the Backup Files

Now, determine the backup location. For this example the backup location is the directory /u01/hbackup/O12C. To get a rough idea of how much space you need, you can run this query:

```
SQL> select sum(bytes) from dba_data_files;
```

Ideally, the backup location should be on a set of disks separate from your live data files. But, in practice, many times you're given a slice of space on a SAN and have no idea about the underlying disk layout. In these situations, you rely on redundancy's being built into the SAN hardware (RAID disks, multiple controllers, and so on) to ensure high availability and recoverability.

Step 3. Identify Which Files Need to Be Backed Up

For this step, you only need to know the locations of the data files:

```
SQL> select name from v$datafile;
```

When you get to step 5, you may want to consider altering tablespaces one at a time into backup mode. If you take that approach, you need to know which data files are associated with which: tablespace:

```
select tablespace_name, file_name
from dba_data_files
order by 1,2;
```

Step 4. Note the Maximum Sequence Number of the Online Redo Logs

To successfully recover using a hot backup, you require, at minimum, all the archive redo logs that were generated during the backup. For this reason, you need to note the archivelog sequence before starting the hot backup:

```
select thread#, max(sequence#)
from v$log
group by thread#
order by thread#;
```

Step 5. Alter the Database/Tablespaces into Backup Mode

You can put all your tablespaces into backup mode at the same time, using the ALTER DATABASE BEGIN BACKUP statement:

```
SQL> alter database begin backup;
```

If it's an active OLTP database, doing this can greatly degrade performance. This is because when a tablespace is in backup mode, Oracle copies a full image of any block (when it's first modified) to the redo stream (see the section "Understanding the Split-Block Issue," later in this chapter, for more details).

The alternative is to alter only one tablespace at a time into backup mode. After the tablespace has been altered into backup mode, you can copy the associated data files (step 6) and then alter the tablespace out of backup mode (step 7). You have to do this for each tablespace:

```
SQL> alter tablespace <tablespace_name> begin backup;
```

Step 6. Copy the Data Files with an OS Utility

Use an OS utility (Linux/Unix cp command) to copy the data files to the backup location. In this example all the data files are in one directory, and they're all copied to the same backup directory:

```
$ cp /u01/dbfile/O12C/*.dbf  /u01/hbackup/O12C
```

Step 7. Alter the Database/Tablespaces out of Backup Mode

After you're finished copying all your data files to the backup directory, you need to alter the tablespaces out of backup mode. This example alters all tablespaces out of backup mode at the same time:

```
SQL> alter database end backup;
```

If you're altering your tablespaces into backup mode one at a time, you need to alter each tablespace out of backup mode after its data files have been copied:

```
SQL> alter tablespace <tablespace_name> end backup;
```

If you don't take the tablespaces out of backup mode, you can seriously degrade performance and compromise the ability to recover your database. You can verify that no data files have an ACTIVE status with the following query:

```
SQL> alter session set nls_date_format = 'DD-MON-RRRR HH24:MI:SS';
SQL> select * from v$backup where status='ACTIVE';
```

■ **Note** Setting the NLS_DATE_FORMAT parameter appropriately will allow you to see the exact date/time when the data file was placed into backup mode. This is useful for determining the starting sequence number of the archivelog needed, in the event that the data file needs to be recovered.

Step 8. Archive the Current Online Redo Log, and Note the Maximum Sequence Number of the Online Redo Logs

The following statement instructs Oracle to archive any unarchived online redo logs and to initiate a log switch. This ensures that an end-of-backup marker is written to the archive redo logs:

```
SQL> alter system archive log current;
```

Also, note the maximum online redo log sequence number. If a failure occurs immediately after the hot backup, you need any archive redo logs generated during the hot backup to fully recover your database:

```
select thread#, max(sequence#)
from v$log
group by thread#
order by thread#;
```

Step 9. Back Up the Control File

For a hot backup, you can't use an OS copy command to make a backup of the control file. Oracle's hot backup procedure specifies that you must use the ALTER DATABASE BACKUP CONTROLFILE statement. This example makes a backup of the control file and places it in the same location as the database backup files:

```
SQL> alter database backup controlfile
     to '/u01/hbackup/O12C/controlbk.ctl' reuse;
```

The REUSE clause instructs Oracle to overwrite the file if it already exists in the backup location.

Step 10. Back Up Any Archive Redo Logs Generated During the Backup

Back up the archive redo logs that were generated during the hot backup. You can do this with an OS copy command:

```
$ cp <archive redo logs generated during backup>  <backup directory>
```

This procedure guarantees that you have the logs, even if a failure should occur soon after the hot backup finishes. Be sure you don't back up an archive redo log that is currently being written to by the archiver process—doing so results in an incomplete copy of that file. Sometimes, DBAs script this process by checking the maximum SEQUENCE# with the maximum RESETLOGS_ID in the V$ARCHIVED_LOG view. Oracle updates that view when it's finished copying the archive redo log to disk. Therefore, any archive redo log file that appears in the V$ARCHIVED_LOG view should be safe to copy.

Scripting Hot Backups

The script in this section covers the minimal tasks associated with a hot backup. For a production environment a hot backup script can be quite complex. The script given here provides you with a baseline of what you should include in a hot backup script. You need to modify these variables in the script for it to work in your environment:

- ORACLE_SID
- ORACLE_HOME
- hbdir

The ORACLE_SID OS variable defines your database name. The ORACLE_HOME OS varriable defines where you installed the Oracle software. The SQL*Plus hbdir variable points to the directory for the hot backups.

```
#!/bin/bash
ORACLE_SID=012C
ORACLE_HOME=/u01/app/oracle/product/12.1.0.1/db_1
PATH=$PATH:$ORACLE_HOME/bin
#
sqlplus -s <<EOF
/ as sysdba
set head off pages0 lines 132 verify off feed off trimsp on
define hbdir=/u01/hbackup/012C
spo hotback.sql
select 'spo &&hbdir/hotlog.txt' from dual;
select 'select max(sequence#) from v\$log;' from dual;
select 'alter database begin backup;' from dual;
select '!cp ' || name || ' ' || '&&hbdir' from v\$datafile;
select 'alter database end backup;' from dual;
select 'alter database backup controlfile to ' || '''' || '&&hbdir'
       || '/controlbk.ctl'  || '''' || ' reuse;' from dual;
select 'alter system archive log current;' from dual;
select 'select max(sequence#) from v\$log;' from dual;
select 'select member from v\$logfile;' from dual;
select 'spo off;' from dual;
spo off;
@@hotback.sql
EOF
```

The script generates a `hotback.sql` script. This script contains the commands for performing the hot backup. Here is a listing of the `hotback.sql` script for a test database:

```
spo /u01/hbackup/O12C/hotlog.txt
select max(sequence#) from v$log;
alter database begin backup;
!cp /u01/dbfile/O12C/system01.dbf /u01/hbackup/O12C
!cp /u01/dbfile/O12C/sysaux01.dbf /u01/hbackup/O12C
!cp /u01/dbfile/O12C/undotbs01.dbf /u01/hbackup/O12C
!cp /u01/dbfile/O12C/users01.dbf /u01/hbackup/O12C
!cp /u01/dbfile/O12C/tools01.dbf /u01/hbackup/O12C
alter database end backup;
alter database backup controlfile to '/u01/hbackup/O12C/controlbk.ctl' reuse;
alter system archive log current;
select max(sequence#) from v$log;
select member from v$logfile;
spo off;
```

You can run this script manually from SQL*Plus, like this:

```
SQL> @hotback.sql
```

■ **Caution** If the previous script fails on a statement before ALTER DATABASE END BACKUP is executed, you must take your database (tablespaces) out of backup mode by manually running ALTER DATABASE END BACKUP from SQL*Plus (as the SYS user).

While you generate the hot backup script, it's prudent to generate a script that you can use to copy the data files from a backup directory. You have to modify the `hbdir` variable in this script to match the location of the hot backups for your environment. Here is a script that generates the copy commands:

```
#!/bin/bash
ORACLE_SID=O12C
ORACLE_HOME=/u01/app/oracle/product/12.1.0.1/db_1
PATH=$PATH:$ORACLE_HOME/bin
#
sqlplus -s <<EOF
/ as sysdba
set head off pages0 lines 132 verify off feed off trimsp on
define hbdir=/u01/hbackup/O12C/
define dbname=$ORACLE_SID
spo hotrest.sql
select '!cp ' || '&&hbdir' || substr(name,instr(name,'/',-1,1)+1)
       || ' ' || name from v\$datafile;
spo off;
EOF
#
exit 0
```

For my environment here is the code generated that can be executed from SQL*Plus to copy the data files back from the backup directory, if a failure should occur:

```
!cp /u01/hbackup/O12C/system01.dbf /u01/dbfile/O12C/system01.dbf
!cp /u01/hbackup/O12C/sysaux01.dbf /u01/dbfile/O12C/sysaux01.dbf
!cp /u01/hbackup/O12C/undotbs01.dbf /u01/dbfile/O12C/undotbs01.dbf
!cp /u01/hbackup/O12C/users01.dbf /u01/dbfile/O12C/users01.dbf
!cp /u01/hbackup/O12C/tools01.dbf /u01/dbfile/O12C/tools01.dbf
```

In this output, you can remove the exclamation point (!) from each line if you prefer to run the commands from the OS prompt. The main idea is that these commands are available in the event of a failure, so you know which files have been backed up to which location and how to copy them back.

■ **Tip** Don't use user-managed hot backup technology for online backups; use RMAN. RMAN doesn't need to place tablespaces in backup mode and automates nearly everything related to backup and recovery.

Understanding the Split-Block Issue

To perform a hot backup, one critical step is to alter a tablespace into backup mode before you copy any of the data files associated with the tablespace, using an OS utility. To understand why you have to alter a tablespace into backup mode, you must be familiar with what is sometimes called the split- (or fractured-) block issue.

Recall that the size of a database block is often different from that of an OS block. For instance, a database block may be sized at 8KB, whereas the OS block size is 4KB. As part of the hot backup, you use an OS utility to copy the live data files. While the OS utility is copying the data files, the possibility exists that database writers are writing to a block simultaneously. Because the Oracle block and the OS block are different sizes, the following may happen:

1. The OS utility copies part of the Oracle block.

2. A moment later, a database writer updates the entire block.

3. A split second later, the OS utility copies the latter half of the Oracle block.

This can result in the OS copy of the block's being inconsistent with what Oracle wrote to the OS. Figure 3-1 illustrates this concept.

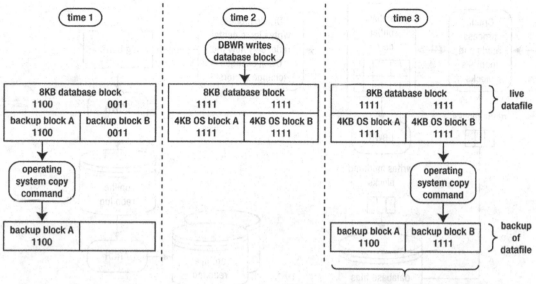

Figure 3-1. *Hot backup split- (or fractured-) block issue*

Looking at Figure 3-1, the block copied to disk at time 3 is corrupt, as far as Oracle is concerned. The first half of the block is from time 1, and the latter half is copied at time 3. When you make a hot backup, you're guaranteeing block-level corruption in the backups of the data files.

To understand how Oracle resolves the split-block issue, first consider a database operating in its normal mode (not in backup mode). The redo information that is written to the online redo logs is only what Oracle needs, to reapply transactions. The redo stream doesn't contain entire blocks of data. Oracle only records a change vector in the redo stream that specifies which block changed and how it was changed. Figure 3-2 shows Oracle operating under normal conditions.

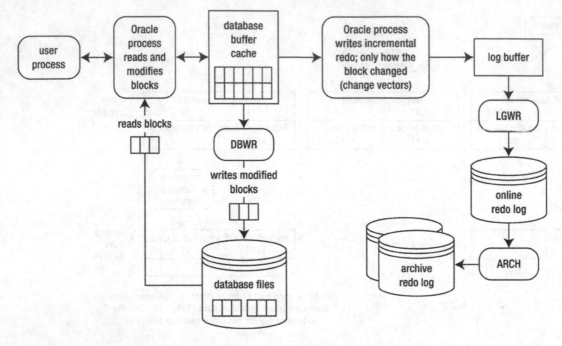

Figure 3-2. *Oracle normally only writes change vectors to the redo stream*

Now, consider what happens during a hot backup. For a hot backup, before you copy the data files associated with a tablespace, you must first alter the tablespace into backup mode. While in this mode, before Oracle modifies a block, the entire block is copied to the redo stream. Any subsequent changes to the block only require that the normal redo-change vectors be written to the redo stream. This is illustrated in Figure 3-3.

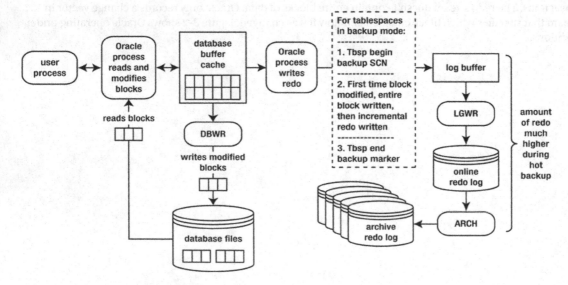

Figure 3-3. *Entire blocks are written to the redo stream*

To understand why Oracle logs the entire block to the redo stream, consider what happens during a restore and recovery. First, the backup files from the hot backup are restored. As explained earlier, these backup files contain corrupt blocks, owing to the split-block issue. But, it doesn't matter, because once Oracle recovers the data files, for any block that was modified during the hot backup, Oracle has an image copy of the block as it was before it was modified. Oracle uses the copy of the block it has in the redo stream as a starting point for the recovery (of that block). This process is illustrated in Figure 3-4.

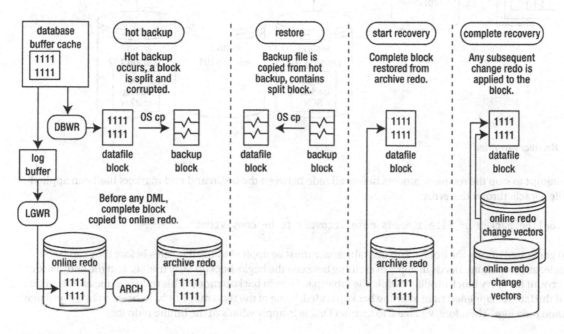

Figure 3-4. *Restore and recovery of a split block*

In this way, it doesn't matter if there are corrupt blocks in the hot backup files. Oracle always starts the recovery process for a block from a copy of the block (as it was before it was modified) in the redo stream.

Understanding the Need for Redo Generated During Backup

What happens if you experience a failure soon after you make a hot backup? Oracle knows when a tablespace was put in backup mode (begin backup system SCN written to the redo stream), and Oracle knows when the tablespace was taken out of backup mode (end-of-backup marker written to the redo stream). Oracle requires every archive redo log generated during that time frame to successfully recover the data files.

Figure 3-5 shows that, at minimum, the archive redo logs from sequence numbers 100 to 102 are required to recover the tablespace. These archive redo logs were generated during the hot backup.

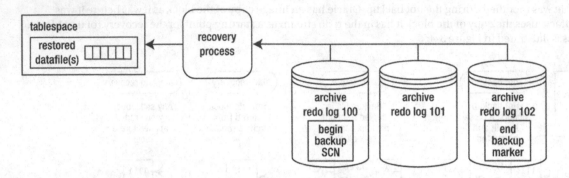

Figure 3-5. *Recovery applied*

If you attempt to stop the recovery process before all redo between the begin and end markers has been applied to the data file, Oracle throws this error:

```
ORA-01195: online backup of file 1 needs more recovery to be consistent
```

All redo generated during the hot backup of a tablespace must be applied to the data files before they can be opened. Oracle, at a minimum, needs to apply everything between the begin-backup SCN marker and the end-backup marker, to account for every block modified while the tablespace was in backup mode. This redo is in the archive redo log files; or, if the failure happened right after the backup ended, some of the redo may not have been archived and may be in the online redo logs. Therefore, you have to instruct Oracle to apply what's in the online redo logs.

Understanding That Data Files Are Updated

Note that, in Figures 3-2 and 3-3, the behavior of the database writer is, for the most part, unchanged throughout the backup procedure. The database writer continues to write blocks to data files, regardless of the backup mode of the database. The database writer doesn't care if a hot backup is taking place; its job is to write blocks from the buffer cache to the data files.

Every once in a while, you run into a DBA who states that the database writer doesn't write to data files during user-managed hot backups. This is a widespread misconception. Use some common sense: if the database writer isn't writing to the data files during a hot backup, then where are the changes being written? If the transactions are being written to somewhere other than the data files, how would those data files be resynchronized after the backup? It doesn't make any sense.

Some DBAs say, "The data file header is frozen, which means no changes to the data file." Oracle does freeze the SCN to indicate the start of the hot backup in the data file header and doesn't update that SCN until the tablespace is taken out of backup mode. This "frozen SCN" doesn't mean that blocks aren't being written to data files during the backup. You can easily demonstrate that a data file is written to during backup mode by doing this:

1. Put a tablespace in backup mode:

    ```
    SQL> alter tablespace users begin backup;
    ```

2. Create a table that has a character field:

    ```
    SQL> create table cc(cc varchar2(20)) tablespace users;
    ```

3. Insert a string into that table:

    ```
    SQL> insert into cc values('DBWR does write');
    ```

4. Force a checkpoint (which ensures that all modified buffers are written to disk):

    ```
    SQL> alter system checkpoint;
    ```

5. From the OS, use the strings and grep commands to search for the string in the data file:

    ```
    $ strings /u01/dbfile/O12C/users01.dbf | grep "DBWR does write"
    ```

6. Here is the output, proving that the database writer did write the data to disk:

    ```
    DBWR does write
    ```

7. Don't forget to take the tablespace out of backup mode:

    ```
    SQL> alter tablespace users end backup;
    ```

Performing a Complete Recovery of an Archivelog Mode Database

The term *complete recovery* means that you can recover all transactions that were committed before a failure occurred. *Complete recovery* doesn't mean you that completely restore and recover the entire database. For instance, if only one data file has experienced media failure, you need to restore and recover only the damaged data file to perform a complete recovery.

■ **Tip**   If you have access to a test or development database, take the time to walk through every step in each of the examples that follow. Going through these steps can teach you more about backup and recovery than any documentation.

The steps outlined here apply to any database backed up while in archivelog mode. It doesn't matter if you made a cold backup or hot backup. The steps to restore and recover data files are the same, as long as the database was in archivelog mode during the backup. For a complete recovery, you need

- to be able to restore the data files that have experienced media failure

- access to all archive redo logs generated since the last backup was started

- intact online redo logs

Here is the basic procedure for a complete recovery:

1. Place the database in mount mode; this prevents normal user transaction processing from reading/writing to data files being restored. (If you're not restoring the SYSTEM or UNDO tablespace, you have the option of opening the database and manually taking the data files offline before restoring them. If you do this, make sure you place the data files online after the recovery is complete.)

2. Restore the damaged data files with an OS copy utility.

3. Issue the appropriate SQL*Plus RECOVER command to apply any information required in the archive redo logs and online redo logs.

4. Alter the database open.

The next several sections demonstrate some common complete restore-and-recovery scenarios. You should be able to apply these basic scenarios to diagnose and recover from any complex situation you find yourself in.

Restoring and Recovering with the Database Offline

This section details a simple restore-and-recovery scenario. Described next are the steps to simulate a failure and then perform a complete restore and recovery. Try this scenario in a development database. Ensure that you have a good backup and that you aren't trying this experiment in a database that contains critical business data.

Before you start this example, create a table, and insert some data. This table and data are selected from the end of the complete recovery process to demonstrate a successful recovery:

```
SQL> create table foo(foo number) tablespace users;
SQL> insert into foo values(1);
SQL> commit;
```

Now, switch the online logs several times. Doing so ensures that you have to apply archive redo logs as part of the recovery:

```
SQL> alter system switch logfile;
```

The forward slash (/) reruns the most recently executed SQL statement:

```
SQL> /
SQL> /
SQL> /
```

Next, simulate a media failure by renaming the data file associated with the USERS tablespace. You can identify the name of this file with this query:

```
SQL> select file_name from dba_data_files where tablespace_name='USERS';

FILE_NAME
----------------------------------
/u01/dbfile/012C/users01.dbf
```

From the OS, rename the file:

```
$ mv /u01/dbfile/O12C/users01.dbf /u01/dbfile/O12C/users01.dbf.old
```

And, attempt to stop your database:

```
$ sqlplus / as sysdba
SQL> shutdown immediate;
```

You should see an error such as this:

```
ORA-01116: error in opening database file ...
```

If this were a real disaster, it would be prudent to navigate to the data file directory, list the files, and see if the file in question was in its correct location. You should also inspect the alert.log file to see if any relevant information is logged there by Oracle.

Now that you've simulated a media failure, the next several steps walk you through a restore and complete recovery.

Step 1. Place Your Database in Mount Mode

Before you place your database in mount mode, you may need to first shut it down, using ABORT:

```
$ sqlplus / as sysdba
SQL> shutdown abort;
SQL> startup mount;
```

Step 2. Restore the Data File from the Backup

The next step is to copy from the backup the data file that corresponds to the one that has had a failure:

```
$ cp /u01/hbackup/O12C/users01.dbf /u01/dbfile/O12C/users01.dbf
```

At this point, it's instructional to ponder what Oracle would do if you attempted to start your database. When you issue the ALTER DATABASE OPEN statement, Oracle inspects the SCN in the control file for each data file. You can examine this SCN by querying V$DATAFILE:

```
SQL> select checkpoint_change# from v$datafile where file#=4;

CHECKPOINT_CHANGE#
------------------
          3543963
```

Oracle compares the SCN in the control file with the SCN in the data file header. You can check the SCN in the data file header by querying V$DATAFILE_HEADER; for example,

```
select file#, fuzzy, checkpoint_change#
from v$datafile_header
where file#=4;

     FILE# FUZ CHECKPOINT_CHANGE#
---------- --- ------------------
         4 YES            3502285
```

Note that the SCN recorded in V$DATAFILE_HEADER is less than the SCN in V$DATAFILE for the same data file. If you attempt to open your database, Oracle throws an error stating that media recovery is required (meaning that you need to apply redo) to synchronize the SCN in the data file with the SCN in the control file. The FUZZY column is set to YES. This indicates that redo must be applied to the data file before it can be opened for use. Here is what happens when you try to open the database at this point:

```
SQL> alter database open;

alter database open;
alter database open
*
ERROR at line 1:
ORA-01113: file 4 needs media recovery...
```

Oracle doesn't let you open the database until the SCN in all data file headers matches the corresponding SCN in the control file.

Step 3. Issue the Appropriate RECOVER Statement

The archive redo logs and online redo logs have the information required to catch up the data file SCN to the control file SCN. You can apply redo to the data file that needs media recovery by issuing one of the following SQL*Plus statements:

- RECOVER DATAFILE
- RECOVER TABLESPACE
- RECOVER DATABASE

Because only one data file in this example needs to be recovered, the RECOVER DATAFILE statement is appropriate. However, keep in mind that you can run any of the previously listed RECOVER statements, and Oracle will figure out what needs to be recovered. In this particular scenario, you may find it easier to remember the name of the tablespace that contains the restored data file(s) than to remember the data file name(s). Next, any data files that need recovery in the USERS tablespace are recovered:

```
SQL> recover tablespace users;
```

At this point, Oracle uses the SCN in the data file header to determine which archive redo log or online redo log to use to begin applying redo. You can view the starting log sequence number that RMAN will use to begin the recovery process via the following query:

```
select
 HXFNM file_name
,HXFIL file_num
,FHTNM tablespace_name
,FHTHR thread
,FHRBA_SEQ sequence
from X$KCVFH
where FHTNM = 'USERS';
```

If all the redo required is in the online redo logs, Oracle applies that redo and displays this message:

```
Media recovery complete.
```

If Oracle needs to apply redo that is only contained in archived redo logs (meaning that the online redo log that contained the appropriate redo has already been overwritten), you're prompted with a recommendation from Oracle as to which archive redo log to apply first:

```
ORA-00279: change 3502285 generated at 11/02/2012 10:49:39 needed for thread 1
ORA-00289: suggestion : /u01/oraarch/012C/1_1_798283209.dbf
ORA-00280: change 3502285 for thread 1 is in sequence #1

Specify log: {<RET>=suggested | filename | AUTO | CANCEL}
```

You can press Enter or Return (<RET>) to have Oracle apply the suggested archive redo log file, specify a file name, specify AUTO to instruct Oracle to apply any suggested files automatically, or type CANCEL to cancel out of the recovery operation.

In this example, specify AUTO. Oracle applies all redo in all archive redo log files and online redo log files to perform a complete recovery:

```
AUTO
```

The last message displayed after all required archive redo and online redo have been applied is this:

```
Log applied.
Media recovery complete.
```

Step 4. Alter Your Database Open

After the media recovery is complete, you can open your database:

```
SQL> alter database open;
```

You can now verify that the transaction you committed just prior to the media failure was restored and recovered:

```
SQL> select * from foo;

     FOO
----------
       1
```

Restoring and Recovering with a Database Online

If you lose a data file associated with a tablespace other than SYSTEM and UNDO, you can restore and recover the damaged data file while leaving the database online. For this to work, any data files being restored and recovered must be taken offline first. You may be alerted to an issue with a data file in which a user is attempting to update a table and sees an error such as this:

```
SQL> insert into foo values(2);

ORA-01116: error in opening database file ...
```

You navigate to the OS directory that contains the data file and determine that it has been erroneously removed by a system administrator.

In this example the data file associated with the USERS tablespace is taken offline and subsequently restored and recovered while the rest of the database remains online. First, place take the data file offline:

```
SQL> alter database datafile '/u01/dbfile/012C/users01.dbf' offline;
```

Now, restore the appropriate data file from the backup location:

```
$ cp /u01/hbackup/012C/users01.dbf /u01/dbfile/012C/users01.dbf
```

In this situation, you can't use RECOVER DATABASE. The RECOVER DATABASE statement attempts to recover all data files in the database, of which the SYSTEM tablespace is part. The SYSTEM tablespace can't be recovered while the database is online. If you use the RECOVER TABLESPACE, all data files associated with the tablespace must be offline. In this case, it's more appropriate to recover at the data file level of granularity:

```
SQL> recover datafile '/u01/dbfile/012C/users01.dbf';
```

Oracle inspects the SCN in the data file header and determines which archive redo log or online redo log to use to start applying redo. If all redo required is in the online redo logs, you see this message:

```
Media recovery complete.
```

If the starting point for redo is contained only in an archive redo log file, Oracle suggests which file to start with:

```
ORA-00279: change 3502285 generated at 11/02/2012 10:49:39 needed for thread 1
ORA-00289: suggestion : /u01/oraarch/012C/1_1_798283209.dbf
ORA-00280: change 3502285 for thread 1 is in sequence #1

Specify log: {<RET>=suggested | filename | AUTO | CANCEL}
```

You can type AUTO to have Oracle apply all required redo in archive redo log files and online redo log files:

```
AUTO
```

If successful, you should see this message:

```
Log applied.
Media recovery complete.
```

You can now bring the data file back online:

```
SQL> alter database datafile '/u01/dbfile/O12C/users01.dbf' online;
```

If successful, you should see this:

```
Database altered.
```

Restoring Control Files

When you're dealing with user-managed backups, you usually restore the control file in one of these situations:

- A control file is damaged, and the file is multiplexed.
- All control files are damaged.

These two situations are covered in the following sections.

Restoring a Damaged Control File When Multiplexed

If you configure your database with more than one control file, you can shut down the database and use an OS command to copy an existing control file to the location of the missing control file. For example, from the initialization file, you know that two control files are used for this database:

```
SQL> show parameter control_files

NAME                        TYPE        VALUE
--------------------------- ----------- ------------------------------
control_files               string      /u01/dbfile/O12C/control01.ctl
                                        ,/u02/dbfile/O12C/control02.ctl
```

Suppose the control02.ctl file has become damaged. Oracle throws this error when querying the data dictionary:

```
ORA-00210: cannot open the specified control file...
```

When a good control file is available, you can shut down the database, move the old/bad control file (this preserves it, in the event that it is later needed for root cause analysis), and copy the existing good control file to the name and location of the bad control file:

```
SQL> shutdown abort;

$ mv /u02/dbfile/O12C/control02.ctl /u02/dbfile/O12C/control02.ctl.old
$ cp /u01/dbfile/O12C/control01.ctl /u02/dbfile/O12C/control02.ctl
```

Now, restart the database:

```
SQL> startup;
```

In this manner, you can restore a control file from an existing control file.

Restoring When All Control Files Are Damaged

If you lose all of your control files, you can restore one from a backup, or you can recreate the control file. As long as you have all your data files and any required redo (archive redo and online redo), you should be able to recover your database completely. The steps for this scenario are as follows:

1. Shut down the database.

2. Restore a control file from the backup.

3. Start the database in mount mode, and initiate database recovery, using the RECOVER DATABASE USING BACKUP CONTROLFILE clause.

4. For a complete recovery, manually apply the redo contained in the online redo logs.

5. Open the database with the OPEN RESETLOGS clause.

In this example all control files for the database were accidentally deleted, and Oracle subsequently reports this error:

```
ORA-00210: cannot open the specified control file...
```

Step 1. Shut Down the Database

First, shut down the database:

```
SQL> shutdown abort;
```

Step 2. Restore the Control File from the Backup

This database was configured with just one control file, which you copy back from the backup location, as shown:

```
$ cp /u01/hbackup/012C/controlbk.ctl /u01/dbfile/012C/control01.ctl
```

If more than one control file is being used, you have to copy the backup control file to each control file and location name listed in the CONTROL_FILES initialization parameter.

Step 3. Start the Database in Mount Mode, and Initiate Database Recovery

Next, start the database in mount mode:

```
SQL> startup mount;
```

After the control file(s) and data files have been copied back, you can perform a recovery. Oracle knows that the control file was from a backup (because it was created with the ALTER DATABASE BACKUP CONTROLFILE statement), so the recovery must be performed with the USING BACKUP CONTROLFILE clause:

```
SQL> recover database using backup controlfile;
```

At this point, you're prompted for the application of archive redo log files:

```
ORA-00279: change 3584431 generated at 11/02/2012 11:48:46 needed for thread 1
ORA-00289: suggestion : /u01/oraarch/O12C/1_8_798283209.dbf
ORA-00280: change 3584431 for thread 1 is in sequence #8

Specify log: {<RET>=suggested | filename | AUTO | CANCEL}
```

Type AUTO to instruct the recovery process to apply all archive redo logs automatically:

```
AUTO
```

The recovery process applies all available archive redo logs. The recovery process has no one way of determining where the archive redo stream ends and therefore tries to apply an archive redo log that doesn't exist, resulting in a message such as this:

```
ORA-00308: cannot open archived log '/u01/oraarch/O12C/1_10_798283209.dbf'
ORA-27037: unable to obtain file status
```

The prior message is to be expected. Now, attempt to open the database:

```
SQL> alter database open resetlogs;
```

Oracle throws the following error in this situation:

```
ORA-01113: file 1 needs media recovery
ORA-01110: data file 1: '/u01/dbfile/O12C/system01.dbf'
```

Step 4. Apply Redo Contained in the Online Redo Logs

Oracle needs to apply more redo to synchronize the SCN in the control file with the SCN in the data file header. In this scenario the online redo logs are still intact and contain the required redo. To apply redo contained in the online redo logs, first identify the locations and names of the online redo log files:

```
select a.sequence#, a.status, a.first_change#, b.member
from v$log a, v$logfile b
where a.group# = b.group#
order by a.sequence#;
```

Here is the partial output for this example:

```
SEQUENCE#  STATUS            FIRST_CHANGE# MEMBER
---------- ----------------  ------------- ------------------------------
         6 INACTIVE                3543960 /u01/oraredo/O12C/redo03a.rdo
         6 INACTIVE                3543960 /u02/oraredo/O12C/redo03b.rdo
         7 INACTIVE                3543963 /u02/oraredo/O12C/redo01b.rdo
         7 INACTIVE                3543963 /u01/oraredo/O12C/redo01a.rdo
         8 CURRENT                 3583986 /u02/oraredo/O12C/redo02b.rdo
         8 CURRENT                 3583986 /u01/oraredo/O12C/redo02a.rdo
```

Now, reinitiate the recovery process:

```
SQL> recover database using backup controlfile;
```

The recovery process prompts for an archive redo log that doesn't exist:

```
ORA-00279: change 3584513 generated at 11/02/2012 11:50:50 needed for thread 1
ORA-00289: suggestion : /u01/oraarch/012C/1_10_798283209.dbf
ORA-00280: change 3584513 for thread 1 is in sequence #10

Specify log: {<RET>=suggested | filename | AUTO | CANCEL}
```

Instead of supplying the recovery process with an archive redo log file, type in the name of a current online redo log file (you may have to attempt each online redo log until you find the one that Oracle needs). This instructs the recovery process to apply any redo in the online redo log:

```
/u01/oraredo/012C/redo01a.rdo
```

You should see this message when the correct online redo log is applied:

```
Log applied.
Media recovery complete.
```

Step 5. Open the Database with RESETLOGS

The database is completely recovered at this point. However, because a backup control file was used for the recovery process, the database must be opened with the RESETLOGS clause:

```
SQL> alter database open resetlogs;
```

Upon success, you should see this:

```
Database altered.
```

Performing an Incomplete Recovery of an Archivelog Mode Database

Incomplete recovery means that you don't restore all transactions that were committed before the failure. With this type of recovery, you're recovering to a point in time in the past, and transactions are lost. This is why incomplete recovery is also known as database point-in-time recovery (DBPITR).

Incomplete recovery doesn't mean that you're restoring and recovering only a subset of data files. In fact, with most incomplete scenarios, you have to restore all data files from the backup as part of the procedure. If you don't want to recover all data files, you first need to take offline any data files you don't intend to participate in the incomplete recovery process. When you initiate the recovery, Oracle will only recover data files that have an ONLINE value in the STATUS column of V$DATAFILE_HEADER.

You may want to perform an incomplete recovery for many different reasons:

- You attempt to perform a complete recovery but are missing the required archive redo logs or unarchived online redo log information.

- You want to restore the database back to a point in time in the past just prior to an erroneous user error (deleted data, dropped table, and so on).

- You have a testing environment in which you have a baseline copy of the database. After the testing is finished, you want to reset the database back to baseline for another round of testing.

You can perform user-managed incomplete recovery three ways:

- Cancel based

- SCN based

- Time based

Cancel based allows you to apply archive redo and halt the process at the boundary, based on an archive redo log file. For instance, say you're attempting to restore and recover your database, and you realize that you're missing an archive redo log. You have to stop the recover process at the point of your last good archive redo log. You initiate cancel-based incomplete recovery with the CANCEL clause of the RECOVER DATABASE statement:

```
SQL> recover database until cancel;
```

If you want to recover up to and including a certain SCN number, use SCN-based incomplete recovery. You may know from the alert log or from the output of LogMiner the point to which you want to restore to a certain SCN. Use the UNTIL CHANGE clause to perform this type of incomplete recovery:

```
SQL> recover database until change 12345;
```

If you know the time at which you want to stop the recovery process, use time-based incomplete recovery. For example, you may know that a table was dropped at a certain time and want to restore and recover the database up to the specified time. The format for a time-based recovery is always as follows: YYYY-MM-DD:HH24:MI:SS. Here is an example:

```
SQL> recover database until time '2012-10-21:02:00:00';
```

When you perform an incomplete recovery, you have to restore all data files that you plan to have online when the incomplete restoration is finished. Here are the steps for an incomplete recovery:

1. Shut down the database.

2. Restore all the data files from the backup.

3. Start the database in mount mode.

4. Apply redo (roll forward) to the desired point, and halt the recovery process (use cancel-, SCN-, or time-based recovery).

5. Open the database with the OPEN RESETLOGS clause.

The following example performs a cancel-based incomplete recovery. If the database is open, shut it down:

```
$ sqlplus / as sysdba
SQL> shutdown abort;
```

Next, copy all data files from the backup (either a cold or hot backup). This example restores all data files from a hot backup. For this example the current control file is intact and doesn't need to be restored. Here is a snippet of the OS copy commands for the database being restored:

```
cp /u01/hbackup/O12C/system01.dbf /u01/dbfile/O12C/system01.dbf
cp /u01/hbackup/O12C/sysaux01.dbf /u01/dbfile/O12C/sysaux01.dbf
cp /u01/hbackup/O12C/undotbs01.dbf /u01/dbfile/O12C/undotbs01.dbf
cp /u01/hbackup/O12C/users01.dbf /u01/dbfile/O12C/users01.dbf
cp /u01/hbackup/O12C/tools01.dbf /u01/dbfile/O12C/tools01.dbf
```

After the data files have been copied back, you can initiate the recovery process. This example performs a cancel-based incomplete recovery:

```
$ sqlplus / as sysdba
SQL> startup mount;
SQL> recover database until cancel;
```

At this point, the Oracle recovery process suggests an archive redo log to apply:

```
ORA-00279: change 3584872 generated at 11/02/2012 12:02:32 needed for thread 1
ORA-00289: suggestion : /u01/oraarch/O12C/1_1_798292887.dbf
ORA-00280: change 3584872 for thread 1 is in sequence #1
```

```
Specify log: {<RET>=suggested | filename | AUTO | CANCEL}
```

Apply the logs up to the point you where want to stop, and then type CANCEL:

```
CANCEL
```

This stops the recovery process. Now, you can open the database with the RESETLOGS clause:

```
SQL> alter database open resetlogs;
```

The database has been opened to a point in time in the past. The recovery is deemed incomplete because not all redo was applied.

■ **Tip** Now would be a good time to get a good backup of your database. This will give you a clean point from which to initiate a restore and recovery should a failure happen soon after you've opened your database.

PURPOSE OF OPEN RESETLOGS

Sometimes, you're required to open your database with the OPEN RESETLOGS clause. You may do this when recreating a control file, performing a restore and recovery with a backup control file, or performing an incomplete recovery. When you open your database with the OPEN RESETLOGS clause, it either wipes out any existing online redo log files or, if the files don't exist, recreates them. You can query the MEMBER column of V$LOGFILE to see which files are involved in an OPEN RESETLOGS operation.

Why would you want to wipe out what's in the online redo logs? Take the example of an incomplete recovery, in which the database is deliberately opened to a point in time in the past. In this situation the SCN information in the online redo logs contains transaction data that will never be recovered. Oracle forces you to open the database with OPEN RESETLOGS to purposely wipe out that information.

When you open your database with OPEN RESETLOGS, you create a new incarnation of your database and reset the log sequence number back to 1. Oracle requires a new incarnation so as to avoid accidentally using any old archive redo logs (associated with a separate incarnation of the database), in the event that another restore and recovery is required.

Summary

Some studies have indicated that airplane pilots who are over dependent on autopilot technology are less able to cope with catastrophic in-flight problems than the pilots who have spent considerable time flying without autopilot assistance. The over-autodependent pilots tend to forget key procedures when serious problems arise, whereas pilots who aren't as dependent on autopilot are more adept at diagnosing and resolving stressful in-flight failures.

Similarly, DBAs who understand how to backup, restore, and recover a database manually, using user-managed techniques, are more proficient at troubleshooting and resolving serious backup and recovery problems than DBAs who only navigate backup and recovery technology via screens. This is why I included this chapter in the book. Understanding what happens at each step and why the step is required is vital for complete knowledge of the Oracle backup and recovery architecture. This awareness translates into key troubleshooting skills when you're using Oracle tools such as RMAN (backup and recovery), Enterprise Manager, and Data Guard (disaster recovery, high availability, and replication).

The user-managed backup and recovery techniques covered in this chapter aren't taught or used much anymore. Most DBAs are (and should be) using RMAN for their Oracle backup and recovery requirements. However, it's critical for you to understand how cold backups and hot backups work. You may find yourself employed in a shop in which old technology has been implemented and needing to restore and recover the database, troubleshoot, or assist in migrating to RMAN. In these scenarios, you must fully understand the old backup technologies.

Now that you have an in-depth understanding of Oracle backup and recovery mechanics, you're ready to investigate RMAN. The next several chapters examine how to configure and use RMAN for backup and recovery.

■■■

Configuring RMAN

As stated earlier in the book, RMAN is Oracle's flagship B&R tool. RMAN is provided by default when you install the Oracle software (for both the Standard Edition and Enterprise Edition). RMAN offers a robust and flexible set of B&R features. The following list highlights some of the most salient qualities:

- Easy-to-use commands for backup, restore, and recovery.

- Ability to track which files have been backed up and where to. Manages the deletion of obsolete backups and archive redo logs.

- Parallelization: Can use multiple processes for backup, restore, and recovery.

- Incremental backups that only back up changes since the previous backup.

- Recovery at the database, tablespace, data file, table, or block level.

- Advanced compression and encryption features.

- Integration with media managers for tape backups.

- Backup validation and testing.

- Cross-platform data conversion.

- Data Recovery Advisor, which assists with diagnosing failures and proposing solutions.

- Ability to detect corrupt blocks in data files.

- Advanced reporting capabilities from the RMAN command line.

The goal of this chapter is to present enough information about RMAN that you can make reasonable decisions about how to implement a solid backup strategy. The basic RMAN components are described first, after which you walk through many of the decision points involved in implementing RMAN.

Understanding RMAN

RMAN consists of many different components. Figure 4-1 shows the interactions of the main RMAN pieces. Refer back to this diagram when reading through this section.

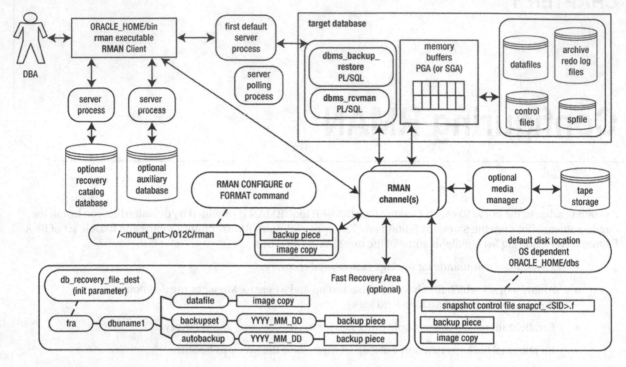

Figure 4-1. *RMAN architectural components*

The following list describes the RMAN architectural components:

DBA: Appears somewhat short and bald in the diagram, which isn't far from the truth (in my case).

Target database: The database being backed up by RMAN. You connect to the target database with the RMAN command-line TARGET parameter (see the next section for more details).

RMAN client: The rman utility from which you issue BACKUP, RESTORE, and RECOVER commands. On most database servers the rman utility is located in the ORACLE_HOME/bin directory (along with all the other Oracle utilities, such as sqlplus and expdp).

Oracle server processes: When you execute the rman client and connect to the target database, two Oracle server background processes are started. The first default server process interacts with the PL/SQL packages to coordinate the backup activities. The secondary polling process occasionally updates Oracle data dictionary structures.

Channel(s): The Oracle server processes for handling I/O between files being backed up (or restored) and the backup device (disk or tape).

PL/SQL packages: RMAN uses two internal PL/SQL packages (owned by SYS) to perform B&R tasks: DBMS_RCVMAN and DBMS_BACKUP_RESTORE. DBMS_RCVMAN accesses information in the control file and passes that to the RMAN server processes. The DBMS_BACKUP_RESTORE package performs most of RMAN's work. For example, this package creates the system calls that direct the channel processes to perform B&R operations.

Memory buffers (PGA or SGA): RMAN uses a memory area in the PGA (and sometimes in the SGA) as a buffer when reading from data files and copying subsequent blocks to back up files.

Auxiliary database: A database to which RMAN restores target database data files for the purpose of duplicating a database, creating a Data Guard standby database, or performing a DBPITR.

Backup/Back up: Can be either a noun or a verb. The physical files (backup) that store the backed up files; or, the act of copying and archiving (backing up) files. Backups can consist of backup sets and backup pieces or image copies.

Backup set: When you run an RMAN BACKUP command, by default, it creates one or more backup sets. A backup set is a logical RMAN construct that groups backup piece files. You can think of the relationship of a backup set to a backup piece as similar to the relationship between a tablespace and a data file: one is a logical construct, the other is a physical file.

Backup piece file: RMAN binary backup files. Each logical backup set consists of one or more backup piece files. These are the physical files that RMAN creates on disk or tape. They're binary, proprietary format files that only RMAN can read or write to. A backup piece can contain blocks from many different data files. Backup piece files are typically smaller than data files, because backup pieces only contain blocks that have been used in the data files.

Image copy: Initiated with the BACKUP AS COPY command. A type of backup in which RMAN creates identical copies of a data file, archive redo log file, or control file. Image copies can be operated on by OS utilities such as the Linux cp and mv commands. Image copies are used as part of incrementally updated image backups. Sometimes, it's preferable to use image copies rather than backup sets if you need to be able to restore quickly.

Recovery catalog: An optional database schema that contains tables used to store metadata information regarding RMAN backup operations. Oracle strongly recommends using a recovery catalog, because it provides more options for B&R.

Media manager: Third-party software that allows RMAN to back up files directly to tape. Backing up to tape is desirable when you don't have enough room to back up directly to disk or when disaster recovery requirements necessitate a backup to storage that can be easily moved offsite.

FRA: An optional disk area that RMAN can use for backups. You can also use the FRA to multiplex control files and online redo logs. You instantiate a fast recovery with the database initialization parameters DB_RECOVERY_FILE_DEST_SIZE and DB_RECOVERY_FILE_DEST.

Snapshot control file: RMAN requires a read-consistent view of the control file when either backing up the control file or synchronizing with the recovery catalog (if it's being used). In these situations, RMAN first creates a temporary copy (snapshot) of the control file. This allows RMAN to use a version of the control file that is guaranteed not to change while backing up the control file or synchronizing with the recovery catalog.

You can make several types of backups with RMAN:

Full backup: All modified blocks associated with the data file are backed up. A full backup is not a backup of the entire database. For example, you can make a full backup of one data file.

Incremental level 0 backup: Backs up the same blocks as a full backup. The only difference between a level 0 backup and a full backup is that you can use a level 0 backup with other incremental backups, but not a full backup.

Incremental level 1 backup: Backs up only blocks that have been modified since the previous backup. Level 1 incremental backups can be either differential or cumulative. A differential level 1 backup is the default and backs up all blocks that have been modified since the last level 0 or level 1 backup. A cumulative level 1 backup backs up all blocks that have changed since the last level 0 backup.

Incrementally updated backup: First creates an image copy of the data files, after which subsequent backups are incremental backups that are merged with the image copy. This is an efficient way to use image copies for backups. Media recoveries using incrementally updated backups are fast because the image copy of the data file is used during the restore.

Block change tracking: Database feature that keeps track of blocks that have changed in the database. A record of the changed blocks is kept in a binary file. RMAN can use the contents of the binary file to improve the performance of incremental backups: instead of having to scan all modified blocks in a data file, RMAN can determine which blocks have changed from the binary block change tracking.

Now that you understand the RMAN architectural components and the types of backups you can make, you're ready to start up RMAN and configure it for your environment.

Starting RMAN

Before you start RMAN and connect to your database, you need to ensure that you have the proper OS variables set and that you have access to an account with sys* privileges. Once those are in place, you can start RMAN and connect to your target database via the rman command-line utility. These are the same conditions that need to be in place before connecting to your database as a privileged user are described earlier in Chapter 1. You may want to review Chapter 1 now if you're not familiar with these conditions.

You can connect to RMAN either through the operating system command-line interface or through Enterprise Manager (EM). Using EM for backup and recovery is out of scope for this book. This book focuses on the command-line interface for its examples.

■ **Tip** Even if you use the screen based Enterprise Manager tool, it's useful to understand the RMAN commands used for backup and recovery operations. This knowledge the foundation for using RMAN regardless of the interface. This awareness is particularly useful when debugging and troubleshooting problems.

The following example assumes you have logged on to a Linux/Unix server using the oracle operating system account assigned to a privileged group, such as dba and have established the required OS variables. You can then invoke RMAN and connect to the target database as follows:

```
$ rman target /
```

Here is a snippet of the output:

```
connected to target database: O12C (DBID=3458744089)
```

If you're using a password file, then you need to specify the username and password that have been granted proper system privileges:

```
$ rman target <user>/<password>
```

If you're accessing your target database remotely via Oracle Net, you will need a password file on the target server and will also need to specify a connection string as follows:

```
$ rman target <user with sys* priv>/<password>@<database connection string>
```

You can also invoke RMAN and then connect to your target database as a second step, from the RMAN prompt:

```
$ rman
RMAN> connect target /
```

To exit RMAN, enter the exit command as follows:

```
RMAN> exit
```

■ **Tip** On Linux systems, when typing in the rman command from the OS prompt, if you get an error, such as "rman: can't open target," make sure your PATH variable includes ORACLE_HOME/bin directory before the /usr/X11R6/bin directory.

(NOT) CALLING RMAN FROM SQL*PLUS

I teach Oracle B&R classes at a local Institute of higher learning. Nearly every term, one of the students asks why the following RMAN command doesn't work:

```
SQL> rman
SP2-0042: unknown command "rman" - rest of line ignored.
```

The answer is short: the rman client is an OS utility, not an SQL*Plus function. You must invoke the rman client from the OS prompt.

Notice that when connecting to RMAN, you do not have to specify the sys* clause (like you do when connecting as a SYSDBA privileged user via SQL*Plus). This is because RMAN always requires that you connect as a user with sys* privileges. Therefore, you must connect to RMAN with either a user who is OS authenticated or a username/password with sys* privileges granted to it (and therefore exists in the password file). This is unlike SQL*Plus, where you have the option of connecting as a non-privileged user. In SQL*Plus, if you want to connect as a user with sys* privileges, you are required to specify a sys* clause when connecting.

If you attempt to connect to RMAN without the proper privileges, you'll receive this error:

```
ORA-01031: insufficient privileges
```

A useful way to troubleshoot the root cause of an ORA-01031 error is to attempt to log in to SQL*Plus with the same authentication information as when trying to connect through RMAN. This will help verify either that you are using an OS-authenticated account or that the username and password are correct. If OS authentication is working, you should be able to log in to SQL*Plus as follows:

```
$ sqlplus / as sysdba
```

If you're using a password file, you can verify that the username and password are correct (and that the user has sysdba privileges) by logging in as shown here:

```
$ sqlplus <username>/<password> as sysdba
```

If you receive an ORA-01031 error from attempting to log in to SQL*Plus, then either you aren't using an OS-authenticated account or your username and password combination does not match what is stored in the password file (for users attempting to connect with sys* privileges).

Once connected to RMAN, you can issue administrative commands, such as startup, shutdown, backup, restore, and recover. For example, if you want to start and stop your database, you can do so from within RMAN as follows:

```
$ rman target /
RMAN> startup;
RMAN> shutdown immediate;
```

This saves you the inconvenience of having to jump back and forth between SQL*Plus and RMAN (when issuing administrative commands).

RUNNING SQL COMMANDS FROM WITHIN RMAN

Starting with Oracle 12c, you can run many SQL commands directly from the RMAN command line. In prior versions of Oracle, when running certain SQL commands from within RMAN, you had to specify the sql clause. For example, say you wanted to run the alter system switch logfile command. Prior to Oracle 12c, you would have to specify that command as shown:

```
RMAN> sql 'alter system switch logfile';
```

In Oracle 12c, you can now run the SQL directly:

```
RMAN> alter system switch logfile;
```

This is a nice ease-of-use enhancement because it eliminates the need for additional clauses and quotes around the command.

RMAN Architectural Decisions

If archiving is enabled for your database (see Chapter 2 for details on archiving), you can use RMAN out of the box to run commands such as this to back up your entire target database:

```
$ rman target /
RMAN> backup database;
```

If you experience a media failure, you can restore all data files, as follows:

```
RMAN> shutdown immediate;
RMAN> startup mount;
RMAN> restore database;
```

After your database is restored, you can fully recover it:

```
RMAN> recover database;
RMAN> alter database open;
```

You're good to go, right? No, not quite. RMAN's default attributes are reasonably set for simple backup requirements. The RMAN out-of-the-box settings may be appropriate for small development or test databases. But, for any type of business critical database, you need to consider carefully where the backups are stored, how long to store backups on disk or tape, which RMAN features are appropriate for the database, and so on. The following sections in this chapter walk you through many of the B&R architectural decisions necessary to implementing RMAN in a production environment. RMAN has a vast and robust variety of options for customizing B&R; and, typically, you don't need to implement many of RMAN's features. However, each time you implement RMAN to back up a production database, you should think through each decision point and decide whether you require an attribute.

Table 4-1 summarizes the RMAN implementation decisions and recommendations. Each of the decision points in the table is elaborated on in subsequent sections. Many DBAs will have differing opinions concerning some of these recommendations; that's fine. The point is that you need to consider each architectural aspect and determine what makes sense for your business requirements.

Table 4-1. *Overview of Architectural Decisions and Recommendations*

Decision Point	Recommendation
1. Running the RMAN client remotely or locally	Run the client locally on the target database server.
2. Specifying the backup user	Use SYS unless you have a security requirement that dictates otherwise.
3. Using online or offline backups	Depends on your business requirements. Most production databases require online backups, which means that you must enable archiving.
4. Setting the archive redo log destination and file format	If you're using an FRA, archive logs are written there with a default format. I prefer to use the LOG_ARCHIVE_DEST_N initialization parameter to specifically set the location outside the FRA.
5. Configuring the RMAN backup location and file format	Depends on your business requirements. Some shops require tape backups. If you're using disk, place the backups in the FRA, or specify a location via channel settings. I prefer not to use an FRA and to explicitly specify the location and file format via a CONFIGURE command.
6. Setting the autobackup of the control file	Always enable autobackup of the control file.
7. Specifying the location of the autobackup of the control file	Either place it in the FRA, or configure a location. I prefer to write the autobackup of the control file to the same location as that of the database backups.

(*continued*)

Table 4-1. (*continued*)

Decision Point	Recommendation
8. Backing up archive redo logs	Depends on your business requirements. For many environments, I back up the archive redo logs on a daily basis, with the same command I use to back up the database.
9. Determining the location for the snapshot control file	Use the default location.
10. Using a recovery catalog	Depends on your business requirements. For many environments, I don't use a recovery catalog. Oracle recommends that you do use a recovery catalog. If the RMAN retention policy is greater than CONTROL_FILE_RECORD_KEEP_TIME, then I recommend that you use a recovery catalog.
11. Using a media manager	This is required for backing up directly to tape.
12. Setting the CONTROL_FILE_RECORD_KEEP_TIME initialization parameter	Usually, the default of 7 days is sufficient.
13. Configuring RMAN's backup retention policy	Depends on your database and business requirements. For many environments, I use a backup retention redundancy of 1 or 2.
14. Configuring the archive redo logs' deletion policy	Depends on your database and business requirements. In many scenarios, applying the backup retention policy to the archive redo logs is sufficient (this is the default behavior).
15. Setting the degree of parallelism	Depends on the available hardware resources and business requirements. For most production servers, on which there are multiple CPUs, I configure a degree of parallelism of 2 or more.
16. Using backup sets or image copies	I prefer backup sets. Backup sets are generally smaller than image copies and easier to manage.
17. Using incremental backups	Use incremental backups for large databases when a small percentage of the database changes between backups and when you want to conserve on disk space. I often use incremental backups in data warehouse–type databases.
18. Using incrementally updated backups	Use this approach if you require image copies of data files.
19. Using block change tracking	Use this to improve the performance of incremental backups. For large, data warehouse–type databases, block change tracking can result in significant time savings for backups.
20. Configuring binary compression	Depends on your business requirements. Compressed backups consume less space but require more CPU resources (and time) for backup and restore operations.
21. Configuring encryption	Depends on your business requirements.
22. Configuring miscellaneous settings	You can set many channel-related properties, such as the backup set size and backup piece size. Configure as needed.
23. Configuring informational output	Configure the OS variable NLS_DATE_FORMAT to display date and time. Use SET ECHO ON and SHOW ALL to display RMAN commands and settings.

1. Running the RMAN Client Remotely or Locally

It's possible to run the rman utility from a remote server and connect to a target database via Oracle Net:

```
$ rman target sys/foo@remote_db
```

This allows you to run RMAN backups on disparate remote servers from one central location. When you run RMAN remotely, the backup files are always created on the target database server.

Whenever possible, I run the rman client locally on the target server and connect, like this:

```
$ rman target /
```

This approach is simple and adequate for most requirements. You don't have to worry about network issues or password files, and there are never compatibility issues with the rman client and the target database. If you run RMAN remotely, you need to be sure the remote rman executable is compatible with the target database. For example, you may establish that the remote rman executable you're running is an Oracle 12c version of the RMAN client and need to determine if it's possible to connect that client to a remote Oracle 9i target database. If you run the rman client locally on the target server, there is never a compatibility issue because the rman client is always the same version as the target database.

2. Specifying the Backup User

As discussed previously, RMAN requires that you use a database user with SYSDBA privileges. Whether I'm running RMAN from the command line or invoking RMAN in a script, in most scenarios, I connect directly as SYS to the target database. For example, here is how I connect to RMAN from the command line:

```
$ rman target /
```

Some DBAs don't use this approach; they opt to set up a user separate from SYS and cite security concerns as a rationale for doing this.

I prefer to use the SYS account directly, because when connecting to RMAN locally on the server, there is no need to specify a username and password. This means that you never have to hard-code usernames and passwords into any backup scripts or specify a username and password on the command line that can be viewed by rogue developers or managers looking over your shoulder.

3. Using Online or Offline Backups

Most production databases have 24-7 availability requirements. Therefore, your only option is online RMAN backups. Your database must be in archivelog mode for online backups. You need to consider carefully to place archive redo logs, how to format them, how often to back them up, and how long to retain them before deletion. These topics are discussed in subsequent sections.

■ **Note** If you make offline backups, you must shut down your database with IMMEDIATE, NORMAL, or TRANSACTIONAL and then place it in mount mode. RMAN needs the database in mount mode so that it can read from and write to the control file.

---

4. Setting the Archive Redo Log Destination and File Format

Enabling archive redo log mode is a prerequisite for making online backups (see Chapter 2 for a full discussion of architectural decisions regarding the archive redo log destination and format and how to enable/disable archivelog mode).

When archivelog mode is enabled, Oracle writes the archive redo logs to one or more of the following locations (you can configure archive redo logs to be written to the FRA as well as to several other locations that you manually set via initialization parameters):

- Default location

- FRA

- Location specified via the LOG_ARCHIVE_DEST_N initialization parameter(s)

If you don't use an FRA, and if you don't explicitly set the archive redo log destination via a LOG_ARCHIVE_DEST_N initialization parameter, then by default the archive redo logs are written to an OS-dependent location. On many Linux/Unix boxes the default location is the ORACLE_HOME/dbs directory. The default file name format for archive redo logs is %t_%s_%r.dbf.

If you enable an FRA (and don't set LOG_ARCHIVE_DEST_N), then, by default, the archive redo logs are written to a directory in the FRA. The default file name format of the of archive redo log files created in the FRA is an OMF format. The files are stored in a subdirectory given the same name as the database's unique name; for example,

/<fra>/<dbuname>/archivelog/<YYYY_MM_DD>/o1_mf_1_1078_68dx5dyj_.arc

Oracle recommends using an FRA. I prefer not to use an FRA because I don't like to be surprised with a hung database when there are issues with the FRA's filling up and not being purged of old files quickly enough. Instead, I use the LOG_ARCHIVE_DEST_N parameter to set the location of the archive redo log files. Here is an example:

log_archive_dest_1='LOCATION=/oraarch1/CHNPRD'

I also prefer to use this format for the default archivelog file name:

log_archive_format='%t_%s_%r.arc'

■ **Tip** Sometimes, DBAs use .dbf as an extension for both data files and archive redo log files. I prefer to use .arc for the archive redo log files. The .arc extension avoids the potentially confusing task of identifying a file as an archive redo log file or a live database data file.

---

5. Configuring the RMAN Backup Location and File Format

When you run a BACKUP command for disk-based backups, RMAN creates backup pieces in one of the following locations:

- Default location

- FRA

- Location specified via the BACKUP...FORMAT command

- Location specified via the CONFIGURE CHANNEL...FORMAT command

Of these choices, I lean toward the last of them; I prefer specifying a target location via a backup channel.

Default Location

If you don't configure any RMAN variables and don't set up an FRA, by default RMAN allocates one disk-based channel and writes the backup files to a default location. For example, you can run the following command without configuring any RMAN parameters:

```
RMAN> backup database;
```

The default location varies by OS. In many Linux/Unix environments the default location is `ORACLE_HOME/dbs`. The default format of the name of the backup files created is an OMF format; for example,

```
<ORACLE_HOME>/dbs/01ln9g7e_1_1
```

■ **Tip** The default location is okay for small development databases. However, for most other environments (especially production), you'll need to plan ahead for how much disk space you'll need for backups and explicitly set the location for the backups via one of the other methods (such as implementing an FRA or `CONFIGURE CHANNEL`).

FRA

When backing up to disk, if you don't explicitly instruct RMAN to write the backups to a specific location (via the `FORMAT` or `CONFIGURE` command), and you're using an FRA, RMAN automatically writes the backup files to directories in the FRA. The files are stored in a subdirectory with the same name as the database's unique name. Also, the default format of the name of the backup files created in the FRA is an OMF format; for example,

```
/<fra>/<dbuname>/backupset/<YYYY_MM_DD>/o1_mf_nnndf_TAG20100907T025402_68czfbdf_.bkp
```

I don't usually use an FRA for the placement of RMAN backups. In many of the environments I work in, there isn't enough disk space on a single mount point to accommodate the entirety of the database backups. In such situations, you need to allocate two or more channels that point to different mount points. Using an FRA in these environments is somewhat unwieldy.

Also, for performance reasons, you may want to instruct RMAN to write to multiple disk locations. If you can ensure that different mount points are based on different physical disks and are written to by separate controllers, you can reduce I/O contention by allocating multiple channels pointing to separate mount points.

When you're using an FRA, RMAN automatically creates separate directories when backing up a database for the first time on a given date. I prefer to have the backups written to one directory and not separate the directories and backups by date. I find it easier to manage, maintain, and troubleshoot the backups if I use one standard directory for each database on each server.

BACKUP...FORMAT

If you've configured an FRA and don't want to place RMAN backup files in the FRA automatically, you can directly specify where you want backups to be placed when you issue the BACKUP command; for example,

```
RMAN> backup database format '/u01/O12C/rman/rman_%U.bkp';
```

Here is a corresponding file generated by RMAN:

```
/u01/O12C/rman/rman_0jnv0557_1_1.bkp
```

The %U instructs RMAN to dynamically construct a unique string for the backup file name. A unique name is required in most situations, because RMAN won't write over the top of a file that already exists. This is important, because if you instruct RMAN to write in parallel, it needs to create unique file names for each channel; for example,

```
RMAN> configure device type disk parallelism 2;
```

Now, when you run the BACKUP command, you see this message:

```
RMAN> backup database format '/u01/O12C/rman/rman_%U.bkp';
```

RMAN allocates multiple channels and writes in parallel to two different backup files. The U% in the format string guarantees that unique file names are created.

CONFIGURE CHANNEL...FORMAT

I don't usually use the BACKUP...FORMAT syntax to specify the location for RMAN backups. I prefer to use the CONFIGURE CHANNEL...FORMAT command. This is because I'm frequently writing to multiple disk locations and need the flexibility to specify directories located on different mount points. Here is a typical configuration specifying CONFIGURE CHANNEL...FORMAT:

```
RMAN> configure device type disk parallelism 3;
RMAN> configure channel 1 device type disk format '/u01/O12C/rman/rman1_%U.bk';
RMAN> configure channel 2 device type disk format '/u02/O12C/rman/rman2_%U.bk';
RMAN> configure channel 3 device type disk format '/u03/O12C/rman/rman3_%U.bk';
```

In these lines of code, you should configure the device-type parallelism degree to match the number of channels that you allocated. RMAN only allocates the number of channels as specified by the degree of parallelism; other configured channels are ignored. For instance, if you specify a degree of parallelism of 2, RMAN allocates only two channels, regardless of the number of channels you configured via the CONFIGURE CHANNEL command.

In this example of configuring three channels, suppose the BACKUP command is issued, like this:

```
RMAN> backup database;
```

RMAN allocates three channels, all on separate mount points (/u01, /u02, /u03), and writes in parallel to the specified locations. RMAN creates as many backup pieces in the three locations as it deems necessary to create a backup of the database.

If you need to unconfigure a channel, do so as follows:

```
RMAN> configure channel 3 device type disk clear;
```

■ **Note**   Also consider what happens if you configure a degree of parallelism higher than the number of preconfigured channels. RMAN will open a channel for each degree of parallelism, and if the number of channels opened is greater than the number of preconfigured channels, for the unconfigured channels, RMAN will write backup files to the FRA (if configured) or the default location.

---

6. Setting the Autobackup of the Control File

You should always configure RMAN to back up the control file automatically after running any RMAN BACKUP or COPY command or after you make physical changes to the database that result in updates to the control file (such as adding/removing a data file). Use the SHOW command to display the current setting of the control file autobackup:

```
RMAN> show controlfile autobackup;
```

Here is some sample output:

```
RMAN configuration parameters for database with db_unique_name O12C are:
CONFIGURE CONTROLFILE AUTOBACKUP ON;
```

The following line of code shows how to enable automatic backup of the control file feature:

```
RMAN> configure controlfile autobackup on;
```

The automatic control file backup always goes into its own backup set. When autobackup of the control file is enabled, if you're using an spfile, it's automatically backed up along with the control file.

If, for any reason, you want to disable automatic backup of the control file, you can do so as follows:

```
RMAN> configure controlfile autobackup off;
```

■ **Note** If autobackup of the control file is off, then any time you back up data file 1 (SYSTEM tablespace data file), RMAN automatically backs up the control file.

---

7. Specifying the Location of the Autobackup of the Control File

When you enable autobackup of the control file, RMAN creates the backup of the control file in one of the following locations:

- Default location
- FRA
- Location specified via the CONFIGURE CONTROLFILE AUTOBACKUP FORMAT command

If you aren't using an FRA, or if you haven't specified a location for the control file autobackups, the control file autobackup is written to an OS-dependent default location. In Linux/Unix environments the default location is ORACLE_HOME/dbs; for example,

```
/u01/app/oracle/product/12.1.0.1/db_1/dbs/c-3423216220-20130109-01
```

If you've enabled an FRA, then RMAN automatically writes the control file autobackup files to directories in the FRA, using an OMF format for the name; for example,

```
/<fra>/<dbuname>/autobackup/<YYYY_MM_DD>/o1_mf_s_729103049_68fho9z2_.bkp
```

I don't usually use the default location or the FRA for control file autobackups. I prefer these backups to be placed in the same directory the database backups are in. Here is an example:

```
RMAN> configure controlfile autobackup format for device type disk to
'/u01/ORA12C/rman/rman_ctl_%F.bk';
```

If you want to set the autobackup format back to the default, do so as follows:

```
RMAN> configure controlfile autobackup format for device type disk clear;
```

8. Backing Up Archive Redo Logs

You should back up your archive redo logs on a regular basis. The archivelog files shouldn't be removed from disk until you've backed them up at least once. I usually like to keep on disk any archive redo logs that have been generated since the last good RMAN backup.

Generally, I instruct RMAN to back up the archive redo logs while the data files are being backed up. This is a sufficient strategy in most situations. Here is the command to back up the archive redo logs along with the data files:

```
RMAN> backup database plus archivelog;
```

Sometimes, if your database generates a great deal of redo, you may need to back up your archive redo logs at a frequency different from that of the data files. DBAs may back up the archive redo logs two or three times a day; after the logs are backed up, the DBAs delete them to make room for more current archivelog files.

In most situations, you don't need any archive redo logs that were generated before your last good backup. For example, if a data file has experienced media failure, you need to restore the data file from a backup and then apply any archive redo logs that were generated during and after the backup of the data file.

On some occasions, you may need archive redo logs that were generated before the last backup. For instance, you may experience a media failure, attempt to restore your database from the last good backup, find corruption in that backup, and therefore need to restore from an older backup. At that point, you need a copy of all archive redo logs that have been generated since that older backup was made.

9. Determining the Location for the Snapshot Control File

RMAN requires a read-consistent view of the control file for the following tasks:

- Synchronizing with the recovery catalog
- Backing up the current control file

RMAN creates a snapshot copy of the current control file that it uses as a read-consistent copy while it's performing these tasks. This ensures that RMAN is working from a copy of the control file that isn't being modified.

The default location of the snapshot control file is OS specific. On Linux platforms the default location/format is ORACLE_HOME/dbs/snapcf_@.f. Note that the default location isn't in the FRA (even if you've implemented an FRA).

You can display the current snapshot control file details, using the SHOW command:

```
RMAN> show snapshot controlfile name;
```

Here is some sample output:

```
CONFIGURE SNAPSHOT CONTROLFILE NAME TO
 '/ora01/app/oracle/product/12.1.0.1/db_1/dbs/snapcf_o12c.f'; # default
```

For most situations the default location and format of the snapshot control file are sufficient. This file doesn't use much space or have any intensive I/O requirements. I recommend that you use the default setting.

If you have a good reason to configure the snapshot control file to a nondefault location, you can do so as follows:

```
RMAN> configure snapshot controlfile name to '/u01/O12C/rman/snapcf.ctl';
```

If you accidentally configure the snapshot control file location to a nonexistent directory, then when running a BACKUP or COPY command, the autobackup of the control file will fail, with this error:

```
ORA-01580: error creating control backup file...
```

You can set the snapshot control file back to the default, like this:

```
RMAN> configure snapshot controlfile name clear;
```

10. Using a Recovery Catalog

RMAN always stores its latest backup operations in the target database control file. You can set up an optional recovery catalog to store metadata regarding RMAN backups. The recovery catalog is a separate schema (usually in a database different from that of the target database) that contains database objects (tables, indexes, and so on) that store the RMAN backup information. The recovery catalog doesn't store RMAN backup pieces—only backup metadata.

The main advantages of using a recovery catalog are as follows:

- Provides a secondary repository for RMAN metadata. If you lose all your control files and backups of your control files, you can still retrieve RMAN metadata from the recovery catalog.

- Stores RMAN metadata for a much longer period than is possible when you just use a control file for the repository.

- Offers access to all RMAN features. Some restore and recovery features are simpler when using a recovery catalog.

The disadvantage of using a recovery catalog is that this is another database you have to set up, maintain, and back up. Additionally, when you start a backup and attempt to connect to the recovery catalog, if the recovery catalog isn't available for any reason (server down, network issues, and so on), you must decide whether you want to continue with the backup without a recovery catalog.

You must also be aware of versioning aspects when using a recovery catalog. You need to make sure the version of the database you use to store the recovery catalog is compatible with the version of the target database. When you upgrade a target database, be sure the recovery catalog is upgraded (if necessary).

■ **Note**   See Chapter 5 for details on how to implement a recovery catalog.

RMAN works fine with or without a recovery catalog. For several of the databases I maintain, I don't use a recovery catalog; this eliminates having to set it up and maintain it. For me, simplicity takes precedence over the features available with the recovery catalog.

However, if you have good business reasons for using a recovery catalog, then implement and use one. The recovery catalog isn't that difficult to set up and maintain, and Oracle recommends that you use it.

11. Using a Media Manager

A media manager is required for RMAN to back up directly to tape. Several vendors provide this feature (for a cost). Media managers are used in large database environments, such as data warehouses, in which you may not have enough room to back up a database to disk. You may also have a disaster recovery requirement to back up directly to tape.

If you have such requirements, then you should purchase a media management package and implement it. If you don't need to back up directly to tape, there's no need to implement a media manager. RMAN works fine backing up directly to disk.

Keep in mind that many shops use RMAN to back up directly to disk and then have the system administrator back up the RMAN backups to tape afterward. If you do this, you have to be sure your RMAN backups aren't running while the tape backups are running (because you may get partial files backed up to tape).

12. Setting the CONTROL_FILE_RECORD_KEEP_TIME Initialization Parameter

The CONTROL_FILE_RECORD_KEEP_TIME initialization parameter specifies the minimum number of days a reusable record in the control file is retained before the record can be overwritten. The RMAN metadata are stored in the reusable section of the control file and therefore are eventually overwritten.

If you're using a recovery catalog, then you don't need to worry about this parameter because RMAN metadata are stored in the recovery catalog indefinitely. Therefore, when you use a recovery catalog, you can access any historical RMAN metadata.

If you're using only the control file as the RMAN metadata repository, then the information stored there will eventually be overwritten. The default value for CONTROL_FILE_RECORD_KEEP_TIME is 7 days:

```
SQL> show parameter control_file_record_keep_time

NAME                                 TYPE        VALUE
------------------------------------ ----------- ---------
control_file_record_keep_time        integer     7
```

You can set the value to anything from 0 to 365 days. Setting the value to 0 means that the RMAN metadata information can be overwritten at any time.

The CONTROL_FILE_RECORD_KEEP_TIME parameter was more critical in older versions of Oracle, in which it wasn't easy to repopulate the control file with RMAN information, in the event that metadata were overwritten. Starting with Oracle 10g, you can use the CATALOG command to quickly make the control file aware of RMAN backup files.

If you run daily backups, then I recommend that you leave this parameter at 7 days. However, if you only back up your database once a month, or if, for some reason, you have a retention policy greater than 7 days, and you're not using a recovery catalog, then you may want to consider increasing the value. The downside to increasing this parameter is that if you have a significant amount of RMAN backup activity, this can increase the size of your control file.

13. Configuring RMAN's Backup Retention Policy

RMAN retention policies allow you to specify how long you want to retain backups. RMAN has two mutually exclusive methods of specifying a retention policy:

- Recovery window
- Number of backups (redundancy)

Recovery Window

With a recovery window, you specify a number of days in the past for which you want to be able recover to any point in that window. For example, if you specify a retention policy window of 5 days, then RMAN doesn't mark as obsolete backups of data files and archive redo logs that are required to be able to restore to any point in that 5-day window:

```
RMAN> configure retention  policy to recovery window of 5 days;
```

For the specified recovery, RMAN may need backups older than the 5-day window because it may need an older backup to start with to be able to recover to the recovery point specified. For example, suppose your last good backup was made 6 days ago, and now you want to recover to 4 days in the past. For this recovery window, RMAN needs the backup from 6 days ago to restore and recover to the point specified.

Redundancy

You can also specify that RMAN keep a minimum number of backups. For instance, if redundancy is set to 2, then RMAN doesn't mark as obsolete the latest two backups of data files and archive redo log files:

```
RMAN> configure retention policy to redundancy 2;
```

I find that a retention policy based on redundancy is easier to work with and more predictable with regard to how long backups are retained. If I set redundancy to 2, I know that RMAN won't mark as obsolete the latest two backups. In contrast, the recovery window retention policy depends on the frequency of the backups and the window length to determine whether a backup is obsolete.

Deleting Backups, Based on Retention Policy

You can report on backups that RMAN has determined to be obsolete per the retention policy, as follows:

```
RMAN> report obsolete;
```

To delete obsolete backups, run the DELETE OBSOLETE command:

```
RMAN> delete obsolete;
```

You're prompted with this:

```
Do you really want to delete the above objects (enter YES or NO)?
```

If you're scripting the procedure, you can specify the delete not to prompt for input:

```
RMAN> delete noprompt obsolete;
```

I usually have the DELETE NOPROMPT OBSOLETE command coded into the shell script that backs up the database. This instructs RMAN to delete any obsolete backups and obsolete archive redo logs, as specified by the retention policy (see the section "Segueing from Decisions to Action," later in this chapter, for an example of how to automate the deleting of obsolete backups with a shell script).

Clearing the Retention Policy

The default retention policy is redundancy of 1. You can completely disable the RMAN retention policy via the TO NONE command.

```
RMAN> configure retention policy to none;
```

When the policy is set to NONE, no backups are ever considered obsolete and therefore cannot be removed via the DELETE OBSOLETE command. This normally is not the behavior you want. You want to let RMAN delete backups per a retention policy based on a window or number of backups.

To set the retention policy back to the default, use the CLEAR command:

```
RMAN> configure retention policy clear;
```

14. Configuring the Archive Redo Logs' Deletion Policy

In most scenarios, I have RMAN delete the archive redo logs based on the retention policy of the database backups. This is the default behavior. You can view the database retention policy, using the SHOW command:

```
RMAN> show retention policy;
CONFIGURE RETENTION POLICY TO REDUNDANCY 1; # default
```

To remove archive redo logs (and backup pieces) based on the database retention policy, run the following:

```
RMAN> delete obsolete;
```

As of Oracle 11g, you can specify an archive redo log deletion policy that is separate from that of the database backups. This deletion policy applies to archive redo logs both outside and in the FRA.

■ **Note**   Prior to Oracle 11g the archive deletion policy only applied to archive redo logs associated with a standby database.

To configure an archive redo log deletion policy, use the CONFIGURE ARCHIVELOG DELETION command. The following command configures the archive redo deletion policy so that archive redo logs aren't deleted until they have been backed up twice to disk:

```
RMAN> configure archivelog deletion policy to backed up 2 times to device type disk;
```

To have RMAN delete obsolete archive redo logs, as defined by the archivelog deletion policy, issue the following command:

```
RMAN> delete archivelog all;
```

■ **Tip** Run the CROSSCHECK command before running the DELETE command. Doing so ensures that RMAN is aware of whether a file is on disk.

To see whether a retention policy has been set specifically for the archive redo log files, use this command:

```
RMAN> show archivelog deletion policy;
```

To clear the archive deletion policy, do this:

```
RMAN> configure archivelog deletion policy clear;
```

15. Setting the Degree of Parallelism

You can significantly increase the performance of RMAN backup and restore operations if your database server is equipped with the hardware to support multiple channels. If your server has multiple CPUs and multiple storage devices (disks or tape devices), then you can improve performance by enabling multiple backup channels.

If you require better performance from backup and restore operations and have hardware that facilitates parallel operations, you should enable parallelism and perform tests to determine the optimal degree. If your hardware can take advantage of parallel RMAN channels, there is little downside to enabling parallelism.

If you have multiple CPUs, but just one storage device location, you can enable multiple channels to write to and read from one location. For example, if you're backing up to an FRA, you can still take advantage of multiple channels by enabling parallelism. Suppose you have four CPUs on a server and want to enable a corresponding degree of parallelism:

```
RMAN> configure device type disk parallelism 4;
```

You can also write to separate locations in parallel by configuring multiple channels associated with different mount points; for example,

```
RMAN> configure device type disk parallelism 4;
RMAN> configure channel 1 device type disk format '/u01/O12C/rman/rman1_%U.bk';
RMAN> configure channel 2 device type disk format '/u02/O12C/rman/rman2_%U.bk';
RMAN> configure channel 3 device type disk format '/u03/O12C/rman/rman3_%U.bk';
RMAN> configure channel 4 device type disk format '/u04/O12C/rman/rman4_%U.bk';
```

This code configures four channels that write to separate locations on disk. When you configure separate channels for different locations, make sure you enable the degree of parallelism to match the number of configured device channels. If you allocate more channels than the specified degree of parallelism, RMAN only writes to the number of channels specified by the degree of parallelism and ignores the other channels.

If you need to clear the degree of parallelism, you can do so as follows:

```
RMAN> configure device type disk clear;
```

Similarly, to clear the channel device types, use the CLEAR command. This example clears channel 4:

```
RMAN> configure channel 4 device type disk clear;
```

16. Using Backup Sets or Image Copies

When you issue an RMAN BACKUP command, you can specify that the backup be one of the following:

- Backup set

- Image copy

A backup set is the default type of RMAN backup. A backup set contains backup pieces, which are binary files that only RMAN can write to or read from. Backup sets are desirable because they're generally smaller than the data files being backed up. If you're using Oracle 10g Release 2 or higher, RMAN automatically attempts to create backup pieces with unused block compression. In this mode, RMAN reads a bitmap to determine which blocks are allocated and only reads from those blocks in the data files. This feature is supported only for disk-based backup sets and Oracle Secure Backup tape backups.

If you're using a database version prior to Oracle 10g Release 2, by default, backup sets are created, using null block compression (sometimes referred to, more aptly, as block skipping). In this mode, RMAN checks blocks in the data file; if the blocks haven't been used, they aren't backed up.

■ **Note** RMAN can also create backup sets using true binary compression. This is the type of compression you get from an OS compression utility (such as zip). Oracle supports several levels of binary compression. The BASIC compression algorithm is available without an additional license. Oracle provides further compression features with the Oracle Advanced Compression option (see the section "Configuring Binary Compression," later in this chapter, for details on how to enable binary compression).

When you create a backup as a backup set, the binary backup piece files can only be manipulated by RMAN processes. Some DBAs view this as a disadvantage because they must use RMAN to back up and restore these files (you have no direct access to or control over the backup pieces). But, these perceptions aren't warranted. Unless you hit a rare bug, RMAN is dependable and works reliably in all backup-and-restore situations.

Contrast the backup set with an image copy. An image copy creates a byte-for-byte identical copy of each data file. The advantage of creating an image copy is that (if necessary) you can manipulate the image copy without using RMAN (as with an OS copy utility). Additionally, in the event of a media failure, an image copy is a fast method of restoring data files, because RMAN only has to copy the file back from the backup location (there is no reconstructing of the data file, because it's an exact copy).

I almost always use backup sets for database backups, rather than image copies. Usually, I require some form of RMAN compression (block skipping). The size of the backup to disk is almost always a concern. Backup sets are more efficient regarding disk space consumption. Because backup sets can take advantage of RMAN compression, there is also less I/O involved, compared with an image copy. In many environments, reducing the I/O so as not to impact other applications is a concern.

However, if you feel that you need direct control over the backup files that RMAN creates, or you're in an environment in which the speed of the restore process is paramount, consider using image copies.

17. Using Incremental Backups

For most of the databases I'm responsible for, I run a daily level 0 backup. I don't usually implement any type of incremental backup strategy.

Incremental backup strategies are appropriate for large databases in which only a small portion of the database blocks change from one backup to the next. If you're in a data warehouse environment, you may want to consider an incremental backup strategy, because it can greatly reduce the size of your backups. For example, you may want to run a weekly level 0 backup and then run a daily level 1 incremental backup.

■ **Note**   See Chapter 5 for details on how to back up a database using incremental backups.

18. Using Incrementally Updated Backups

Incrementally updated backups are an efficient way to implement an image copy backup strategy. This technique instructs RMAN to first create image copies of data files; then, the next time the backup runs, instead of creating a fresh set of image copies, RMAN makes an incremental backup (changes to blocks since the image copy was created) and applies that incremental backup to the image copies.

If you have the disk space available for full image copies of your database and you want the flexibility to use the image copies directly, in the event of a media failure, consider this backup strategy.

One potential disadvantage of this approach is that if you're required to restore and recover to some point in the past, you can only restore and recover to the point at which the image copies were last updated with the incremental backup.

■ **Note**   See Chapter 5 for details on how to back up a database using incrementally updated backups.

19. Using Block Change Tracking

This feature keeps track of when a database block changes. The idea is that if you're using an incremental backup strategy, you can enhance performance, because by implementing this feature, RMAN doesn't have to scan each block (under the high-water mark) in the data files to determine whether it needs to be backed up. Rather, RMAN only has to access the block change tracking file to find which blocks have changed since the last backup and directly access those blocks. If you work in a large, data warehouse environment and are using an incremental backup strategy, consider enabling block change tracking to enhance performance.

■ **Note**   See Chapter 5 for details on how to implement block change tracking.

20. Configuring Binary Compression

You can configure RMAN to use true binary compression when generating backup sets. You can enable compression in one of two ways:

- Specify AS COMPRESSED BACKUPSET with the BACKUP command.
- Use a one-time CONFIGURE command.

Here is an example of backing up with compression when issuing the BACKUP command:

```
RMAN> backup as compressed backupset database;
```

In this example, compression is configured for the disk device:

```
RMAN> configure device type disk backup type to compressed backupset;
```

113

If you need to clear the device-type compression, issue this command:

```
RMAN> configure device type disk clear;
```

I've found the default compression algorithm to be quite efficient. For a typical database the backups are usually approximately four to five times smaller than the regular backups. Of course, your compression results may vary, depending on your data.

Why not compress all backups? Compressed backups consume more CPU resources and take longer to create and restore from, but they result in less I/O, spread out over a longer period. If you have multiple CPUs, and the speed of making a backup isn't an issue, then you should consider compressing your backups.

You can view the type of compression enabled, using the SHOW command:

```
RMAN> show compression algorithm;
```

Here is some sample output:

```
CONFIGURE COMPRESSION ALGORITHM 'BASIC' AS OF RELEASE 'DEFAULT'
OPTIMIZE FOR LOAD TRUE ; # default
```

The basic compression algorithm doesn't require an extra license from Oracle. If you're using Oracle 11g Release 2 or higher, and if you have a license for the Advanced Compression option, then you have available three additional configurable levels of binary compression; for example,

```
RMAN> configure compression algorithm 'HIGH';
RMAN> configure compression algorithm 'MEDIUM';
RMAN> configure compression algorithm 'LOW';
```

In my experience the prior compression algorithms are very efficient, both in compression ratios and time taken to create backups.

You can query V$RMAN_COMPRESSION_ALGORITHM to view details regarding the compression algorithms available for your release of the database. To reset the current compression algorithm to the default of BASIC, use the CLEAR command:

```
RMAN> configure compression algorithm clear;
```

21. Configuring Encryption

You may be required to encrypt backups. Some shops especially require this for backups that contain sensitive data and that are stored offsite. To use encryption when backing up, you must use the Oracle Enterprise Edition, possess a license for the Advanced Security option, and use Oracle 10g Release 2 or higher.

If you've configured a security wallet (see the *Oracle Advanced Security Administrator's Guide*, which can be freely downloaded from the Technology Network area of the Oracle website (http://otn.oracle.com, for details), you can configure transparent encryption for backups, as shown:

```
RMAN> configure encryption for database on;
```

Any backups that you make now will be encrypted. If you need to restore from a backup, it's automatically unencrypted (assuming the same security wallet is in place as when you encrypted the backup). To disable encryption, use the CONFIGURE command:

```
RMAN> configure encryption for database off;
```

You can also clear the encryption setting with CLEAR:

```
RMAN> configure encryption for database clear;
```

You can query V$RMAN_ENCRYPTION_ALGORITHMS to view details regarding the encryption algorithms available for your release of the database.

RUNNING SQL FROM WITHIN RMAN

Starting with Oracle 12c, you can run SQL statements (and see the results) directly from within RMAN:

```
RMAN> select * from v$rman_encryption_algorithms;
```

Prior to 12c, you could run the prior SQL statement with the RMAN sql command, but no results would be displayed:

```
RMAN> sql 'select * from v$rman_encryption_algorithms';
```

The RMAN sql command was meant more for running commands such as ALTER SYTEM:

```
RMAN> sql 'alter system switch logfile';
```

Now, in 12c, you can run the SQL directly:

```
RMAN> alter system switch logfile;
```

This ability to run SQL from within RMAN is a really nice enhancement; it allows you to see the results of SQL queries and eliminates the need for specifying the sql keyword as well as for placing quotation marks around the SQL command itself.

---

22. Configuring Miscellaneous Settings

RMAN provides a flexible number of channel configuration commands. You will occasionally need to use them, depending on special circumstances and the requirements for your database. Here are some of the options:

- Maximum backup set size
- Maximum backup piece size
- Maximum rate
- Maximum open files

By default the maximum backup set size is unlimited. You can use the MAXSETSIZE parameter with the CONFIGURE or BACKUP command to specify the overall maximum backup set size. Make sure the value of this parameter is at least as great as the largest data file being backed up by RMAN. Here is an example:

```
RMAN> configure maxsetsize to 2g;
```

Sometimes, you may want to limit the overall size of a backup piece because of physical limitations of storage devices. Use the MAXPIECESIZE parameter of the CONFIGURE CHANNEL or ALLOCATE CHANNEL command do this; for example,

```
RMAN> configure channel device type disk maxpiecesize = 2g;
```

If you need to set the maximum number of bytes that RMAN reads each second on a channel, you can do so, using the RATE parameter. This configures the maximum read rate for channel 1 to 200MB per second:

```
configure channel 1 device type disk rate 200M;
```

If you have a limit on the number of files you can have open simultaneously, you can specify a maximum open files number via the MAXOPENFILES parameter:

```
RMAN> configure channel 1 device type disk maxopenfiles 32;
```

You may need to configure any of these settings when you need to make RMAN aware of some OS or hardware limitation. You'll rarely need to use these parameters but should know of them.

23. Configuring Informational Output

A good practice is to always set the OS NLS_DATE_FORMAT variable (before running RMAN) so that both the date and time information are displayed in the RMAN log instead of just the date, which is the default:

```
export NLS_DATE_FORMAT='dd-mon-yyyy hh24:mi:ss'
```

This is useful during troubleshooting, especially when RMAN fails, because we can use the exact date/time information for when the RMAN error occurred and compare it with the alert.log and OS/MML logs to verify what other events occurred in the database/server.

Also consider executing SET ECHO ON to ensure that RMAN commands are displayed within the log before the command is executed. Execute SHOW ALL as well to display the current settings of RMAN variables. These settings are useful when troubleshooting and tuning.

CLEARING ALL RMAN CONFIGURATIONS

There is no CLEAR ALL command for resetting all RMAN configurations back to the default values. However, you can easily simulate this by running a script that contains CONFIGURE...CLEAR commands:

```
CONFIGURE RETENTION POLICY clear;
CONFIGURE BACKUP OPTIMIZATION clear;
CONFIGURE DEFAULT DEVICE TYPE clear;
CONFIGURE CONTROLFILE AUTOBACKUP clear;
CONFIGURE CONTROLFILE AUTOBACKUP FORMAT FOR DEVICE TYPE DISK clear;
CONFIGURE DEVICE TYPE DISK clear;
CONFIGURE DATAFILE BACKUP COPIES FOR DEVICE TYPE DISK clear;
CONFIGURE CHANNEL 1 DEVICE TYPE DISK clear;
CONFIGURE CHANNEL 2 DEVICE TYPE DISK clear;
CONFIGURE CHANNEL 3 DEVICE TYPE DISK clear;
CONFIGURE ARCHIVELOG BACKUP COPIES FOR DEVICE TYPE DISK clear;
```

```
CONFIGURE MAXSETSIZE clear;
CONFIGURE ENCRYPTION FOR DATABASE clear;
CONFIGURE ENCRYPTION ALGORITHM clear;
CONFIGURE COMPRESSION ALGORITHM clear;
CONFIGURE RMAN OUTPUT clear; # 12c
CONFIGURE ARCHIVELOG DELETION POLICY clear;
CONFIGURE SNAPSHOT CONTROLFILE NAME clear;
```

Depending on what you've set (and the version of your database), you may need to set additional configurations.

Segueing from Decision to Action

Now that you have a good understanding of what types of decisions you should make before implementing RMAN, it's instructional to view a script that implements some of these components. I mainly work with Linux/Unix servers. In these environments, I use shell scripts to automate the RMAN backups. These shell scripts are automated through a scheduling utility such as cron.

This section contains a typical shell script for RMAN backups. The shell script has line numbers in the output for reference in the discussion of the architectural decisions I made when writing the script. (If you copy the script, take out the line numbers before running it.)

Following is the script. Table 4-2 details every RMAN architectural decision point covered in this chapter, how it's implemented (or not) in the shell script, and the corresponding line number in the shell script. The script doesn't cover every aspect of how to use RMAN. If you use the script, be sure to modify it to meet the requirements and RMAN standards for your own environment:

```
1 #!/bin/bash
2 #-----------------------------------------------
3 PRG=`basename $0`
4 USAGE="Usage: ${PRG}"
5 if [ $# -gt 0 ]; then
6    echo "${USAGE}"
7    exit 1
8 fi
9 export ORACLE_SID=O12C
10 export ORACLE_HOME=/orahome/app/oracle/product/12.1.0.1/db_1
11 export PATH=$PATH:$ORACLE_HOME/bin
12 BOX=`uname -a | awk '{print$2}'`
13 MAILX='/bin/mailx'
14 MAIL_LIST='dkuhn@gmail.com'
15 export NLS_DATE_FORMAT='dd-mon-yyyy hh24:mi:ss'
16 date
17 #-----------------------------------------------
18 LOCKFILE=/tmp/$PRG.lock
19 if [ -f $LOCKFILE ]; then
20   echo "lock file exists, exiting..."
21   exit 1
22 else
23   echo "DO NOT REMOVE, $LOCKFILE" > $LOCKFILE
24 fi
25 #-----------------------------------------------
26 rman nocatalog <<EOF
27 connect target /
```

```
28 set echo on;
29 show all;
30 crosscheck backup;
31 crosscheck copy;
32 configure controlfile autobackup on;
33 configure controlfile autobackup format for device type disk to
   '/u01/O12C/rman/O12C_ctl_%F.bk';
34 configure retention policy to redundancy 1;
35 configure           device type disk parallelism 2;
36 configure channel 1 device type disk format '/u01/O12C/rman/O12C_%U.bk';
37 configure channel 2 device type disk format '/u02/O12C/rman/O12C_%U.bk';
38 backup as compressed backupset incremental level=0 database plus archivelog;
39 delete noprompt obsolete;
40 EOF
41 #------------------------------------------------
42 if [ $? -ne 0 ]; then
43   echo "RMAN problem..."
44   echo "Check RMAN backups" | $MAILX -s "RMAN issue: $ORACLE_SID on $BOX" $MAIL_LIST
45 else
46   echo "RMAN ran okay..."
47 fi
48 #------------------------------------------------
49 if [ -f $LOCKFILE ]; then
50   rm $LOCKFILE
51 fi
52 #------------------------------------------------
53 date
54 exit 0
```

Table 4-2. Implementation of Architectural Decisions

Decision Point	Implementation in Script	Line Number in Script
1. Running the RMAN client remotely or locally	Running script locally on the database server	Line 26, connecting locally (not a network connection)
2. Specifying the backup user	Using SYS to connect	Line 27, starting rman connecting with forward slash (/)
3. Using online or offline backups	Online backup	N/A. Database is assumed to be up during the backup
4. Setting the archive redo log destination and file format	LOG_ARCHIVE_DEST_N and LOG_ARCHIVE_ FORMAT initialization parameters set outside the script in a database parameter file	N/A; set outside the script
5. Configuring the RMAN backup location and file format	Using the CONFIGURE command directly in the script	Lines 33–37

(*continued*)

Table 4-2. (continued)

Decision Point	Implementation in Script	Line Number in Script
6. Setting the autobackup of the control file	Enabled in the script	Line 32
7. Specifying the location of the autobackup of the control file	Placed in the same directory as the backups	Line 33
8. Backing up archive redo logs	Backing up with the rest of the database; specifically, using the PLUS ARCHIVELOG clause	Line 38
9. Determining the location for the snapshot control file	Using the default location	N/A
10. Using a recovery catalog	Not using	Line 26, connecting as nocatalog
11. Using a media manager	Not using	Lines 35–37, device type disk
12. Setting the CONTROL_FILE_RECORD_KEEP_TIME initialization parameter	Using the default	N/A
13. Configuring RMAN's backup retention policy	Configuring to a redundancy of 1, cross-checking, and deleting obsolete backups and archive redo log files	Line 34, configuring; lines 30 and 31 cross-check; line 39, using RMAN to delete old files
14. Configuring the archive redo logs' deletion policy	Using the same retention policy applied to the backups	N/A
15. Setting the degree of parallelism	Setting a degree of 2	Lines 35–37
16. Using backup sets or image copies	Using backup sets	Line 38
17. Using incremental backups	Incremental level 0, the same as a full backup	Line 38
18. Using incrementally updated backups	Not using	N/A
19. Using block change tracking	Not using	N/A
20. Configuring binary compression	Using basic compression	Line 38
21. Configuring encryption	Not using	N/A
22. Configuring miscellaneous settings	Not using	N/A
23. Configuring informational output	Setting	Lines 15, 28, and 29

A few aspects of this script need further discussion. Lines 9, 10, and 11 set the required OS variables by hard-coding the required OS variables into the script (see Chapter 1 for details on sourcing OS variables). I generally prefer not to hard-code variables into a script like this, but did so here to provide a simple example of how to script RMAN to backup your database. You'll find that many DBAs do hard-code these variables into scripts.

Line 15 sets the NLS_DATE_FORMAT OS variable to a value that includes hours, minutes, and seconds. This ensures that when RMAN runs commands that are appropriate, it displays the date output with a time component. This can be invaluable when you're debugging and diagnosing issues. By default, RMAN displays only the date component. Knowing just the date when a command ran is rarely enough information to determine the timing of the commands as they were executed. At minimum, you need to see hours and minutes (along with the date).

Lines 18–24 check for the existence of a lock file. You don't want to run this script if it's already running. The script checks for the lock file, and, if it exists, the script exits. After the backup has finished, the lock file is removed (lines 49–51).

Line 28 sets the ECHO parameter to on. This instructs RMAN to display in the output the command before running it. This can be invaluable for debugging issues. Line 29 displays all the configurable variables. This also comes in handy for troubleshooting issues because you can see what the RMAN variables were set to before any commands are executed.

Lines 32–37 use the CONFIGURE command. These commands run each time the script is executed. Why do that? You only need to run a CONFIGURE command once, and it's stored in the control file—you don't have to run it again, right? That is correct. However, I've occasionally been burned when a DBA with poor habits configured a setting for a database and didn't tell anybody, and I didn't discover the misconfiguration until I attempted to make another backup. I strongly prefer to place the CONFIGURE commands in the script so that the behavior is the same, regardless of what another DBA may have done outside the script. The CONFIGURE settings in the script also act as a form of documentation: I can readily look at the script and determine how settings have been configured.

Lines 30 and 31 run CROSSCHECK commands. Why do that? Sometimes, files go missing, or a rogue DBA may remove archive redo log files from disk with an OS command outside RMAN. When RMAN runs, if it can't find files that it thinks should be in place, it throws an error and stops the backup. I prefer to run the CROSSCHECK command and let RMAN reconcile which files it thinks should be on disk with those that are actually on disk. This keeps RMAN running smoothly.

You run DELETE NOPROMPT OBSOLETE on line 39. This removes all backup files and archive redo log files that have been marked as OBSOLETE by RMAN, as defined by the retention policy. This lets RMAN manage which files should be kept on disk. I prefer to run the DELETE command after the backup has finished (as opposed to running it before the backup). The retention policy is defined as 1, so if you run DELETE after the backup, RMAN leaves one backup copy on disk. If you run DELETE before the backup, RMAN leaves one copy of the backup on disk. After the backup runs, there are be two copies of the backup on disk, which I don't have room for on this server.

You can execute the shell script from the Linux/Unix scheduling utility cron, as follows:

```
0 16 * * * $HOME/bin/rmanback.bsh >$HOME/bin/log/INVPRDRMAN.log 2>&1
```

The script runs daily at 1600 hours military time on the database server. A log file is created (INVPRDRMAN.log) to capture any output and errors associated with the RMAN job.

Again, the script in this section is basic; you'll no doubt want to enhance and modify it to meet your requirements. This script gives you a starting point, with concrete RMAN recommendations and how to implement them.

Summary

RMAN is Oracle's flagship B&R tool. If you're still using the older, user-managed backup technologies, then I strongly recommend that you switch to RMAN. RMAN contains a powerful set of features that are unmatched by any other backup tool available. RMAN is easy to use and configure. It will save you time and effort and give you peace of mind when you're implementing a rock-solid B&R strategy.

If you're new to RMAN, it may not be obvious which features should always be enabled and implemented and, likewise, which aspects you'll rarely need. This chapter contains a checklist that walks you through each architectural decision point. You may disagree with some of my conclusions, or some recommendations may not meet your business requirements—that's fine. The point is that you should carefully consider each component and how to implement the features that make sense.

The chapter ended with a real-world example of a script used to implement RMAN in a production environment. Now that you have a good idea of RMAN's features and how to use them, you're ready to start making backups. The next chapter deals with RMAN backup scenarios.

CHAPTER 5

■ ■ ■

RMAN Backups and Reporting

Chapter 4 provided the details on configuring RMAN and using specialized features to control the behavior of RMAN. After you consider which features you require, you're ready to create backups. RMAN can back up the following types of files:

- Data files
- Control files
- Archived redo log files
- spfiles
- Backup pieces

For most scenarios, you will use RMAN to back up data files, control files, and archive redo log files. If you have the autobackup of the control file feature enabled, then RMAN will automatically back up the control file and the spfile (if you're using one) when a BACKUP or COPY command is issued. You can also back up the backup piece files that RMAN has created.

RMAN does not back up Oracle Net files, password files, block change tracking files, flashback logs, or the Oracle binary files (files created when you installed Oracle). If required, you should put in place OS backups that include those files.

Also note that RMAN does not back up online redo log files. If you were to back up the online redo log files, it would be pointless to restore them. The online redo log files contain the latest redo generated by the database. You would not want to overwrite them from a backup with old redo information. When your database is in archivelog mode, the online redo log files contain the most recently generated transactions required to perform complete recovery.

This chapter details many of the features related to running the RMAN BACKUP command. Also covered are creating a recovery catalog and techniques for logging output and reporting on RMAN backup operations. This chapter begins by discussing a few common practices used to enhance what is displayed in the RMAN output when running commands.

Preparing to Run RMAN Backup Commands

Before I run RMAN backups, I usually set a few things so as to enhance what is shown in the output. You don't need to set these variables every time you log in and run an RMAN command. However, when troubleshooting or debugging issues, it's almost always a good idea to perform the following tasks:

- Set NLS_DATE_FORMAT OS variable
- Set ECHO
- Show RMAN variables

The bulleted items are discussed in the following sections.

121

Setting NLS_DATE_FORMAT

Before running any RMAN job, I set the OS variable NLS_DATE_FORMAT to include a time (hours, minutes, seconds) component; for example,

```
$ export NLS_DATE_FORMAT='dd-mon-yyyy hh24:mi:ss'
```

Additionally, if I have a shell script that calls RMAN, I put the prior line directly in the shell script (see the shell script at the end of Chapter 4 for an example):

```
NLS_DATE_FORMAT='dd-mon-yyyy hh24:mi:ss'
```

This ensures that when RMAN displays a date, it always includes the hours, minutes, and seconds as part of the output. By default, RMAN only includes the date component (DD-MON-YY) in the output. For instance, without setting NLS_DATE_FORMAT, when starting a backup, here is what RMAN displays:

```
Starting backup at 04-SEP-14
```

When you set the NLS_DATE_FORMAT OS variable to include a time component, the output will look like this instead:

```
Starting backup at 04-sep-2014 16:43:04
```

When troubleshooting, it's essential to have a time component so that you can determine how long a command took to run or how long a command was running before a failure occurred. Oracle Support will almost always ask you to set this variable to include the time component before capturing output and sending it to them.

The only downside to setting the NLS_DATE_FORMAT is that if you set it to a value unknown to RMAN, connectivity issues can occur. For example, here the NLS_DATE_FORMAT is set to an invalid value:

```
$ export NLS_DATE_FORMAT='dd-mon-yyyy hh24:mi:sd'
$ rman target /
```

When set to an invalid value, you get this error when logging in to RMAN:

```
RMAN-03999: Oracle error occurred while converting a date: ORA-01821:
```

To unset the NLS_DATE_FORMAT variable, set it to a blank value, like so:

```
$ export NLS_DATE_FORMAT=''
```

Setting ECHO Setting ECHO

Another value that I always set in any RMAN scripts is the ECHO command, seen here:

```
RMAN> set echo on;
```

This instructs RMAN to display the command that it's running in the output, so you can see what RMAN command is running. along with any relevant error or output messages associated with the command. This is especially important when you're running RMAN commands within scripts, because you're not directly typing in a command (and may not know what command was issued within the shell script). For example, without SET ECHO ON, here is what is displayed in the output for a command:

```
Starting backup at...
```

With SET ECHO ON, this output shows the actual command that was run:

```
backup datafile 4;
Starting backup at...
```

From the prior output, you can see which command is running, when it started, and so on.

Showing Variables

Another good practice is to run the SHOW ALL command within any script, as follows:

```
RMAN> show all;
```

This displays all the RMAN configurable variables. When troubleshooting, you may not be aware of something that another DBA has configured. This gives you a snapshot of the settings as they were when the RMAN session executed.

Running Backups

Before you run an RMAN backup, make sure you read Chapter 4 for details on how to configure RMAN with settings for a production environment. For production databases, I mainly run RMAN from a shell script similar to the one shown at the end of Chapter 4. Within the shell script, I configure every aspect of RMAN that I want to use for a particular database. If you run RMAN out of the box, with its default settings, you will be able to back up your database. However, these settings will not be adequate for most production database applications.

Backing Up the Entire Database

If you're not sure where RMAN will be backing up your database files, you need to read Chapter 4, because it describes how to configure RMAN to create the backup files in the location of your choice. Here is how I usually configure RMAN to write to specific locations on disk (note that the CONFIGURE command must be executed before you run the BACKUP command):

```
RMAN> configure channel 1 device type disk format '/u01/O12C/rman/rman1_%U.bk';
```

After a backup location is configured, I almost always use a command similar to the one shown next to back up the entire database:

```
RMAN> backup incremental level=0 database plus archivelog;
```

This command ensures that RMAN will back up all data files in the database, all available archive redo logs generated prior to the backup, and all archive redo logs generated during the backup. This command also ensures that you have all the data files and archive redo logs that would be required to restore and recover your database.

If you have the autobackup of the control file feature enabled, run this command next:

```
RMAN> configure controlfile autobackup on;
```

The last task RMAN does as part of the backup is to generate a backup set that contains a backup of the control file. This control file will contain all information regarding the backup that took place and any archive redo logs that were generated during the backup.

■ **Tip**   Always enable the autobackup of the control file feature.

There are many nuances to the RMAN BACKUP command. For production databases, I usually back up the database with the BACKUP INCREMENTAL LEVEL=0 DATABASE PLUS ARCHIVELOG command. That's generally sufficient. However, you will encounter many situations in which you need to run a backup that uses a specific RMAN feature, or you might troubleshoot an issue requiring that you be aware of the other ways to invoke an RMAN backup. These aspects are discussed in the next several sections.

Full Backup vs. Incremental Level=0

The term *RMAN full backup* sometimes causes confusion. A more apt way of phrasing this task would be *RMAN backing up all modified blocks within one or more data files*. The term *full* does not mean that all blocks are backed up or that all data files are backed up. It simply means that all blocks that would be required to rebuild a data file (in the event of a failure) are being backed up. You can take a full backup of a single data file, and the contents of that backup piece may be quite a bit smaller than the data file itself.

The term *RMAN level 0 incremental backup* doesn't exactly describe itself very well, either. A level 0 incremental backup is backing up the same blocks as a full backup. In other words, the following two commands back up the same blocks in a database:

```
RMAN> backup as backupset full database;
RMAN> backup as backupset incremental level=0 database;
```

The only difference between the prior two commands is that an incremental level 0 backup can be used in conjunction with other incremental backups, whereas a full backup cannot participate in an incremental backup strategy. Therefore, I almost always prefer to use the INCREMENTAL LEVEL=0 syntax (as opposed to a full backup); it gives me the flexibility to use the level 0 incremental backup along with subsequent incremental level 1 backups.

Backup Sets vs. Image Copies

The default backup mode of RMAN instructs it to back up only blocks that have been used in a data file; these are known as backup sets. RMAN can also make byte-for-byte copies of the data files; these are known as image copies. Creating a backup set is the default type of backup that RMAN creates. The next command creates a backup set backup of the database:

```
RMAN> backup database;
```

If you prefer, you can explicitly place the AS BACKUPSET command when creating backups:

```
RMAN> backup as backupset database;
```

You can instruct RMAN to create image copies by using the AS COPY command. This command creates image copies of every data file in the database:

```
RMAN> backup as copy database;
```

Because image copies are identical copies of the data files, they can be directly accessed by the DBA with OS commands. For example, say you had a media failure, and you didn't want to use RMAN to restore an image copy. You could use an OS command to copy the image copy of a data file to a location where it could be used by the database. In contrast, a backup set consists of binary files that only the RMAN utility can write to or read from.

I prefer to use backup sets when working with RMAN. The backup sets tend to be smaller than the data files and can have true binary compression applied to them. Also, I don't find it inconvenient to use RMAN as the mechanism for creating backup files that only RMAN can restore. Using RMAN with backup sets is efficient and very reliable.

Backing Up Tablespaces

RMAN has the ability to back up at the database level (as shown in the prior section), the tablespace level, or, even more granularly, at the data file level. When you back up a tablespace, RMAN backs up any data files associated with the tablespaces(s) that you specify. For instance, the following command will back up all the data files associated with the SYSTEM and SYSAUX tablespaces:

```
RMAN> backup tablespace system, sysaux;
```

One scenario in which I back up at the tablespace level is if I've recently created a new tablespace and want to take a backup of just the data files associated with the newly added tablespace. Note that when B&R issues, it's often more efficient to work with one tablespace (because it's generally much faster to back up one tablespace than the entire database).

Backing Up Data Files

You may occasionally need to back up individual data files. For example, when troubleshooting issues with backups, it's often helpful to attempt to successfully backup one data file. You can specify data files by file name or by file number, as follows:

```
RMAN> backup datafile '/u01/dbfile/O12C/system01.dbf';
```

In this example, file numbers are specified:

```
RMAN> backup datafile 1,4;
```

Here are some other examples of backing up data files, using various features:

```
RMAN> backup as copy datafile 4;
RMAN> backup incremental level 1 datafile 4;
```

■ **Tip** Use the RMAN REPORT SCHEMA command to list tablespace, data file name, and data file number information.

Backing Up the Control File

The most reliable way to back up the control file is to configure the autobackup feature:

```
RMAN> configure controlfile autobackup on;
```

This command ensures that the control file is automatically backed up when a BACKUP or COPY command is issued. I usually enable the autobackup of the control file feature and then never have to worry about explicitly issuing a separate command to back up the control file. When in this mode the control file is always created in its own backup set and backup piece after the data file backup pieces have been created.

If you need to back up the control file manually, you can do so like this:

```
RMAN> backup current controlfile;
```

The location of the backup is either a default OS location, the FRA (if using), or a manually configured location. As shown in Chapter 4, I prefer to set the location of the control file backup piece to the same location as that of the data file backups:

```
RMAN> configure controlfile autobackup format for device type disk to
'/u01/O12C/rman/rman_ctl_%F.bk';
```

Backing up the spfile

If you have enabled the autobackup of the control file feature, the spfile will be backed up automatically (along with the control file) anytime a BACKUP or COPY command is issued. If you need to back up the spfile manually, use the following command:

```
RMAN> backup spfile;
```

The location of the file that contains the backup of the spfile is dependent on what you have configured for the autobackup of the control file (see the previous section for an example). By default, if you don't use an FRA, and you haven't explicitly configured a location via a channel, then for Linux/Unix servers, the backup goes to the ORACLE_HOME/dbs directory.

■ **Note** RMAN can only back up the spfile if the instance was started using a spfile.

Backing Up Archive Redo Logs

I don't usually back up the archive redo logs separately from the database backups. As mentioned earlier, I normally back up the database files and the archive redo log files by using the following command:

```
RMAN> backup incremental level=0 database plus archivelog;
```

However, you will occasionally find yourself in a situation in which you need to take a special, one-off backup of the archive redo logs. You can issue the following command to back up the archive redo logs files:

```
RMAN> backup archivelog all;
```

If you have a mount point that is nearly full, and you determine that you want to back up the archive redo logs (so that they exist in a backup file), but then you want to immediately delete the files (that were just backed up) from disk, you can use the following syntax to back up the archive redo logs and then have RMAN delete them from the storage media:

```
RMAN> backup archivelog all delete input;
```

Listed next are some other ways in which you can back up the archive redo log files:

```
RMAN> backup archivelog sequence 300;
RMAN> backup archivelog sequence between 300 and 400 thread 1;
RMAN> backup archivelog from time "sysdate-7" until time "sysdate-1";
```

If an archive redo log has been removed from disk manually via an OS delete command, RMAN will throw the following error when attempting to back up the nonexistent archive redo log file:

```
RMAN-06059: expected archived log not found, loss of archived log compromises recoverability
```

In this situation, first run a CROSSCHECK command to let RMAN know which files are physically available on disk:

```
RMAN> crosscheck archivelog all;
```

Backing Up FRA

If you use an FRA, one nice RMAN feature is that you can back up all the files in that location with one command. If you're using a media manager and have a tape backup channel enabled, you can back up everything in the FRA to tape, like this:

```
RMAN> backup device type sbt_tape recovery area;
```

You can also back up the FRA to a location on disk. Use the TO DESTINATION command to accomplish this:

```
RMAN> backup recovery area to destination '/u01/O12C/fra_back';
```

RMAN will automatically create directories as required beneath the directory specified by the TO DESTINATION command.

■ **Note**   The format of the subdirectory under the directory TO_DESTINATION is db_uniuqe_name/backupset/ YYYY_MM_DD.

RMAN will back up full backups, incremental backups, control file autobackups, and archive redo log files. Keep in mind that flashback logs, online redo log files, and the current control file are not backed up.

Excluding Tablespaces from Backups

Suppose you have a tablespace that contains noncritical data, and you don't ever want to back it up. RMAN can be configured to exclude such tablespaces from the backup. To determine if RMAN is currently configured to exclude any tablespaces, run this command:

```
RMAN> show exclude;
RMAN configuration parameters for database with db_unique_name O12C are:
RMAN configuration has no stored or default parameters
```

Use the EXCLUDE command to instruct RMAN as to which tablespaces not to back up:

```
RMAN> configure exclude for tablespace users;
```

Now, for any database-level backups, RMAN will exclude the data files associated with the USERS tablespace. You can instruct RMAN to back up all data files and any excluded tablespaces with this command:

```
RMAN> backup database noexclude;
```

You can clear the exclude setting via the following command:

```
RMAN> configure exclude for tablespace users clear;
```

Backing Up Data Files Not Backed Up

Suppose you have just added several data files to your database, and you want to ensure that you have a backup of them. You can issue the following command to instruct Oracle to back up data files that have not yet been backed up:

```
RMAN> backup database not backed up;
```

You can also specify a time range for such files that have not yet been backed up. Say you discover that your backups have not been running for the last several days, and you want to back up everything that hasn't been backed up within the last 24 hours. The following command backs up all data files that have not been backed up within the last day:

```
RMAN> backup database not backed up since time='sysdate-1';
```

The prior command is also useful if, for any reason (a power failure in the data center, your backup directory's becoming full during backups, and so on), your backups aborted. After you have resolved the issue that caused your backup job to fail, you can issue the previous command, and RMAN will back up only the data files that have not been backed up in the specified time period.

Skipping Read-Only Tablespaces

Because data in read-only tablespaces can't change, you may only want to back up read-only tablespaces once and then skip them in subsequent backups. Use the SKIP READONLY command to achieve this:

```
RMAN> backup database skip readonly;
```

Keep in mind that when you skip read-only tablespaces, you'll need to keep available a backup that contains these tablespaces. As long as you only issue the RMAN command DELETE OBSOLETE, the RMAN backup set containing the read-only tablespaces will be retained and not deleted, even if that RMAN backup set contains other read-write tablespaces.

Skipping Offline or Inaccessible Files

Suppose you have one data file that is missing or corrupt, and you don't have a backup of it, so you can't restore and recover it. You can't start your database in this situation:

```
SQL> startup;
ORA-01157: cannot identify/lock data file 6 - see DBWR trace file
ORA-01110: data file 6: '/u01/dbfile/ 012C/reg_data01.dbf'
```

In this scenario, you'll have to take the data file offline before you can start your database:

```
SQL> alter database datafile '/u01/dbfile/012C/reg_data01.dbf' offline for drop;
```

Now, you can open your database:

```
SQL> alter database open;
```

Suppose you then attempt to run an RMAN backup:

```
RMAN> backup database;
```

The following error is thrown when RMAN encounters a data file that it can't back up:

```
RMAN-03002: failure of backup command at ...
RMAN-06056: could not access datafile 6
```

In this situation, you'll have to instruct RMAN to exclude the offline data file from the backup. The SKIP OFFLINE command instructs RMAN to ignore data files with an offline status:

```
RMAN> backup database skip offline;
```

If a file has gone completely missing, use SKIP INACCESSIBLE to instruct RMAN to ignore files that are not available on disk. This might happen if the data file was deleted using an OS command. Here is an example of excluding inaccessible data files from the RMAN backup:

```
RMAN> backup database skip inaccessible;
```

You can skip read-only, offline, and inaccessible data files with one command:

```
RMAN> backup database skip readonly skip offline skip inaccessible;
```

When dealing with offline and inaccessible files, you should figure out why the files are offline or inaccessible and try to resolve any issues.

Backing Up Large Files in Parallel

Normally, RMAN will only use one channel to back up a single data file. When you enable parallelism, it allows RMAN to spawn multiple processes to back up multiple files. However, even when parallelism is enabled, RMAN will not use parallel channels simultaneously to back up one data file.

Starting with Oracle 11g, you can instruct RMAN to use multiple channels to back up one data file in parallel. This is known as a multisection backup. This feature can speed up the backups of very large data files. Use the SECTION SIZE parameter to make a multisection backup. The following example configures two parallel channels to back up one file:

```
RMAN> configure device type disk parallelism 2;
RMAN> configure channel 1 device type disk format '/u01/O12C/rman/r1%U.bk';
RMAN> configure channel 2 device type disk format '/u02/O12C/rman/r2%U.bk';
RMAN> backup section size 2500M datafile 10;
```

When this code runs, RMAN will allocate two channels to back up the specified data file in parallel.

■ **Note**   If you specify a section size greater than the size of the data file, RMAN will not back up the file in parallel.

Adding RMAN Backup Information to the Repository

Suppose you've had to re-create your control file. The process of re-creating the control file wipes out any information regarding RMAN backups. However, you want to make the newly created control file aware of RMAN backups sitting on disk. In this situation, use the CATALOG command to populate the control file with RMAN metadata. For example, if all the RMAN backup files are kept in the /u01/O12C/rman directory, you can make the control file aware of these backups files in the directory, as follows:

```
RMAN> catalog start with '/u01/O12C/rman';
```

This instructs RMAN to look for any backup pieces, image copies, control file copies, and archive redo logs in the specified directory, and, if found, to populate the control file with the appropriate metadata. For this example two backup piece files are found in the given directory:

```
searching for all files that match the pattern /u01/O12C/rman

List of Files Unknown to the Database
=======================================
File Name: /u01/O12C/rman/r1otlns9Oo_1_1.bk
File Name: /u01/ O12C/rman/r1xyklnrveg_1_1.bk

Do you really want to catalog the above files (enter YES or NO)?
```

If you enter YES, then metadata regarding the backup files will be added to the control file. In this way, the CATALOG command allows you to make the RMAN repository (control file and recovery catalog) aware of files that RMAN can work with for B&R.

You can also instruct RMAN to catalog any files in the FRA that the control file isn't currently aware of, like this:

```
RMAN> catalog recovery area;
```

Additionally, you can catalog specific files. This example instructs RMAN to add metadata to the control file for a specific backup piece file:

```
RMAN> catalog backuppiece '/u01/O12C/rman/r159nv562v_1_1.bk';
```

Taking Backups of Pluggable Databases

Starting with Oracle 12c, you can create pluggable databases within a root container database. If you're using this option, there are a few features to be aware of in regard to backups:

- While connected to the root container, you can back up all the data files within the database or just the root database data files; a specific pluggable database; or specific tablespaces or data files, or a combination of these.

- While connected to a pluggable database, you can only back up data files associated with that database.

The bulleted items are detailed in the following two sections.

While Connected to the Root Container

Suppose you're connected to the root container as SYS and want to back up all data files (including any data files with associated pluggable databases). First, verify that you are indeed connected to the root container as SYS:

```
RMAN> SELECT SYS_CONTEXT('USERENV', 'CON_ID')        AS con_id,
      SYS_CONTEXT('USERENV', 'CON_NAME')        AS cur_container,
      SYS_CONTEXT('USERENV', 'CURRENT_SCHEMA') AS cur_user
      FROM DUAL;
```

Here is some sample output:

```
CON_ID              CUR_CONTAINER          CUR_USER
------------------- ---------------------- --------------------
1                   CDB$ROOT               SYS
```

Now, to back up all data files, both in the root container and in any associated pluggable databases, do so as follows:

```
RMAN> backup database;
```

If you want to back up only the data files associated with the root container, then specify ROOT:

```
RMAN> backup database root;
```

You can also back up a specific pluggable database:

```
RMAN> backup pluggable database salespdb;
```

Additionally, you can back up specific tablespaces within a pluggable database:

```
RMAN> backup tablespace SALESPDB:SALES;
```

And, you can specify the file name to back up any data file within the root container or associated pluggable databases:

```
RMAN> backup datafile '/ora01/app/oracle/oradata/CDB/salespdb/sales01.dbf';
```

While Connected to a Pluggable Database

First, start RMAN, and connect to the pluggable database you want to back up. You must connect as a user with SYSDBA or SYSBACKUP privileges. Also, there must be a listener running and a password file in place. This example connects to the SALESPDB pluggable database:

```
$ rman target sys/foo@salespdb
```

Once connected to a pluggable database, you can only back up data files specific to that database. Therefore, for this example, the following command takes a backup of just data files associated with the SALESPDB pluggable database:

```
RMAN> backup database;
```

This example backs up the data files associated with the pluggable database SYSTEM tablespace:

```
RMAN> backup tablespace system;
```

I should emphasize again that when you are connected directly to a pluggable database, you can only back up data files associated with that database. You can't back up data files associated with the root container or with any other pluggable databases within the container. Figure 5-1 illustrates this concept. A connection as SYSDBA to the SALESPDB pluggable database can only back up and view data files related to that database. The SYSDBA connection can't see outside its pluggable box in regard to data files and RMAN backups of data files. In contrast, the SYSDBA connection to the root container can back up all data files (root, seed, and all pluggable databases) as well as access RMAN backups that were initiated from a connection to a pluggable database.

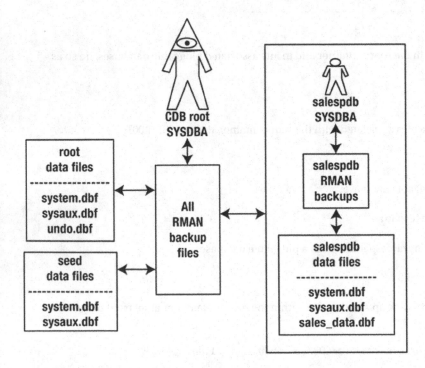

Figure 5-1. *Purview of a SYSDBA connection to root container vs. a SYSDBA connection to a pluggable database*

Creating Incremental Backups

RMAN has three separate and distinct incremental backup features:

- Incremental-level backups

- Incrementally updating backups

- Block change tracking

With incremental-level backups, RMAN only backs up the blocks that have been modified since a previous backup. Incremental backups can be applied to the entire database, tablespaces, or data files. Incremental-level backups are the most commonly used incremental feature with RMAN.

Incrementally updating backups is a separate feature from incremental-level backups. These backups take image copies of the data files and then use incremental backups to update the image copies. This gives you an efficient way to implement and maintain image copies as part of your backup strategy. You only take the image copy backup once, and then use incremental backups to keep the image copies updated with the most recent transactions.

Block change tracking is another feature designed to speed up the performance of incremental backups. The idea here is that an OS file is used to record which blocks have changed since the last backup. RMAN can use the block change tracking file to quickly identify which blocks need to be backed up when performing incremental backups. This feature can greatly improve the performance of incremental backups.

Taking Incremental-Level Backups

RMAN implements incremental backups through levels. Starting with Oracle 10g, there are only two documented levels of incremental backups: level 0 and level 1. Prior versions of Oracle offer five levels, 0–4. These levels (0–4) are still available but are not specified in the Oracle documentation. You must first take a level 0 incremental backup to establish a baseline, after which you can take a level 1 incremental backup.

■ **Note** A full backup backs up the same blocks as a level 0 backup. However, you can't use a full backup with incremental backups. Furthermore, you have to start an incremental backup strategy with a level 0 backup. If you attempt to take a level 1 backup, and no level 0 exists, RMAN will automatically take a level 0 backup.

Here is an example of taking an incremental level 0 backup:

```
RMAN> backup incremental level=0 database;
```

Suppose for the next several backups you want to back up only the blocks that have changed since the last incremental backup. This line of code takes a level 1 backup:

```
RMAN> backup incremental level=1 database;
```

There are two different types of incremental backups: differential and cumulative. Which type you use depends on your requirements. Differential backups (the default) are smaller but take more time to recover from. Cumulative backups are larger than differential backups but require less recovery time.

A differential incremental level 1 backup instructs RMAN to back up blocks that have changed since the last level 1 or level 0 backup, whereas a cumulative incremental level 1 backup instructs RMAN to back up blocks that have changed since the last level 0 backup. Cumulative incremental backups, in effect, ignore any level 1 incremental backups.

■ **Note** The RMAN incremental level 0 backups are used to restore the data files, whereas the RMAN incremental level 1 backups are used to recover the data files.

When using incremental backups, I almost always use the default, of differential. Usually, I don't worry about the differences between differential and cumulative backups. If you require cumulative backups, you must specify the key word CUMULATIVE. Here is an example of taking a cumulative level 1 backup:

```
RMAN> backup incremental level=1 cumulative database;
```

Here are some examples of taking incremental backups at a more granular level than the database:

```
RMAN> backup incremental level=0 tablespace sysaux;
RMAN> backup incremental level=1 tablespace sysaux plus archivelog;
RMAN> backup incremental from scn 4343352 datafile 3;
```

Making Incrementally Updating Backups

The basic idea behind an incrementally updating backup is to create image copies of data files and then use incremental backups to update the image copies. In this manner, you have image copies of your database that are kept somewhat current. This can be an efficient way to combine image copy backups with incremental backups.

To understand how this backup technique works, you'll need to inspect the commands that perform an incrementally updating backup. The following lines of RMAN code are required to enable this feature:

```
run{recover copy of database with tag 'incupdate';
backup incremental level 1 for recover of copy with tag 'incupdate' database;}
```

In the first line a tag is specified (this example uses incupdate). You can use whatever you want for the tag name; the tag name lets RMAN associate the backup files being used each time the commands are run. This code will perform as follows the first time you run the script:

- RECOVER COPY generates a message saying there's nothing for it to do.

- If no image copies exist, the BACKUP INCREMENTAL creates an image copy of the database data files.

You should see messages such as this in the output when the RECOVER COPY and BACKUP INCREMENTAL commands run the first time:

```
no copy of datafile 1 found to recover
...
no parent backup or copy of datafile 1 found
...
```

The second time you run the incrementally updating backup, it does as follows:

- RECOVER COPY again generates a message saying it has nothing to do.

- BACKUP INCREMENTAL makes an incremental level 1 backup and assigns it the tag name specified; this backup will subsequently be used by the RECOVER COPY command.

The third time you run the incrementally updating backup, it does this:

- Now that an incremental backup has been created, the RECOVER COPY applies the incremental backup to the image copies.

- BACKUP INCREMENTAL makes an incremental level 1 backup and assigns it the tag name specified; this backup will subsequently be used by the RECOVER COPY command.

Going forward, each time you run the two lines of code, you will have a regularly repeating backup pattern. If you use image copies for backups, you might consider using an incrementally updating backup strategy, because with it, you avoid creating entire image copies whenever the backup runs. The image copies are updated each time the backup runs with the incremental changes from the previous backup.

Using Block Change Tracking

Block change tracking is the process in which a binary file is used to record changes to database data file blocks. The idea is that incremental backup performance can be improved because RMAN can use the block change tracking file to pinpoint which blocks have changed since the last backup. This saves a great deal of time because otherwise RMAN would have to scan all the blocks that had been backed up to determine if they'd changed since the last backup.

Listed next are the steps for enabling block change tracking:

1. If not already enabled, set the DB_CREATE_FILE_DEST parameter to a location (that already exists on disk); for example,

   ```
   SQL> alter system set db_create_file_dest='/u01/O12C/bct' scope=both;
   ```

2. Enable block change tracking via the ALTER DATABASE command:

   ```
   SQL> alter database enable block change tracking;
   ```

This example creates a file with an OMF name in the directory specified by DB_CREATE_FILE_DEST. In this example the file created is given this name:

```
/u01/O12C/bct/O12C/changetracking/o1_mf_8h0wmng1_.chg
```

You can also enable block change tracking by directly specifying a file name, which does not require that DB_CREATE_FILE_DEST be set; for example,

```
SQL> alter database enable block change tracking using file '/u01/O12C/bct/btc.bt';
```

You can verify the details of block change tracking by running the following query:

```
SQL> select * from v$block_change_tracking;
```

For space-planning purposes, the size of the block change tracking file is approximately 1/30,000 the size of the total size of the blocks being tracked in the database. Therefore, the size of the block change tracking file is proportional to the size of the database and not to the amount of redo generated.

To disable block change tracking, run this command:

```
SQL> alter database disable block change tracking;
```

■ **Note** When you disable block change tracking, Oracle will automatically delete the block change tracking file.

Checking for Corruption in Data Files and Backups

You can use RMAN to check for corruption in data files, archive redo logs, and control files. You can also verify whether a backup set is restorable. The RMAN VALIDATE command is used to perform these types of integrity checks. There are three ways you can run the VALIDATE command:

- VALIDATE
- BACKUP...VALIDATE
- RESTORE...VALIDATE

■ **Note** The stand-alone VALIDATE command is available in Oracle 11g and higher. The BACKUP...VALIDATE and RESTORE...VALIDATE commands are available in Oracle 10g and higher.

Using VALIDATE

The VALIDATE command can be used stand-alone to check for missing files or physical corruption in database data files, archive redo log files, control files, spfiles, and backup set pieces. For example, this command will validate all data files and the control files:

```
RMAN> validate database;
```

You can also validate just the control file, as follows:

```
RMAN> validate current controlfile;
```

You can validate the archive redo log files, like so:

```
RMAN> validate archivelog all;
```

You may want to combine all the prior integrity checks into one command, as shown:

```
RMAN> validate database include current controlfile plus archivelog;
```

Under normal conditions the VALIDATE command only checks for physical corruption. You can specify that you also want to check for logical corruption by using the CHECK LOGICAL clause:

```
RMAN> validate check logical database include current controlfile plus archivelog;
```

VALIDATE has a variety of uses. Here are a few more examples:

```
RMAN> validate database skip offline;
RMAN> validate copy of database;
RMAN> validate tablespace system;
RMAN> validate datafile 3 block 20 to 30;
RMAN> validate spfile;
RMAN> validate backupset <primary_key_value>;
RMAN> validate recovery area;
```

If you're using the Oracle 12c pluggable database feature, you can validate specific databases within the container. While connected as SYS to the root container, validate any associated pluggable databases:

```
RMAN> validate pluggable database salespdb;
```

If RMAN detects any corrupt blocks, the V$DATABASE_BLOCK_CORRUPTION is populated. This view contains information on the file number, block number, and number of blocks affected. You can use this information to perform a block-level recovery (see Chapter 6 for more details).

■ **Note**   Physical corruption is a change to a block, such that its contents don't match the physical format that Oracle expects. By default, RMAN checks for physical corruption when backing up, restoring, and validating data files. With logical corruption, a block is in the correct format, but the contents aren't consistent with what Oracle expects, such as in a row piece or an index entry.

Using BACKUP...VALIDATE

The BACKUP...VALIDATE command is very similar to the VALIDATE command, in that it can check to see if data files are available and if the data files contain any corrupt blocks; for example,

```
RMAN> backup validate database;
```

This command doesn't actually create any backup files; it only reads the data files and checks for corruption. Like the VALIDATE command, BACKUP VALIDATE, by default, only checks for physical corruption. You can instruct it to check as well for logical corruption, as shown:

```
RMAN> backup validate check logical database;
```

Here are some variations of the BACKUP...VALIDATE command:

```
RMAN> backup validate database current controlfile;
RMAN> backup validate check logical database current controlfile plus archivelog;
```

Also like the VALIDATE command, BACKUP...VALIDATE will populate V$DATABASE_BLOCK_CORRUPTION if it detects any corrupt blocks. The information in this view can be used to determine which blocks can potentially be restored by block-level recovery (see Chapter 6 for more details).

Using RESTORE...VALIDATE

The `RESTORE...VALIDATE` command is used to verify backup files that would be used in a restore operation. This command validates backup sets, data file copies, and archive redo log files:

```
RMAN> restore validate database;
```

No actual files are restored when using `RESTORE...VALIDATE`. This means that you can run the command while the database is online and available.

Using a Recovery Catalog

When you use a recovery catalog, it's possible to create the recovery catalog user in the same database, on the same server, as your target database. However, that approach isn't recommended because you don't want the availability of your target database or of the server on which the target database resides to affect the recovery catalog. Therefore, you should create the recovery catalog database on a server different from that of your target database.

Creating a Recovery Catalog

When I use a recovery catalog, I prefer to have a dedicated database that is used only for the recovery catalog. This ensures that the recovery catalog isn't affected by any maintenance or downtime required by another application (and vice versa).

Listed next are the steps for creating a recovery catalog:

1. Create a database on a server different from that of your target database, to be used for the recovery catalog. Make sure the database is adequately sized. I've found that Oracle's recommended sizes are usually much too small. Here are some adequate recommendations:

   SYSTEM tablespace: 500MB

   SYSAUX tablespace: 500MB

   TEMP tablespace: 500MB

   UNDO tablespace: 500MB

   Online redo logs: 25MB each; three groups, multiplexed with two members per group

   RECCAT tablespace: 500MB

2. Create a tablespace to be used by the recovery catalog user. I recommend giving the tablespace a name such as `RECCAT` so that it's readily identifiable as the tablespace that contains the recovery catalog metadata:

```
CREATE TABLESPACE reccat
  DATAFILE '/u01/dbfile/O12C/reccat01.dbf' SIZE 500M
  EXTENT MANAGEMENT LOCAL UNIFORM SIZE 128k
  SEGMENT SPACE MANAGEMENT AUTO;
```

3. Create a user that will own the tables and other objects used to store the target database metadata. I recommend giving the recovery catalog user a name such as RCAT so that it's readily identifiable as the user that owns the recovery catalog objects. Also, grant the RECOVERY_CATALOG_OWNER role to the RCAT user as well as CREATE SESSION:

```
CREATE USER rcat IDENTIFIED BY foo
TEMPORARY TABLESPACE temp
DEFAULT TABLESPACE reccat
QUOTA UNLIMITED ON reccat;
--
GRANT RECOVERY_CATALOG_OWNER TO rcat;
GRANT CREATE SESSION TO rcat;
```

4. Connect through RMAN as RCAT, and create the recovery catalog objects:

```
$ rman catalog rcat/foo
```

5. Now, run the CREATE CATALOG command:

```
RMAN> create catalog;
RMAN> exit;
```

6. This command may take a few minutes to run. When it's finished, you can verify that the tables were created with the following query:

```
$ sqlplus rcat/foo
SQL> select table_name from user_tables;
```

7. Here is a small sample of the output:

```
TABLE_NAME
-----------------------------
DB
NODE
CONF
DBINC
```

Registering a Target Database

Now, you can register a target database with the recovery catalog. Log in to the target database server. Ensure that you can establish Oracle Net connectivity to the recovery catalog database. For instance, one approach is to populate the TNS_ADMIN/tnsnames.ora file with an entry that points to the remote database. On the target database server, register the recovery catalog, as follows:

```
$ rman target / catalog rcat/foo@rcat
```

When you connect, you should see verification that you're connecting to both the target and the recovery catalog:

```
connected to target database: O12C (DBID=3423216220)
connected to recovery catalog database
```

Next, run the REGISTER DATABASE command:

```
RMAN> register database;
```

Now, you can run backup operations and have the metadata about the backup tasks written to both the control file and the recovery catalog. Make sure you connect to the recovery catalog, along with the target database, each time you run RMAN commands:

```
$ rman target / catalog rcat/foo@rcat
RMAN> backup database;
```

Backing Up the Recovery Catalog

Make certain you include a strategy for backing up and recovering the recovery catalog database. For the most protection, be sure the recovery catalog database is in archivelog mode, and use RMAN to back up the database.

You can also use a tool such as Data Pump to take a snapshot of the database. The downside to using Data Pump is that you can potentially lose some information in the recovery catalog that was created after the Data Pump export.

Keep in mind that if you experience a complete failure on your recovery catalog database server, you can still use RMAN to back up your target databases; you just can't connect to the recovery catalog. Therefore, any scripts that instruct RMAN to connect to the target and the recovery catalog must be modified.

Also, if you completely lose a recovery catalog and don't have a backup, one option is to re-create it from scratch. As soon as you re-create it, you reregister the target databases with the recovery catalog. You lose any long-term historical recovery catalog metadata.

Synchronizing the Recovery Catalog

You may have an issue with the network that renders the recovery catalog inaccessible. In the meantime, you connect to your target database and perform backup operations. Sometime later, the network issues are resolved, and you can again connect to the recovery catalog.

In this situation, you need to resynchronize the recovery catalog with the target database so that the recovery catalog is aware of any backup operations that aren't stored in it. Run the following command to ensure that the recovery catalog has the most recent backup information:

```
$ rman target / catalog rcat/foo@rcat
RMAN> resync catalog;
```

Keep in mind that you have to resynchronize the catalog only if, for some reason, you're performing backup operations without connecting to the catalog. Under normal conditions, you don't have to run the RESYNC command.

Recovery Catalog Versions

I recommend that you create a recovery catalog for each version of the target databases that you're backing up. Doing so will save you some headaches with compatibility issues and upgrades. I've found it easier to use a recovery catalog when the database version of the rman client is the same version used when creating the catalog.

Yes, having multiple versions of the recovery catalog can cause some confusion. However, if you're in an environment in which you have several different versions of the Oracle database, then multiple recovery catalogs may be more convenient.

Dropping a Recovery Catalog

If you determine that you're not using a recovery catalog and that you no longer need the data, you can drop it. To do so, connect to the recovery catalog database as the catalog owner, and issue the DROP CATALOG command:

```
$ rman catalog rcat/foo
RMAN> drop catalog;
```

You're prompted as follows:

```
recovery catalog owner is RCAT
enter DROP CATALOG command again to confirm catalog removal
```

If you enter the DROP CATALOG command again, all the objects in the recovery catalog are removed from the recovery catalog database.

The other way to drop a catalog is to drop the owner. To do so, connect to the recovery catalog as a user with DBA privileges, and issue the DROP USER statement:

```
$ sqlplus system/manager
SQL> drop user rcat cascade;
```

SQL*Plus doesn't prompt you twice; it does as you instructed and drops the user and its objects. Again, the only reason to do this is when you're certain you don't need the recovery catalog or its data any longer. Use caution when dropping a user or the recovery catalog: I recommend that you take a Data Pump export of the recovery catalog owner before dropping it.

Logging RMAN Output

When troubleshooting RMAN output or checking the status of a backup job, it's essential to have a record of what RMAN ran and the status of each command. There are several methods for logging RMAN output. Some are built-in aspects of the Linux/Unix OS. Others are RMAN-specific features:

- Linux/Unix redirect output to file

- Linux/Unix logging commands

- RMAN SPOOL LOG command

- V$RMAN_OUTPUT view

These logging features are discussed in the next sections.

Redirecting Output to a File

I run almost all RMAN backup jobs from shell scripts. The shell scripts are usually run automatically from a scheduling tool such as cron. When running RMAN commands in this fashion, I always capture the output by instructing the shell command to redirect standard output messaging and standard error messaging to a log file. This is done with the redirection (>) character. This example runs a shell script (rmanback.bsh) and redirects both standard output and standard error output to a log file named rmanback.log:

```
$ rmanback.bsh 1>/home/oracle/bin/log/rmanback.log 2>&1
```

Here, 1> instructs standard output to be redirected to the specified file. The 2>&1 instructs the shell script to send standard error output to the same location as standard output.

■ **Tip**   For further details on how DBAs use shell scripts and Linux features, see *Linux Recipes for Oracle DBAs* by Darl Kuhn (Apress, 2008).

Capturing Output with Linux/Unix Logging Commands

You can instruct Linux/Unix to create a log file to capture any output that is also being displayed on your screen. This can be done in one of two ways:

- tee
- script

Capturing Output with tee

When you start RMAN, you can send the output you see on your screen to an OS text file, using the tee command:

```
$ rman | tee /tmp/rman.log
```

Now, you can connect to the target database and run commands. All the output seen on your screen will be logged to the /tmp/rman.log file:

```
RMAN> connect target /
RMAN> backup database;
RMAN> exit;
```

The tee party session stops writing to the log file when you exit RMAN.

Capturing Output with script

The script command is useful because it instructs the OS to log any output that appears at the terminal to a log file. To capture all output, run the script command before connecting to RMAN:

```
$ script /tmp/rman.log
Script started, file is /tmp/rman.log
$ rman target /
RMAN> backup database;
RMAN> exit;
```

To end a script session, press Ctrl+D, or type exit. The tmp/rman.log file will contain all output that was displayed on your screen. The script command is useful when you need to capture all the output from a particular time range. For example, you may be running RMAN commands, exiting from RMAN, running SQL*Plus commands, and so on. The script session lasts from the point at which you start script to the point at which you press Ctrl+D.

Logging Output to a File

An easy way to capture RMAN output is to use the SPOOL LOG command to send the output to a file. This example spools a log file from within RMAN:

```
RMAN> spool log to '/tmp/rmanout.log'
RMAN> set echo on;
RMAN> <run RMAN commands>
RMAN> spool log off;
```

By default the SPOOL LOG command will overwrite an existing file. If you want to append to the log file, use the keyword APPEND:

```
RMAN> spool log to '/tmp/rmanout.log' append
```

You can also direct output to a log file when starting RMAN on the command line, which will overwrite an existing file:

```
$ rman target / log /tmp/rmanout.log
```

You can also append to the log file, as follows:

```
$ rman target / log /tmp/rmanout.log append
```

When you use SPOOL LOG as shown in the previous examples, the output goes to a file and not to your terminal. Therefore, I hardly ever use SPOOL LOG when running RMAN interactively. The command is mainly a tool for capturing output when running RMAN from scripts.

Querying for Output in the Data Dictionary

If you don't capture any RMAN output, you can still view the most recent RMAN output by querying the data dictionary. The V$RMAN_OUTPUT view contains messages recently reported by RMAN:

```
select sid, recid, output
from v$rman_output
order by recid;
```

The V$RMAN_OUTPUT view is an in-memory object that holds up to 32,768 rows. Information in this view is cleared out when you stop and restart your database. The view is handy when you're using the RMAN SPOOL LOG command to spool output to a file and cannot view what is happening at your terminal.

RMAN Reporting

There are several different methods for reporting on the RMAN environment:

- LIST command
- REPORT command
- Query metadata via data dictionary views

When first learning RMAN, the difference between the LIST and REPORT commands may seem confusing because the distinction between the two is not clear-cut. In general, I use the LIST command to view information about existing backups and the REPORT command to determine which files need to be backed or to display information on obsolete or expired backups.

I use SQL queries for specialized reports (not available via LIST or REPORT) or for automating reports. For example, I'll generally implement an automated check via a shell script and SQL that reports whether the RMAN backups have run within the last day.

Using LIST

When investigating issues with RMAN backups, usually one of the first tasks I undertake is connecting to the target database and running the LIST BACKUP command. This command allows you to view backup sets, backup pieces, and the files included in the backup:

```
RMAN> list backup;
```

The command shows all RMAN backups recorded in the repository. You may want to spool the backups to an output file so that you can save the output and then use an OS editor to search through and look for specific strings in the output.

To get a summarized view of backup information, use the LIST BACKUP SUMMARY command:

```
RMAN> list backup summary;
```

You can also use the LIST command to report just image copy information:

```
RMAN> list copy;
```

To list all files that have been backed up, and the associated backup set, issue the following command:

```
RMAN> list backup by file;
```

These commands display archive redo logs on disk:

```
RMAN> list archivelog all;
RMAN> list copy of archivelog all;
```

And, this command lists the backups of the archive redo logs (and which archive redo logs are contained in which backup pieces):

```
RMAN> list backup of archivelog all;
```

There are a great many ways in which you can run the LIST command (and, likewise, the REPORT command, covered in the next section). The prior methods are the ones you'll run most of the time. See the *Oracle Database Backup and Recovery Reference Guide*, available from the Technology Network area of the Oracle web site (http://otn.oracle.com), for a complete list of options.

Using REPORT

The RMAN REPORT command is useful for reporting on a variety of details. You can quickly view all the data files associated with a database, as follows:

```
RMAN> report schema;
```

The REPORT command provides detailed information about backups marked obsolete via the RMAN retention policy; for example,

```
RMAN> report obsolete;
```

You can report on data files that need to be backed up, as defined by the retention policy, like this:

```
RMAN> report need backup;
```

There are several ways to report on data files that need to be backed up. Here are some other examples:

```
RMAN> report need backup redundancy 2;
RMAN> report need backup redundancy 2 datafile 2;
```

The REPORT command may also be used for data files that have never been backed up or that may contain data created from a NOLOGGING operation. For example, say you have direct-path loaded data into a table, and the data file in which the table resides has not been backed up. The following command will detect these conditions:

```
RMAN> report unrecoverable;
```

Using SQL

There are a number of data dictionary views available for querying about backup information. Table 5-1 describes RMAN-related data dictionary views. These views are available regardless of your use of a recovery catalog (the information in these views is derived from the control file).

Table 5-1. *Description of RMAN Backup Data Dictionary Views*

View Name	Information Provided
V$RMAN_BACKUP_JOB_DETAILS	RMAN backup jobs
V$BACKUP	Backup status of online data files placed in backup mode (for hot backups)
V$BACKUP_ARCHIVELOG_DETAILS	Archive logs backed up
V$BACKUP_CONTROLFILE_DETAILS	Control files backed up
V$BACKUP_COPY_DETAILS	Control file and data file copies
V$BACKUP_DATAFILE	Control files and data files backed up
V$BACKUP_DATAFILE_DETAILS	Data files backed up in backup sets, image copies, and proxy copies
V$BACKUP_FILES	Data files, control files, spfiles, and archive redo logs backed up
V$BACKUP_PIECE	Backup piece files
V$BACKUP_PIECE_DETAILS	Backup piece details
V$BACKUP_SET	Backup sets
V$BACKUP_SET_DETAILS	Backup set details

Sometimes, DBAs new to RMAN have a hard time grasping the concept of backups, backup sets, backup pieces, and data files and how they relate. I find the following query useful when discussing RMAN backup components. This query will display backup sets, the backup pieces with the set, and the data files that are backed up within the backup pieces:

```
SET LINES 132 PAGESIZE 100
BREAK ON REPORT ON bs_key ON completion_time ON bp_name ON file_name
COL bs_key      FORM 99999 HEAD "BS Key"
COL bp_name     FORM a40   HEAD "BP Name"
COL file_name FORM a40    HEAD "Datafile"
--
SELECT
 s.recid                  bs_key
,TRUNC(s.completion_time) completion_time
,p.handle                 bp_name
,f.name                   file_name
FROM v$backup_set      s
    ,v$backup_piece    p
    ,v$backup_datafile d
    ,v$datafile        f
WHERE p.set_stamp = s.set_stamp
AND    p.set_count = s.set_count
AND    d.set_stamp = s.set_stamp
AND    d.set_count = s.set_count
AND    d.file#     = f.file#
ORDER BY
 s.recid
,p.handle
,f.name;
```

The output here has been shortened to fit on the page:

```
S Key COMPLETIO BP Name                                      Datafile
------ --------- ------------------------------------------- -----------------------------------
    11 28-SEP-14 /u01/O12C/rman/O12C_Ocpjkl6h_1_1.bk          /u01/dbfile/O12C/inv_mgmt_data01.dbf
                                                              /u01/dbfile/O12C/reg_index01.dbf
                                                              /u01/dbfile/O12C/tools01.dbf
                                                              /u01/dbfile/O12C/undotbs01.dbf
                                                              /u01/dbfile/O12C/users01.dbf
```

Sometimes, it's useful to report on the performance of RMAN backups. The following query reports on the time taken for an RMAN backup per session.

```
COL hours               FORM 9999.99
COL time_taken_display FORM a20
SET LINESIZE 132
--
SELECT
 session_recid
,compression_ratio
,time_taken_display
,(end_time - start_time) * 24 as hours
```

```
,TO_CHAR(end_time,'dd-mon-yy hh24:mi') as end_time
FROM v$rman_backup_job_details
ORDER BY end_time;
```

Here is some sample output:

```
SESSION_RECID COMPRESSION_RATIO TIME_TAKEN_DISPLAY     HOURS END_TIME
------------- ----------------- --------------------   -------- ------------------------
            3        2.03556203 00:00:18                   .00 28-sep-14 11:03
            6        7.81358269 00:00:25                   .01 28-sep-14 11:06
           14        10.7638918 00:00:19                   .01 28-sep-14 11:07
```

The contents of V$RMAN_BACKUP_JOB_DETAILS are summarized by a session connection to RMAN. Therefore, the report output is more accurate if you connect to RMAN (establishing a session) and then exit out of RMAN after the backup job is complete. If you remain connected to RMAN while running multiple backup jobs, the query output reports on all backup activity while connected (for that session).

You should have an automated method of detecting whether or not RMAN backups are running and if data files are being backed up. One reliable method of automating such a task is to embed SQL into a shell script and then run the script on a periodic basis from a scheduling utility such as cron.

I typically run two basic types of checks regarding the RMAN backups:

- Have the RMAN backups run recently?

- Are there any data files that have not been backed up recently?

The following shell script checks for these conditions. You'll need to modify the script and provide it with a username and password for a user that can query the data dictionary objects referenced in the script and also change the e-mail address of where messages are sent. When running the script, you'll need to pass in two variables: the Oracle SID and the threshold number of past days that you want to check for the last time the backups ran or for when a data file was backed up.

```
#!/bin/bash
#
if [ $# -ne 2 ]; then
  echo "Usage: $0 SID threshold"
  exit 1
fi
# source oracle OS variables
export ORACLE_SID=O12C
export ORACLE_HOME=/orahome/app/oracle/product/12.1.0.1/db_1
export PATH=$PATH:$ORACLE_HOME/bin
crit_var=$(sqlplus -s <<EOF
/ as sysdba
SET HEAD OFF FEEDBACK OFF
SELECT COUNT(*) FROM
(SELECT (sysdate - MAX(end_time)) delta
 FROM v\$rman_backup_job_details) a
WHERE a.delta > $2;
EOF)
#
if [ $crit_var -ne 0 ]; then
  echo "rman backups not running on $1" | mailx -s "rman problem" dkuhn@gmail.com
```

```
else
  echo "rman backups ran ok"
fi
#-----------------------------------------------
crit_var2=$(sqlplus -s <<EOF
/ as sysdba
SET HEAD OFF FEEDBACK OFF
SELECT COUNT(*)
FROM
(
SELECT name
FROM v\$datafile
MINUS
SELECT DISTINCT
 f.name
FROM v\$backup_datafile d
    ,v\$datafile          f
WHERE d.file#    = f.file#
AND   d.completion_time > sysdate - $2);
EOF)
#
if [ $crit_var2 -ne 0 ]; then
  echo "datafile not backed up on $1" | mailx -s "backup problem" dkuhn@gmail.com
else
  echo "datafiles are backed up..."
fi
#
exit 0
```

For example, to check if backups have been running successfully within the past 2 days, run the script (named rman_chk.bsh):

```
$ rman_chk.bsh 012c 2
```

The prior script is basic but effective. You can enhance it as required for your RMAN environment.

Summary

RMAN offers many flexible and feature-rich options for backups. By default, RMAN backs up only blocks that have been modified in the database. The incremental features allow you to back up only blocks that have been modified since the last backup. These incremental features are particularly useful in reducing the size of backups in large database environments, in which only a small percentage of data in the database changes from one backup to the next.

You can instruct RMAN to back up every block in each data file via an image copy. An image copy is a block-for-block identical copy of the data file. Image copies have the advantage of being able to restore the backup files directly from the backup (without using RMAN). You can use the incrementally updated backup feature to implement an efficient hybrid of image copy backups and incremental backups.

RMAN contains built-in commands for reporting on many aspects of backups. The LIST command reports on backup activity. The REPORT command is useful for determining which files need to be backed up, as dictated by the retention policy.

After you've successfully configured RMAN and created backups, you are in a position to be able to restore and recover your database in the event of a media failure. Restore and recovery topics are detailed in the next chapter.

CHAPTER 6

■ ■ ■

RMAN Restore and Recovery

A couple of years ago, I was out on a long Saturday morning bike ride. About halfway through the ride, my cell phone rang. It was one of the data center operational support technicians. He told me that a mission critical database server was acting strange and that I should log in as soon as possible and make sure things were okay. I told him that I was about 15 minutes from being able to log in. So, I scurried home as fast as I could to check out the production box. When I got home and logged in to the database server, I tried to start SQL*Plus and immediately got an error indicating that the SQL*Plus binary file had corruption. Great. I couldn't even log in to SQL*Plus. This was not good.

■ **Mental Note**   Ensure that all bicycle rides are taken out of range of cell phone coverage. – Ed.

I had the SA restore the Oracle binaries from an OS backup. I started SQL*Plus. The database had crashed, so I attempted to start it. The output indicated that there was a media failure with all the data files. After some analysis it was discovered that there had been some filesystem issues and that all these files on disk were corrupt:

- Data files
- Control files
- Archive redo logs
- Online redo log files
- RMAN backup pieces

This was almost a total disaster. My director asked about our options. I responded, "All we have to do is restore the database from our last tape backup, and we'll lose whatever data are in archive redo logs that haven't been backed up to tape yet."

The storage administrators were called in and instructed to restore the last set of RMAN backups that had been written to tape. About 15 minutes later, we could hear the tape guys talking to each other in hushed voices. One of them said, "We are sooooo hosed. We don't have any tape backups of RMAN for any databases on this box."

That was a dark moment. The worst case scenario was to rebuild the database from DDL scripts and lose 3 years of production data. Not a very palatable option.

After looking around the production box, I discovered that the prior production support DBA (who, ironically, had just been let go a few days before, owing to budget cuts) had implemented a job to copy the RMAN backups to another server in the production environment. The RMAN backups on this other server were intact. I was able to restore and recover the production database from these backups. We lost about a day's worth of data (between corrupt archive logs and downtime, in which no incoming transactions were allowed), but we were able to get the database restored and recovered approximately 20 hours after the initial phone call. That was a long day.

Most situations in which you need to restore and recover will not be as bad as the one just described. However, the previous scenario does highlight the need for

- a backup strategy

- a DBA with B&R skills

- a restore-and-recovery strategy, including a requirement to test the restore and recovery periodically

This chapter walks you through restore and recovery, using RMAN. The chapter covers many of the common tasks you will have to perform when dealing with media failures.

Determining if Media Recovery Is Required

The term media recovery means the restoration of files that have been lost or damaged, owing to the failure of the underlying storage media (usually a disk of some sort) or accidental removal of files. Usually, you know that media recovery is required through an error such as the following:

```
ORA-01157: cannot identify/lock data file 1 - see DBWR trace file
ORA-01110: data file 1: '/u01/dbfile/O12C/system01.dbf'
```

The error may be displayed on your screen when performing DBA tasks, such as stopping and starting the database. Or, you might see such an error in a trace file or the alert.log file. If you don't notice the issue right away, with a severe media failure, the database will stop processing transactions, and users will start calling you.

To understand how Oracle determines that media recovery is required, you must first understand how Oracle determines that everything is okay. When Oracle shuts down normally (IMMEDIATE, TRANSACTIONAL, NORMAL), part of the shutdown process is to flush all modified blocks (in memory) to disk, mark the header of each data file with the current SCN, and update the control file with the current SCN information.

Upon startup, Oracle checks to see if the SCN in the control file matches the SCN in the header of the data files. If there is a match, then Oracle attempts to open the data files and online redo log files. If all files are available and can be opened, Oracle starts normally. The following query compares the SCN in the control file (for each data file) with the SCN in the data file header:

```
SET LINES 132
COL name            FORM a40
COL status          FORM A8
COL file#           FORM 9999
COL control_file_SCN FORM 999999999999999
COL datafile_SCN    FORM 999999999999999
--
SELECT
 a.name
,a.status
,a.file#
,a.checkpoint_change# control_file_SCN
,b.checkpoint_change# datafile_SCN
,CASE
   WHEN ((a.checkpoint_change# - b.checkpoint_change#) = 0) THEN 'Startup Normal'
   WHEN ((b.checkpoint_change#) = 0)                        THEN 'File Missing?'
   WHEN ((a.checkpoint_change# - b.checkpoint_change#) > 0) THEN 'Media Rec. Req.'
```

```
  WHEN ((a.checkpoint_change# - b.checkpoint_change#) < 0) THEN 'Old Control File'
  ELSE 'what the ?'
END datafile_status
FROM v$datafile          a -- control file SCN for datafile
    ,v$datafile_header b -- datafile header SCN
WHERE a.file# = b.file#
ORDER BY a.file#;
```

If the control file SCN values are greater than the data file SCN values, then media recovery is most likely required. This would be the case if you restored a data file from a backup, and the SCN in the restored data file had an SCN less than the data file in the current control file.

■ **Tip** The V$DATAFILE_HEADER view uses the physical data file on disk as its source. The V$DATAFILE view uses the control file as its source.

You can also directly query the V$DATAFILE_HEADER for more information. The ERROR and RECOVER columns report any potential problems. For example, a YES or null value in the RECOVER column indicates that there is a problem:

```
SQL> select file#, status, error, recover from v$datafile_header;
```

Here is some sample output:

```
FILE# STATUS  ERROR                REC
----- ------- -------------------- ---
    1 ONLINE  FILE NOT FOUND
    2 ONLINE                       NO
    3 ONLINE                       NO
```

Determining What to Restore

Media recovery requires that you perform manual tasks to get your database back in one piece. These tasks usually involve a combination of RESTORE and RECOVER commands. You will have to issue an RMAN RESTORE command if, for some reason (accidental deleting of files, disk failure, and so on), your data files have experienced media failure.

How the Process Works

When you issue the RESTORE command, RMAN automatically decides how to extract the data files from any of the following available backups:

- Full database backup

- Incremental level-0 backup

- Image copy backup generated by BACKUP AS COPY command

After the files are restored from a backup, you are required to apply redo to them via the RECOVER command. When you issue the RECOVER command, Oracle examines the SCNs in the affected data files and determines whether any of them need to be recovered. If the SCN in the data file is less than the corresponding SCN in the control file, then media recovery will be required.

Oracle retrieves the data file SCN and then looks for the corresponding SCN in the redo stream to establish where to start the recovery process. If the starting recovery SCN is in the online redo log files, the archived redo log files are not required for recovery.

During a recovery, RMAN automatically determines how to apply redo. First, RMAN applies any incremental backups available that are greater than level 0, such as the incremental level 1. Next, any archived redo log files on disk are applied. If the archived redo log files do not exist on disk, RMAN attempts to retrieve them from a backup set.

To be able to perform a complete recovery, all the following conditions need to be true:

- Your database is in archivelog mode.

- You have a good baseline backup of your database.

- You have any required redo that has been generated since the backup (archived redo log files, online redo log files, or incremental backups that RMAN can use for recovery instead of applying redo).

There are a wide variety of restore-and-recovery scenarios. How you restore and recover depends directly on your backup strategy and which files have been damaged. Listed next are the general steps to follow when facing a media failure:

1. Determine which files need to be restored.

2. Depending on the damage, set your database mode to nomount, mount, or open.

3. Use the RESTORE command to retrieve files from RMAN backups.

4. Use the RECOVER command for data files requiring recovery.

5. Open your database.

Your particular restore-and-recovery scenario may not require that all the previous steps be performed. For instance, you may just want to restore your spfile, which doesn't require a recovery step.

The first step in the restore-and-recovery process is to determine which files have experienced media failure. You can usually determine which files need to be restored from the following sources:

- Error messages displayed on your screen, either from RMAN or SQL*Plus

- Alert.log file and corresponding trace files

- Data dictionary views

If you're using Oracle 11g or higher, then in addition to the previously listed methods, you should consider the Data Recovery Advisor for obtaining information about the extent of a failure and corresponding corrective action.

Using Data Recovery Advisor

The Data Recovery Advisor tool was introduced in Oracle 11g. In the event of a media failure, this tool will display the details of the failure, recommend corrective actions, and perform the recommended actions if you specify that it do so. It's like having another set of eyes to provide feedback when in a restore-and-recovery situation. There are four modes to Data Recovery Advisor:

- Listing failures

- Suggesting corrective action

- Running commands to repair failures

- Changing the status of a failure

The Data Recovery Advisor is invoked from RMAN. You can think of the Data Recovery Advisor as a set of RMAN commands that can assist you when dealing with media failure.

Listing Failures

When using the Data Recovery Advisor, the LIST FAILURE command is used to display any issues with the data files, control files, or online redo logs:

```
RMAN> list failure;
```

■ **Tip** If you suspect there's a media failure, yet the Data Recovery Advisor is not reporting any issues, run the VALIDATE DATABASE command to verify that the database is intact.

If there are no detected failures, you'll see a message indicating that there are no failures. Here is some sample output indicating that there may be an issue with a data file:

```
List of Database Failures
=========================

Failure ID Priority Status    Time Detected Summary
---------- -------- --------- ------------- -------
6222       CRITICAL OPEN      12-JAN-14     System datafile 1:
'/u01/dbfile/O12C/system01.dbf' is missing
```

To display more information about the failure, use the DETAIL clause:

```
RMAN> list failure 6222 detail;
```

Here is the additional output for this example:

```
Impact: Database cannot be opened
```

With this type of failure, the prior output indicates that the database can't be opened.

Suggesting Corrective Action

The ADVISE FAILURE command gives advice about how to recover from potential problems detected by the Data Recovery Advisor. If you have multiple failures with your database, you can directly specify the failure ID to get advice on a given failure, like so:

```
RMAN> advise failure 6222;
```

Here is a snippet of the output for this particular issue:

```
Optional Manual Actions
========================
1. If file /u01/dbfile/O12C/system01.dbf was unintentionally renamed or moved,
restore it

Automated Repair Options
========================
Option Repair Description
------ -------------------
1      Restore and recover datafile 1
  Strategy: The repair includes complete media recovery with no data loss
  Repair script: /ora01/app/oracle/diag/rdbms/O12C/O12C/hm/reco_4116328280.hm
```

In this case, the Data Recovery Advisor created a script that can be used to potentially fix the problem. The contents of the repair script can be viewed with an OS utility; for example,

```
$ cat /ora01/app/oracle/diag/rdbms/O12C/O12C/hm/reco_4116328280.hm
```

Here are the contents of the script for this example:

```
# restore and recover datafile
restore ( datafile 1 );
recover datafile 1;
sql 'alter database datafile 1 online';
```

After reviewing the script, you can decide to run the suggested commands manually, or you can have the Data Recovery Advisor run the script via the REPAIR command (see the next section for details).

Repairing Failures

If you have identified a failure and viewed the recommended advice, you can proceed to the repair work. If you want to inspect what the REPAIR FAILURE command will do without actually running the commands, use the PREVIEW clause:

```
RMAN> repair failure preview;
```

Before you run the REPAIR FAILURE command, ensure that you first run the LIST FAILURE and ADVISE FAILURE commands from the same connected session. In other words, the RMAN session that you're in must run the LIST and ADVISE commands within the same session before running the REPAIR command.

If you're satisfied with the repair suggestions, then run the REPAIR FAILURE command:

```
RMAN> repair failure;
```

You'll be prompted at this point for confirmation:

```
Do you really want to execute the above repair (enter YES or NO)?
```

Type YES to proceed:

```
YES
```

If all goes well, you should see a final message such as this in the output:

```
repair failure complete
```

■ **Note**   You can run the Data Recovery Advisor commands from the RMAN command prompt or from Enterprise Manager.

In this way, you can use the RMAN commands LIST FAILURE, ADVISE FAILURE, and REPAIR FAILURE to resolve media failures.

Changing the Status of a Failure

One last note on the Data Recovery Advisor: if you know that you've had a failure and that it isn't critical (e.g., a data file missing from a tablespace that is no longer used), then use the CHANGE FAILURE command to alter the priority of a failure. In this example, there's a missing data file that belongs to a noncritical tablespace. First, obtain the failure priority via the LIST FAILURE command:

```
RMAN> list failure;
```

Here is some sample output:

```
Failure ID Priority Status    Time Detected Summary
---------- -------- --------- ------------- -------
5          HIGH     OPEN      12-JAN-14     One or more non-system datafiles
                                            are missing
```

Next, change the priority from HIGH to LOW with the CHANGE FAILURE command:

```
RMAN> change failure 5 priority low;
```

You will be prompted to confirm that you really do want to change the priority:

```
Do you really want to change the above failures (enter YES or NO)?
```

If you do want to change the priority, then type YES, and press the Enter key. If you run the LIST FAILURE command again, you'll see that the priority has now been changed to LOW:

```
RMAN> list failure low;
```

Using RMAN to Stop/Start Oracle

You can use RMAN to stop and start your database with methods that are almost identical to those available through SQL*Plus. When performing restore and recovery operations, it's often more convenient to stop and start your database from within RMAN. The following RMAN commands can be used to stop and start your database:

- SHUTDOWN
- STARTUP
- ALTER DATABASE

Shutting Down

The SHUTDOWN command works the same from RMAN as it does from SQL*Plus. There are four types of shutdown: ABORT, IMMEDIATE, NORMAL, and TRANSACTIONAL. I usually first attempt to stop a database using SHUTDOWN IMMEDIATE; if that doesn't work, don't hesitate to use SHUTDOWN ABORT. Here are some examples:

```
RMAN> shutdown immediate;
RMAN> shutdown abort;
```

If you don't specify a shutdown option, NORMAL is the default. Shutting down a database with NORMAL is rarely viable, as this mode waits for currently connected users to disconnect at their leisure. I never use NORMAL when shutting down a database.

Starting Up

As with SQL*Plus, you can use a combination of STARTUP and ALTER DATABASE commands with RMAN to step the database through startup phases, like this:

```
RMAN> startup nomount;
RMAN> alter database mount;
RMAN> alter database open;
```

Here is another example:

```
RMAN> startup mount;
RMAN> alter database open;
```

If you want to start the database with restricted access, use the DBA option:

```
RMAN> startup dba;
```

■ **Tip** Starting with Oracle 12c, you can run all SQL statements directly from within RMAN without having to specify the RMAN sql command.

Complete Recovery

As discussed in Chapter 3, the term *complete recovery* means that you can restore all transactions that were committed before a failure occurred. *Complete recovery* doesn't mean that you are restoring and recovering all data files in your database. For instance, you are performing a complete recovery if you have a media failure with one data file, and you restore and recover the one data file. For complete recovery, the following conditions must be true:

- Your database is in archivelog mode.

- You have a good baseline backup of the data files that have experienced media failure.

- You have any required redo that has been generated since the last backup.

- All archive redo logs start from the point at which the last backup began.

- Any incremental backups that RMAN can use for recovery are available (if using).

- Online redo logs that contain transactions that have not yet been archived are available.

If you've experienced a media failure, and you have the required files to perform a complete recovery, then you can restore and recover your database.

Testing Restore and Recovery

You can determine which files RMAN will use for restore and recovery before you actually perform the restore and recovery. You can also instruct RMAN to verify the integrity of the backup files that will be used for the restore and recovery.

Previewing Backups Used for Recovery

Use the RESTORE...PREVIEW command to list the backups and archive redo log files that RMAN will use to restore and recover database data files. The RESTORE...PREVIEW command does not actually restore any files. Rather, it lists the backup files that will be used for a restore operation. This example previews in detail the backups required for restore and recovery for the entire database:

```
RMAN> restore database preview;
```

You can also preview require backup files at a summarized level of detail:

```
RMAN> restore database preview summary;
```

Here is a snippet of the output:

```
List of Backups
===============
Key     TY LV S Device Type Completion Time #Pieces #Copies Compress Tag
------- -- -- - ----------- --------------- ------- ------- -------- ---
12      B  0  A DISK        28-SEP-14       1       1       YES      TAG20140928T110657
11      B  0  A DISK        28-SEP-14       1       1       YES      TAG20140928T110657
```

Here are some more examples of how to preview backups required for restore and recovery:

```
RMAN> restore tablespace system preview;
RMAN> restore archivelog from time 'sysdate -1' preview;
RMAN> restore datafile 1, 2, 3 preview;
```

Validating Backup Files Before Restoring

There are several levels of verification that you can perform on backup files without actually restoring anything. If you just want RMAN to verify that the files exist and check the file headers, then use the RESTORE...VALIDATE HEADER command, as shown:

```
RMAN> restore database validate header;
```

This command only validates the existence of backup files and checks the file headers. You can further instruct RMAN to verify the integrity of blocks within backup files required to restore the database data files via the RESTORE...VALIDATE command (sans the HEADER clause). Again, RMAN will not restore any data files in this mode:

```
RMAN> restore database validate;
```

This command only checks for physical corruption within the backup files. You can also check for logical corruption (along with physical corruption), as follows:

```
RMAN> restore database validate check logical;
```

Here are some other examples of using RESTORE...VALIDATE:

```
RMAN> restore datafile 1,2,3 validate;
RMAN> restore archivelog all validate;
RMAN> restore controlfile validate;
RMAN> restore tablespace system validate;
```

Testing Media Recovery

The prior sections covered reporting and verifying the restore operations. You can also instruct RMAN to verify the recovery process via the RECOVER...TEST command. Before performing a test recovery, you need to ensure that the data files being recovered are offline. Oracle will throw an error for any online data files being recovered in test mode.

In this example the tablespace USERS is restored first, and then a trial recovery is performed:

```
RMAN> connect target /
RMAN> startup mount;
RMAN> restore tablespace users;
RMAN> recover tablespace users test;
```

If there are any missing archive redo logs that are required for recovery, the following error is thrown:

```
RMAN-06053: unable to perform media recovery because of missing log
RMAN-06025: no backup of archived log for thread 1 with sequence 6...
```

If the testing of the recovery succeeded, you'll see messages such as the following, indicating that the application of redo was tested but not applied:

```
ORA-10574: Test recovery did not corrupt any data block
ORA-10573: Test recovery tested redo from change 4586939 to 4588462
ORA-10572: Test recovery canceled due to errors
ORA-10585: Test recovery can not apply redo that may modify control file
```

Here are some other examples of testing the recovery process:

```
RMAN> recover database test;
RMAN> recover tablespace users, tools test;
RMAN> recover datafile 1,2,3 test;
```

Restoring and Recovering the Entire Database

The RESTORE DATABASE command will restore every data file in your database. The exception to this is when RMAN detects that data files have already been restored; in that case, it will not restore them again. If you want to override that behavior, use the FORCE command.

When you issue the RECOVER DATABASE command, RMAN will automatically apply redo to any data files that need recovery. The recovery process includes applying changes found in the following files:

- Incremental backup pieces (applicable only if using incremental backups)

- Archived redo log files (generated since the last backup or incremental backup applied)

- Online redo log files (current and unarchived)

You can open your database after the restore-and-recovery process is complete. Complete database recovery works only if you have good backups of your database and access to all redo generated after the backup was taken. You need all the redo required to recover the database data files. If you don't have all the required redo, then you'll most likely have to perform an incomplete recovery (see the section "Incomplete Recovery," later in this chapter).

■ **Note** Your database has to be at least mounted to restore data files, using RMAN. This is because RMAN reads information from the control file during the restore-and-recovery process.

You can perform a complete database-level recovery with either the current control file or a backup control file.

Using the Current Control File

You must first put your database in mount mode to perform a database-wide restore and recovery. This is because Oracle won't allow you to operate your database in open mode while data files associated with the SYSTEM tablespace are being restored and recovered. In this situation, start up the database in mount mode, issue the RESTORE and RECOVER commands, and then open the database, like so:

```
$ rman target /
RMAN> startup mount;
RMAN> restore database;
RMAN> recover database;
RMAN> alter database open;
```

If everything goes as expected, the last message you should see is this:

```
Statement processed
```

Using the Backup Control File

This technique uses an autobackup of the control file retrieved from the FRA (see the section "Restoring a Control File," later in this chapter, for more examples of how to restore your control file). In this scenario the control file is first retrieved from a backup before restoring and recovering the database:

```
$ rman target /
RMAN> startup nomount;
RMAN> restore controlfile from autobackup;
RMAN> alter database mount;
RMAN> restore database;
RMAN> recover database;
RMAN> alter database open resetlogs;
```

If successful, the last message you should see is this:

```
Statement processed
```

Restoring and Recovering Tablespaces

Sometimes you'll have a media failure that's localized to a particular tablespace or set of tablespaces. In this situation, it's appropriate to restore and recover at the tablespace level of granularity. The RMAN RESTORE TABLESPACE and RECOVER TABLESPACE commands will restore and recover all data files associated with the specified tablespace(s).

Restoring Tablespaces While the Database Is Open

If your database is open, then you must take offline the tablespace you want to restore and recover. You can do this for any tablespace except SYSTEM and UNDO. This example restores and recovers the USERS tablespace while the database is open:

```
$ rman target /
RMAN> sql 'alter tablespace users offline immediate';
RMAN> restore tablespace users;
RMAN> recover tablespace users;
RMAN> sql 'alter tablespace users online';
```

After the tablespace is brought online, you should see a message such as this:

```
sql statement: alter tablespace users online
```

Starting with Oracle 12c, you can run SQL statements directly, without the RMAN sql command and associated quotation marks; for example,

```
$ rman target /
RMAN> alter tablespace users offline immediate;
RMAN> restore tablespace users;
RMAN> recover tablespace users;
RMAN> alter tablespace users online;
```

Restoring Tablespaces While the Database Is in Mount Mode

Usually when performing a restore and recovery, DBAs will shut down the database and restart it in mount mode in preparation for performing the recovery. Placing a database in mount mode ensures that no users are connecting to the database and that no transactions are transpiring.

Also, if you're restoring and recovering the SYSTEM tablespace, then you must start the database in mount mode. Oracle doesn't allow for restoring and recovering the SYSTEM tablespace data files while the database is open. This next example restores the SYSTEM tablespace while the database is in mount mode:

```
$ rman target /
RMAN> shutdown immediate;
RMAN> startup mount;
RMAN> restore tablespace system;
RMAN> recover tablespace system;
RMAN> alter database open;
```

If successful, the last message you should see is this:

```
Statement processed
```

Restoring Read-Only Tablespaces

RMAN will restore read-only tablespaces along with the rest of the database when you issue a RESTORE DATDABASE command. For example, the following command will restore all data files (including those in read-only mode):

```
RMAN> restore database;
```

Prior to Oracle 11g, you were required to issue RESTORE DATABASE CHECK READONLY to instruct RMAN to restore read-only tablespaces along with tablespaces in read-write mode. This is no longer a requirement in Oracle 11g and higher.

■ **Note**   If you are using a backup that was created after the read-only tablespace was placed in read-only mode, then no recovery is necessary for the read-only data files. In this situation no redo has been generated for the read-only tablespace since it was backed up.

Restoring Temporary Tablespaces

Starting with Oracle 10g, you don't have to restore or re-create missing locally managed temporary tablespace temp files. When you open your database for use, Oracle automatically detects and re-creates locally managed temporary tablespace temp files.

When Oracle automatically re-creates a temporary tablespace, it will log a message to your target database alert.log such as this:

```
Re-creating tempfile <your temporary tablespace filename>
```

If, for any reason, your temporary tablespace becomes unavailable, you can also re-create it yourself. Because there are never any permanent objects in temporary tablespaces, you can simply re-create them as needed. Here is an example of how to create a locally managed temporary tablespace:

```
CREATE TEMPORARY TABLESPACE temp TEMPFILE
'/u01/dbfile/012C/temp01.dbf' SIZE 1000M
EXTENT MANAGEMENT
LOCAL UNIFORM SIZE 512K;
```

If your temporary tablespace exists, but the temporary data files are missing, you can just add them, as shown:

```
alter tablespace temp
add tempfile '/u01/dbfile/012C/temp02.dbf' SIZE 5000M REUSE;
```

Restoring and Recovering Data Files

A data file–level restore and recovery works well when a media failure is confined to a small set of data files. With data file–level recoveries, you can instruct RMAN to restore and recover either with data file name or data file number. For data files not associated with the SYSTEM or UNDO tablespaces, you have the option of restoring and recovering while the database remains open. While the database is open, however, you must first take offline any data files being restored and recovered.

Restoring and Recovering Data Files While the Database Is Open

Use the RESTORE DATAFILE and RECOVER DATAFILE commands to restore and recover at the data file level. When your database is open, you're required to take offline any data files that you're attempting to restore and recover. This example restores and recovers data files while the database is open:

```
RMAN> sql 'alter database datafile 4, 5 offline';
RMAN> restore datafile 4, 5;
RMAN> recover datafile 4, 5;
RMAN> sql 'alter database datafile 4, 5 online';
```

■ **Tip**   Use the RMAN REPORT SCHEMA command to list data file names and file numbers. You can also query the NAME and FILE# columns of V$DATAFILE to take names and numbers.

You can also specify the name of the data file that you want to restore and recover; for example,

```
RMAN> sql "alter database datafile ''/u01/dbfile/012C/users01.dbf'' offline";
RMAN> restore datafile '/u01/dbfile/012C/users01.dbf';
RMAN> recover datafile '/u01/dbfile/012C/users01.dbf';
RMAN> sql "alter database datafile ''/u01/dbfile/012C/users01.dbf'' online";
```

■ **Note**   When using the RMAN sql command, if there are single quotation marks within the SQL statement, then you are required to use double quotation marks to enclose the entire SQL statement and two single quotation marks where you would ordinarily use just one quotation double mark.

As mentioned earlier, starting with Oracle 12c, you can run SQL commands directly, without the RMAN sql command and associated quotation marks; for example,

```
RMAN> alter database datafile 4 offline;
RMAN> restore datafile 4;
RMAN> recover datafile 4;
RMAN> alter database datafile 4 online;
```

Here are the corresponding 12c examples, with the data file names:

```
RMAN> alter database datafile '/u01/dbfile/O12C/users01.dbf' offline;
RMAN> restore datafile '/u01/dbfile/O12C/users01.dbf';
RMAN> recover datafile '/u01/dbfile/O12C/users01.dbf';
RMAN> alter database datafile '/u01/dbfile/O12C/users01.dbf' online;
```

Restoring and Recovering Data Files While the Database Is Not Open

In this scenario the database is first shut down and then started in mount mode. You can restore and recover any data file in your database while the database is not open. This example shows the restoring of data file 1, which is associated with the SYSTEM tablespace:

```
$ rman target /
RMAN> shutdown abort;
RMAN> startup mount;
RMAN> restore datafile 1;
RMAN> recover datafile 1;
RMAN> alter database open;
```

You can also specify the file name when performing a data file recovery:

```
$ rman target /
RMAN> shutdown abort;
RMAN> startup mount;
RMAN> restore datafile '/u01/dbfile/O12C/system01.dbf';
RMAN> recover datafile '/u01/dbfile/O12C/system01.dbf';
RMAN> alter database open;
```

Restoring Data Files to Nondefault Locations

Sometimes a failure will occur that renders the disks associated with a mount point inoperable. In these situations, you will need to restore and recover the data files to a location different from the one where they originally resided. Another typical need for restoring data files to nondefault locations is that you're restoring to a different database server, on which the mount points are completely different from those of the server on which the backup originated.

Use the SET NEWNAME and SWITCH commands to restore data files to nondefault locations. Both of these commands must be run from within an RMAN run{} block. You can think of using SET NEWNAME and SWITCH as a way to rename data files (similar to the SQL*Plus ALTER DATABASE RENAME FILE statement).

This example changes the location of data files when doing a restore and recover. First, place the database in mount mode:

```
$ rman target /
RMAN> startup mount;
```

Then, run the following block of RMAN code:

```
run{
set newname for datafile 4 to '/u02/dbfile/012C/users01.dbf';
set newname for datafile 5 to '/u02/dbfile/012C/users02.dbf';
restore datafile 4, 5;
switch datafile all; # Updates repository with new datafile location.
recover datafile 4, 5;
alter database open;
}
```

This is a partial listing of the output:

```
datafile 4 switched to datafile copy
input datafile copy RECID=79 STAMP=804533148 file name=/u02/dbfile/012C/users01.dbf
datafile 5 switched to datafile copy
input datafile copy RECID=80 STAMP=804533148 file name=/u02/dbfile/012C/users02.dbf
```

If the database is open, you can place the data files offline and then set their new names for restore and recovery, as follows:

```
run{
sql 'alter database datafile 4, 5 offline';
set newname for datafile 4 to '/u02/dbfile/012C/users01.dbf';
set newname for datafile 5 to '/u02/dbfile/012C/users02.dbf';
restore datafile 4, 5;
switch datafile all; # Updates repository with new datafile location.
recover datafile 4, 5;
sql 'alter database datafile 4, 5 online';
}
```

Starting with Oracle 12c, you no longer need to specify the RMAN `sql` command when running SQL statements, such as `ALTER DATABASE`; for example,

```
run{
alter database datafile 4, 5 offline;
set newname for datafile 4 to '/u02/dbfile/012C/users01.dbf';
set newname for datafile 5 to '/u02/dbfile/012C/users02.dbf';
restore datafile 4, 5;
switch datafile all; # Updates repository with new datafile location.
recover datafile 4, 5;
alter database datafile 4, 5 online;
}
```

Performing Block-Level Recovery

Block-level corruption is rare and is usually caused by some sort of I/O error. However, if you do have an isolated corrupt block within a large data file, it's nice to have the option of performing a block-level recovery. Block-level recovery is useful when a small number of blocks are corrupt within a data file. Block recovery is not appropriate if the entire data file needs media recovery.

RMAN will automatically detect corrupt blocks whenever a BACKUP, VALIDATE, or BACKUP VALIDATE command is run. Details on corrupt blocks can be viewed in the V$DATABASE_BLOCK_CORRUPTION view. In the following example the regular backup job has reported a corrupt block in the output:

```
ORA-19566: exceeded limit of 0 corrupt blocks for file...
```

Querying the V$DATABASE_BLOCK_CORRUPTION view indicates which file contains corruption:

```
SQL> select * from v$database_block_corruption;

     FILE#     BLOCK#     BLOCKS CORRUPTION_CHANGE# CORRUPTIO     CON_ID
---------- ---------- ---------- ------------------ --------- ----------
         4         20          1                  0 ALL ZERO           0
```

Your database can be either mounted or open when performing block-level recovery. You do not have to take offline the data file being recovered. You can instruct RMAN to recover all blocks reported in V$DATABASE_BLOCK_CORRUPTION, as shown:

```
RMAN> recover corruption list;
```

If successful, the following message is displayed:

```
media recovery complete...
```

Another way to recover the block is to specify the data file and block number, like so:

```
RMAN> recover datafile 4 block 20;
```

It's preferable to use the RECOVER CORRUPTION LIST syntax because it will clear out any blocks recovered from the V$DATABASE_BLOCK_CORRUPTION view.

■ **Note** RMAN can't perform block-level recovery on block 1 (data file header) of the data file.

Block-level media recovery allows you to keep your database available and also reduces the mean time to recovery, as only the corrupt blocks are offline during the recovery. Your database must be in archivelog mode for performing block-level recoveries. Starting with Oracle 11g, RMAN can restore the block from the flashback logs (if available). If the flashback logs are not available, then RMAN will attempt to restore the block from a full backup, a level-0 backup, or an image copy backup generated by the BACKUP AS COPY command. After the block has been restored, any required archived redo logs must be available to recover the block. RMAN can't perform block media recovery using incremental level-1 (or higher) backups.

■ **Note** If you're using Oracle 10g or Oracle9i, use the BLOCKRECOVER command to perform block media recovery.

Restoring a Container Database and Its Associated Pluggable Databases

Starting with Oracle 12c, you can create pluggable databases within one container database. When dealing with container and associated pluggable databases, there are three basic scenarios:

- All data files have experienced media failure (container root data files as well as all associated pluggable database data files).

- Just the data files associated with the container root database have experienced media failure.

- Only data files associated with a pluggable database have experienced media failure.

The prior scenarios are covered in the following sections.

Restoring and Recovering All Data Files

To restore and recover all data files associated with a container database (this includes the root container, the seed container, and all associated pluggable databases), use RMAN to connect to the container database as a user with sysdba or sysbackup privileges. Because the data files associated with the root system tablespace are being restored, the database must be started in mount mode (and not open):

```
$ rman target /
RMAN> startup mount;
RMAN> restore database;
RMAN> recover database;
RMAN> alter database open;
```

Keep in mind that when you open a container database, this does not, by default, open the associated pluggable databases. You can do that from the root container, as follows:

```
RMAN> alter pluggable database all open;
```

Restoring and Recovering Root Container Data Files

If just data files associated with the root container have been damaged, then you can restore and recover at the root level. In this example the root container's system data file is being restored, so the database must not be open. The following commands instruct RMAN to restore only the data files associated with the root container database, via the keyword root:

```
$ rman target /
RMAN> startup mount;
RMAN> restore database root;
RMAN> recover database root;
RMAN> alter database open;
```

In the prior code the restore database root command instructs RMAN to restore only data files associated with the root container database. After the container database is opened, you must open any associated pluggable databases. You can do so from the root container, as shown:

```
RMAN> alter pluggable database all open;
```

You can check the status of your pluggable databases via this query:

```
SQL> select name, open_mode from v$pdbs;
```

Restoring and Recovering a Pluggable Database

You have two options for restoring and recovering a pluggable database:

- Connect as the container root user, and specify the pluggable database to be restored and recovered.

- Connect directly to the pluggable database as a privileged pluggable-level user, and issue RESTORE and RECOVER commands.

This first example connects to the root container and restores and recovers the data files associated with the salespdb pluggable database. For this to work, the pluggable database must not be open (because the pluggable database's system data files are also being restored and recovered):

```
$ rman target /
RMAN> alter pluggable database salespdb close;
RMAN> restore pluggable database salespdb;
RMAN> recover pluggable database salespdb;
RMAN> alter pluggable database salespdb open;
```

You can also connect directly to a pluggable database and perform restore and recovery operations. When connected directly to the pluggable database, the user only has access to the data files associated with the pluggable database:

```
$ rman target sys/foo@salespdb
RMAN> shutdown immediate;
RMAN> restore database;
RMAN> recover database;
RMAN> alter database open;
```

■ **Note** When you're connected directly to a pluggable database, you can't specify the name of the pluggable database as part of the RESTORE and RECOVER commands. In this situation, you'll get an RMAN-07536: command not allowed when connected to a Pluggable Database error.

The prior code only affects data files associated with the pluggable database to which you are connected. The pluggable database needs to be closed for this to work. However, the root container database can be open or mounted. Also, you must use a backup that was taken while connected to the pluggable database as a privileged user. The privileged pluggable database user can't access backups of data files initiated by the root container database privileged user.

Restoring Archive Redo Log Files

RMAN will automatically restore any archived redo log files that it needs during a recovery process. You normally don't need to restore archived redo log files manually. However, you may want to do so if any of the following situations apply:

- You need to restore archived redo log files in anticipation of later performing a recovery; the idea is that if the archived redo log files are already restored, it will speed the recovery operation.

- You're required to restore the archived redo log files to a nondefault location, either because of media failure or because of storage space issues.

- You need to restore specific archived redo log files in order to inspect them via LogMiner.

If you've enabled an FRA, then RMAN will, by default, restore archived redo log files to the destination defined by the initialization parameter DB_RECOVERY_FILE_DEST. Otherwise, RMAN uses the LOG_ARCHIVE_DEST_N initialization parameter (where N is usually 1) to determine where to restore the archived redo log files.

If you restore archived redo log files to a nondefault location, RMAN knows the location they were restored to and automatically finds these files when you issue any subsequent RECOVER commands. RMAN will not restore archived redo log files that it determines are already on disk. Even if you specify a nondefault location, RMAN will not restore an archived redo log file to disk if the file already exists. In this situation, RMAN simply returns a message stating that the archived redo log file has already been restored. Use the FORCE option to override this behavior.

If you are uncertain of the sequence numbers to use during a restore of log files, you can query the V$LOG_HISTORY view.

■ **Tip**   Keep in mind that you can't restore an archive redo log that you never backed up. Also, you can't restore an archive redo log if the backup file containing the archive redo log is no longer available. Run the LIST ARCHIVELOG ALL command to view archive redo logs currently on disk, and LIST BACKUP OF ARCHIVELOG ALL to verify which archive redo log files are in available RMAN backups.

Restoring to the Default Location

The following command will restore all archived redo log files that RMAN has backed up:

```
RMAN> restore archivelog all;
```

If you want to restore from a specified sequence, use the FROM SEQUENCE clause. You may want to run this query first to establish the most recent log files and sequence numbers that have been generated:

```
SQL> select sequence#, first_time from v$log_history order by 2;
```

This example restores all archived redo log files from sequence 68:

```
RMAN> restore archivelog from sequence 68;
```

If you want to restore a range of archived redo log files, use the FROM SEQUENCE and UNTIL SEQUENCE clauses or the SEQUENCE BETWEEN clause, as shown. The following commands restore archived redo log files from sequence 68 through sequence 78, using thread 1:

```
RMAN> restore archivelog from sequence 68 until sequence 78 thread 1;
RMAN> restore archivelog sequence between 68 and 78 thread 1;
```

By default, RMAN won't restore an archived redo log file if it is already on disk. You can override this behavior if you use the FORCE, like so:

```
RMAN> restore archivelog from sequence 1 force;
```

Restoring to a Nondefault Location

Use the SET ARCHIVELOG DESTINATION clause if you want to restore archived redo log files to a location different from the default. The following example restores to the nondefault location /u01/archtemp. The option of the SET command must be executed from within an RMAN run{} block.

```
run{
set archivelog destination to '/u01/archtemp';
restore archivelog from sequence 8 force;
}
```

Restoring a Control File

If you are missing one control file, and you have multiple copies, then you can shut down your database and simply restore the missing or damaged control file by copying a good control file to the correct location and name of the missing control file (see Chapter 2 for details).

Listed next are three typical scenarios when restoring a control file:

- Using a recovery catalog
- Using an autobackup
- Specifying a backup file name

Using a Recovery Catalog

When you're connected to the recovery catalog, you can view backup information about your control files even while your target database is in nomount mode. To list backups of your control files, use the LIST command, as shown:

```
$ rman target / catalog rcat/foo@rcat
RMAN> startup nomount;
RMAN> list backup of controlfile;
```

If you're missing all your control files, and you're using a recovery catalog, then issue the STARTUP NOMOUNT and the RESTORE CONTROLFILE commands:

```
RMAN> startup nomount;
RMAN> restore controlfile;
```

RMAN restores the control files to the location defined by your CONTROL_FILES initialization parameter. You should see a message indicating that your control files have been successfully copied back from an RMAN backup piece. You can now alter your database into mount mode and perform any additional restore and recovery commands required for your database.

■ **Note**   When you restore a control file from a backup, you're required to perform media recovery on your entire database and open your database with the OPEN RESETLOGS command, even if you didn't restore any data files. You can determine whether your control file is a backup by querying the CONTROLFILE_TYPE column of the V$DATABASE view.

Using an Autobackup

When you enable the autobackup of your control file and are using an FRA, restoring your control file is fairly simple. First, connect to your target database, then issue a STARTUP NOMOUNT command, followed by the RESTORE CONTROLFILE FROM AUTOBACKUP command, like this:

```
$ rman target /
RMAN> startup nomount;
RMAN> restore controlfile from autobackup;
```

RMAN restores the control files to the location defined by your CONTROL_FILES initialization parameter. You should see a message indicating that your control files have been successfully copied back from an RMAN backup piece. Here is a snippet of the output:

```
channel ORA_DISK_1: control file restore from AUTOBACKUP complete
```

You can now alter your database into mount mode and perform any additional restore and recovery commands required for your database.

Specifying a Backup File Name

When restoring a database to a different server, these are generally the first few steps in the process take a backup of the target database, copy to the remote server, and then restore the control file from the RMAN backup. In these scenarios, I usually know the name of the backup piece that contains the control file. Here is an example in which you instruct RMAN to restore a control file from a specific backup piece file:

```
RMAN> startup nomount;
RMAN> restore controlfile from
'/u01/O12C/rman/rman_ctl_c-3423216220-20130113-01.bk';
```

The control file will be restored to the location defined by the CONTROL_FILES initialization parameter.

Restoring the spfile

You might want to restore a spfile for several different reasons:

- You accidentally set a value in the spfile that keeps your instance from starting.

- You accidentally deleted the spfile.

- You are required to see what the spfile looked like at some point in time in the past.

One scenario (this has happened to me more than once) is that you're using a spfile, and one of the DBAs on your team does something inexplicable, such as this:

```
SQL> alter system set processes=1000000 scope=spfile;
```

The parameter is changed in the spfile on disk, but not in memory. Sometime later, the database is stopped for some maintenance. When attempting to start the database, you can't even get the instance to start in a nomount state. This is because a parameter has been set to a ridiculous value that will consume all the memory on the box. In this scenario the instance may hang, or you may see one or more of the following messages:

```
ORA-01078: failure in processing system parameters
ORA-00838: Specified value of ... is too small
```

If you have an RMAN backup available that has a copy of the spfile as it was before it was modified, you can simply restore the spfile. If you are using a recovery catalog, here is the procedure for restoring the spfile:

```
$ rman target / catalog rcat/foo@rcat
RMAN> startup nomount;
RMAN> restore spfile;
```

- If you're not using a recovery catalog, there are a number of ways to restore your spfile. The approach you take depends on several variables, such as whether you're using an FRA

- you've configured a channel backup location for the autobackup

- you're using the default location for autobackups

I'm not going to show every detail of these scenarios. Usually, I determine the location of the backup piece that contains the backup of the spfile and do the restore, like this:

```
RMAN> startup nomount force;
RMAN> restore spfile to '/tmp/spfile.ora'
    from '/u01/O12C/rman/rman_ctl_c-3423216220-20130113-00.bk';
```

You should see a message such as this:

```
channel ORA_DISK_1: SPFILE restore from AUTOBACKUP complete
```

In this example the spfile is restored to the /tmp directory. Once restored, you can copy the spfile to ORACLE_HOME/dbs, with the proper name. For my environment (database name: O12C) this would be as follows:

```
$ cp /tmp/spfile.ora $ORACLE_HOME/dbs/spfileo12c.ora
```

■ **Note** For a complete description of all possible `spfile` and control file restore scenarios, see *RMAN Recipes for Oracle Database 12c*.

Incomplete Recovery

The term *incomplete database recovery* means that you can't recover all committed transactions. *Incomplete* means that you do not apply all redo to restore up to the point of the last committed transaction that occurred in your database. In other words, you are restoring and recovering to a point in time in the past. For this reason, incomplete database recovery is also called database point-in-time recovery (DBPITR). Typically, you perform incomplete database recovery for one of the following reasons:

- You don't have all the redo required to perform a complete recovery. You're missing either the archived redo log files or the online redo log files that are required for complete recovery. This situation could arise because the required redo files are damaged or missing.

- You purposely want to roll back the database to a point in time in the past. For example, you would do this if somebody accidentally truncated a table, and you intentionally wanted to roll back the database to just before the truncate table command was issued.

Incomplete database recovery consists of two : restore and recovery. The restore step re-creates data files, and the recover step applies redo up to the specified point in time. The restore process can be initiated from RMAN in a couple of different ways:

- `RESTORE DATABASE UNTIL`

- `FLASHBACK DATABASE`

For the majority of incomplete database recovery circumstances, you use the `RESTORE DATABASE UNTIL` command to instruct RMAN to retrieve data files from the RMAN backup files. This type of incomplete database recovery is the main focus of this section of the chapter. The Flashback Database feature is covered in the section "Flashing Back a Database," later in this chapter.

The `UNTIL` portion of the `RESTORE DATABASE` command instructs RMAN to retrieve data files from a point in time in the past, based on one of the following methods:

- Time

- SCN

- Log sequence number

- Restore point

The RMAN `RESTORE DATABASE UNTIL` command will retrieve all data files from the most recent backup set or image copy. RMAN will automatically determine from the `UNTIL` clause which backup set contains the required data files. If you omit the `UNTIL` clause of the `RESTORE DATABASE` command, RMAN will retrieve data files from the latest available backup set or image copy. In some situations this may be the behavior you desire. I recommend that you use the `UNTIL` clause to ensure that RMAN restores from the correct backup set. When you issue the `RESTORE DATABASE UNTIL` command, RMAN will establish how to extract the data files from any of the following types of backups:

- Full database backup

- Incremental level-0 backup

- Image copy backup generated by the `BACKUP AS COPY` command

You can't perform an incomplete database recovery on a subset of your database's online data files. When performing incomplete database recovery, all the checkpoint SCNs for all online data files must be synchronized before you can open your database with the ALTER DATABASE OPEN RESETLOGS command. You can view the data file header SCNs and the status of each data file via this SQL query:

```
select file#, status, fuzzy,
error, checkpoint_change#,
to_char(checkpoint_time,'dd-mon-rrrr hh24:mi:ss') as checkpoint_time
from v$datafile_header;
```

■ **Note** The FUZZY column V$DATAFILE_HEADER contains data files that have one or more blocks with an SCN value greater than or equal to the checkpoint SCN in the data file header. If a data file is restored and has a FUZZY value of YES, then media recovery is required.

The only exception to this rule of not performing an incomplete recovery on a subset of online database files is a tablespace point-in-time recovery (TSPITR), which uses the RECOVER TABLESPACE UNTIL command. TSPITR is used in rare situations; it restores and recovers only the tablespace(s) you specify. For more details on TSPITR, see *RMAN Recipes for Oracle Database 12c*.

The recovery portion of an incomplete database recovery is always initiated with the RECOVER DATABASE UNTIL command. RMAN will automatically recover your database up to the point specified with the UNTIL clause. Just like the RESTORE command, you can recover up to time, change/SCN, log sequence number, or restore point. When RMAN reaches the specified point, it will automatically terminate the recovery process.

■ **Note** Regardless of what you specify in the UNTIL clause, RMAN will convert that into a corresponding UNTIL SCN clause and assign the appropriate SCN. This is to avoid any timing issues, particularly those caused by Daylight Saving Time.

During a recovery, RMAN will automatically determine how to apply redo. First, RMAN will apply any incremental backups available. Next, any archived redo log files on disk will be applied. If the archived redo log files do not exist on disk, then RMAN will attempt to retrieve them from a backup set. If you want to apply redo as part of an incomplete database recovery, the following conditions must be true:

- Your database is in archivelog mode.
- You have a good backup of all data files.
- You have all redo required to restore up to the specified point.

■ **Tip** Starting with Oracle 10g, you can perform parallel media recovery by using the RECOVER DATABASE PARALLEL command.

When performing an incomplete database recovery with RMAN, you must have your database in mount mode. RMAN needs the database in mount mode to be able to read and write to the control file. Also, with an incomplete database recovery, any SYSTEM tablespace data files are always recovered. Oracle will not allow your database to be open while restoring the SYSTEM tablespace data file(s).

■ **Note**   After incomplete database recovery is performed, you are required to open your database with the ALTER DATABASE OPEN RESETLOGS command.

Depending on the scenario, you can use RMAN to perform a variety of incomplete recovery methods. The next section discusses how to determine what type of incomplete recovery to perform.

Determining the Type of Incomplete Recovery

Time-based restore and recovery is commonly used when you know the approximate date and time to which you want to recover your database. For instance, you may know approximately the time you want to stop the recovery process, but not a particular SCN.

Log sequence–based and cancel-based recovery work well in situations in which you have missing or damaged log files. In such scenarios, you can recover only up to your last good archived redo log file.

SCN-based recovery works well if you can pinpoint the SCN at which you want to stop the recovery process. You can retrieve SCN information from views such as V$LOG and V$LOG_HISTORY. You can also use tools such as LogMiner to retrieve the SCN of a particular SQL statement.

Restore point recoveries work only if you have established restore points. In these situations, you restore and recover up to the SCN associated with the specified restore point.

TSPITR is used in situations in which you need to restore and recover just a few tablespaces. You can use RMAN to automate many of the tasks associated with this type of incomplete recovery.

Performing Time-Based Recovery

To restore and recover your database back to a point in time in the past, you can use either the UNTIL TIME clause of the RESTORE and RECOVER commands or the SET UNTIL TIME clause within a run{} block. RMAN will restore and recover the database up to, but not including, the specified time. In other words, RMAN will restore any transactions committed prior to the time specified. RMAN automatically stops the recovery process when it reaches the time you specified.

The default date format that RMAN expects is YYYY-MM-DD:HH24:MI:SS. However, I recommend using the TO_DATE function and specifying a format mask. This eliminates ambiguities with different national date formats and having to set the OS NLS_DATE_FORMAT variable. The following example specifies a time when issuing the restore and recover commands:

```
$ rman target /
RMAN> startup mount;
RMAN> restore database until time
    "to_date('15-jan-2015 12:20:00', 'dd-mon-rrrr hh24:mi:ss')";
RMAN> recover database until time
    "to_date('15-jan-2015 12:20:00', 'dd-mon-rrrr hh24:mi:ss')";
RMAN> alter database open resetlogs;
```

If everything goes well, you should see output such as this:

```
Statement processed
```

Performing Log Sequence-Based Recovery

Usually this type of incomplete database recovery is initiated because you have a missing or damaged archived redo log file. If that's the case, you can recover only up to your last good archived redo log file, because you can't skip a missing archived redo log.

How you determine which archived redo log file to restore up to (but not including) will vary. For example, if you are physically missing an archived redo log file, and RMAN can't find it in a backup set, you'll receive a message such as this when trying to apply the missing file:

```
RMAN-06053: unable to perform media recovery because of missing log
RMAN-06025: no backup of archived log for thread 1 with sequence 19...
```

Based on the previous error message, you would restore up to (but not including) log sequence 19.

```
$ rman target /
RMAN> startup mount;
RMAN> restore database until sequence 19;
RMAN> recover database until sequence 19;
RMAN> alter database open resetlogs;
```

If successful, you should see output such as this:

```
Statement processed
```

■ **Note** Log sequence–based recovery is similar to user-managed cancel-based recovery. See Chapter 3 for details on a user-managed cancel-based recovery.

Performing SCN-Based Recovery

SCN-based incomplete database recovery works in situations in which you know the SCN value at which you want to end the restore-and-recovery session. RMAN will recover up to, but not including, the specified SCN. RMAN automatically terminates the restore process when it reaches the specified SCN.

You can view your database SCN information in several ways:

- Using LogMiner to determine an SCN associated with a DDL or DML statement
- Looking in the alert.log file
- Looking in your trace files
- Querying the FIRST_CHANGE# column of VLOG, VLOG_HISTORY and V$ARCHIVED_LOG

After establishing the SCN to which you want to restore, use the UNTIL SCN clause to restore up to, but not including, the SCN specified. The following example restores all transactions that have an SCN that is less than 95019865425:

```
$ rman target /
RMAN> startup mount;
RMAN> restore database until scn 95019865425;
RMAN> recover database until scn 95019865425;
RMAN> alter database open resetlogs;
```

If everything goes well, you should see output such as this:

```
Statement processed
```

Restoring to a Restore Point

There are two types of restore points: normal and guaranteed. The main difference between a guaranteed restore point and a normal restore point is that a guaranteed restore point is not eventually aged out of the control file; a guaranteed restore point will persist until you drop it. Guaranteed restore points do require an FRA. However, for incomplete recovery using a guaranteed restore point, you do not have to have flashback database enabled.

You can create a normal restore point using SQL*Plus, as follows:

```
SQL> create restore point MY_RP;
```

This command creates a restore point, named MY_RP, that is associated with the SCN of the database at the time the command was issued. You can view the current SCN of your database, as shown:

```
SQL> select current_scn from v$database;
```

You can view restore point information in the V$RESTORE_POINT view, like so:

```
SQL> select name, scn from v$restore_point;
```

The restore point acts like a synonym for the particular SCN. The restore point allows you to restore and recover to an SCN without having to specify a number. RMAN will restore and recover up to, but not including, the SCN associated with the restore point.

This example restores and recovers to the MY_RP restore point:

```
$ rman target /
RMAN> startup mount;
RMAN> restore database until restore point MY_RP;
RMAN> recover database until restore point MY_RP;
RMAN> alter database open resetlogs;
```

Restoring Tables to a Previous Point

Starting with Oracle 12c, you can restore individual tables from RMAN backups via the RECOVER TABLE command. This gives you with the ability to restore and recover a table back to a point in time in the past.

The table-level restore feature uses a temporary auxiliary instance and the Data Pump utility. Both the auxiliary instance and Data Pump create temporary files when restoring the table. Before initiating a table-level restore, first create two directories: one to hold files used by the auxiliary instance and one to store a Data Pump dump file:

```
$ mkdir /tmp/oracle
$ mkdir /tmp/recover
```

The prior two directories are referenced within the RECOVER TABLE command via the AUXILIARY DESTINATION and DATAPUMP DESTINATION clauses. In the following bit of code, the INV table, owned by MV_MAINT, is restored as it was at a prior SCN:

```
recover table mv_maint.inv
until scn 4689805
auxiliary destination '/tmp/oracle'
datapump destination '/tmp/recover';
```

Providing that RMAN backups are available that contain the state of the table at the specified SCN, a table-level restore and recovery is performed.

■ **Note** You can also restore a table to an SCN, a point in time, or a log sequence number.

When RMAN performs a table-level recovery, it automatically creates a temporary auxiliary database, uses Data Pump to export the table, and then imports the table back into the target database as it was at the specified restore point. After the restore is finished, the auxiliary database is dropped, and Data Pump dump file is removed.

■ **Tip** Although the RECOVER TABLE command is a nice enhancement, I would recommend that, if you have an accidentally dropped table, you first explore using the Flashback Table to Before Drop feature to restore the table. Or, if the table was erroneously deleted from, then use the Flashback Table feature to restore the table back to a point in time in the past. If neither of the prior options are viable, then consider using the RMAN Recover Table feature.

Flashing Back a Table

Prior to Oracle 10g, if a table was accidentally dropped, you had to do the following to restore the table:

1. Restore a backup of the database to a test database.
2. Perform an incomplete recovery up to the point in time at which the table was dropped.
3. Export the table.
4. Import the table into the production database.

This process can be time-consuming and resource intensive. It requires extra server resources as well as time and effort from a DBA.

To simplify recovery of an accidentally dropped table, Oracle introduced the Flashback Table feature. Oracle offers two different types of Flashback Table operations:

- FLASHBACK TABLE TO BEFORE DROP quickly undrops a previously dropped table. This feature uses a logical container named the recycle bin.

- FLASHBACK TABLE flashes back to a recent point in time to undo the effects of undesired DML statements. You can flash back to an SCN, a timestamp, or a restore point.

Oracle introduced FLASHBACK TABLE TO BEFORE DROP to allow you to quickly recover a dropped table. As of Oracle 10g, when you drop a table, if you don't specify the PURGE clause, Oracle doesn't drop the table—instead, the table is renamed. Any tables you drop (that Oracle renames) are placed in the recycle bin. The recycle bin provides you with an efficient way to view and manage dropped objects.

■ **Note** To use the Flashback Table feature, you don't need to implement an FRA, nor do you need Flashback Database to be enabled.

The FLASHBACK TABLE TO BEFORE DROP operation only works if your database has the recycle bin feature enabled (which it is by default). You can check the status of the recycle bin, as follows:

```
SQL> show parameter recyclebin

NAME                                 TYPE        VALUE
------------------------------------ ----------- -------
recyclebin                           string      on
```

FLASHBACK TABLE TO BEFORE DROP

When you drop a table, if you don't specify the PURGE clause, Oracle renames the table with a system-generated name. Because the table isn't really dropped, you can use FLASHBACK TABLE TO BEFORE DROP to instruct Oracle to rename the table with its original name. Here is an example. Suppose the INV table is accidentally dropped:

```
SQL> drop table inv;
```

Verify that the table has been renamed by viewing the contents of the recycle bin:

```
SQL> show recyclebin;
ORIGINAL NAME    RECYCLEBIN NAME                  OBJECT TYPE  DROP TIME
---------------- -------------------------------- ------------ -----------
INV      BIN$BCRjF6KSbi/gU7fQTwrP+Q==$0 TABLE    2014-09-28:11:26:15
```

The SHOW RECYCLEBIN statement shows only tables that have been dropped. To get a more complete picture of renamed objects, query the RECYCLEBIN view:

```
SQL> select object_name, original_name, type from recyclebin;
```

Here is the output:

```
OBJECT_NAME                          ORIGINAL_NAME         TYPE
------------------------------------ --------------------- ----------
BIN$BCRjF6KSbi/gU7fQTwrP+Q==$0       INV                   TABLE
BIN$BCRjF6KRbi/gU7fQTwrP+Q==$0       INV_TRIG              TRIGGER
BIN$BCRjF6KQbi/gU7fQTwrP+Q==$0       INV_PK                INDEX
```

In this output the table also has a primary key that was renamed when the object was dropped. To undrop the table, do this:

```
SQL> flashback table inv to before drop;
```

The prior command restores the table to its original name. This statement, however, doesn't restore the index to its original name:

```
SQL> select index_name from user_indexes where table_name='INV';

INDEX_NAME
---------------------------------
BIN$BCRjF6KQbi/gU7fQTwrP+Q==$0
```

In this scenario, you have to rename the index:

```
SQL> alter index "BIN$BCRjF6KQbi/gU7fQTwrP+Q==$0" rename to inv_pk;
```

You also have to rename any trigger objects in the same manner. If referential constraints were in place before the table was dropped, you must manually re-create them.

If, for some reason, you need to flash back a table to a name different from the original name, you can do so as follows:

```
SQL> flashback table inv to before drop rename to inv_bef;
```

Flashing Back a Table to a Previous Point in Time

If a table was erroneously deleted from, you have the option of flashing back the table to a previous point in time. The Flashback Table feature uses information in the undo tablespace to restore the table. The point in time in the past depends on your undo tablespace retention period, which specifies the minimum time that undo information is kept.

If the required flashback information isn't in the undo tablespace, you receive an error such as this:

```
ORA-01555: snapshot too old
```

In other words, to be able to flash back to a point in time in the past, the required information in the undo tablespace must not have been overwritten.

FLASHBACK TABLE TO SCN

Suppose you're testing an application feature, and you want to quickly restore a table back to a specific SCN. As part of the application testing, you record the SCN before testing begins:

```
SQL> select current_scn from v$database;

CURRENT_SCN
-----------
    4760099
```

You perform some testing and then want to flash back the table to the SCN previously recorded. First, ensure that row movement is enabled for the table:

```
SQL> alter table inv enable row movement;
SQL> flashback table inv to scn 4760089;
```

The table should now reflect transactions that were committed as of the historical SCN value specified in the FLASHBACK statement.

FLASHBACK TABLE TO TIMESTAMP

You can also flash back a table to a prior point in time. For example, to flash back a table to 15 minutes in the past, first enable row movement, and then use FLASHBACK TABLE:

```
SQL> alter table inv enable row movement;
SQL> flashback table inv to timestamp(sysdate-1/96) ;
```

179

The timestamp you provide must evaluate to a valid format for an Oracle timestamp. You can also explicitly specify a time, as follows:

```
SQL> flashback table inv to timestamp
    to_timestamp('14-jan-15 12:07:33','dd-mon-yy hh24:mi:ss');
```

FLASHBACK TABLE TO RESTORE POINT

A restore point is a name associated with a timestamp or an SCN in the database. You can create a restore point that contains the current SCN of the database, as shown:

```
SQL> create restore point point_a;
```

Later, if you decide to flash back a table to that restore point, first enable row movement:

```
SQL> alter table inv enable row movement;
SQL> flashback table inv to restore point point_a;
```

The table should now contain transactions as they were at the SCN associated with the specified restore point.

Flashing Back a Database

The Flashback Database feature allows you to perform an incomplete recovery back to a point in time in the past. Flashback Database uses information stored in flashback logs; it doesn't rely on restoring database files (as do cold backup, hot backup, and RMAN).

■ **Tip**   Flashback Database isn't a substitute for a backup of your database. If you experience a media failure with a data file, you can't use Flashback Database to flash back to before the failure. If a data file is damaged, you have to restore and recover, using a physical backup (hot, cold, or RMAN).

The Flashback Database feature may be desirable in situations in which you want to consistently reset your database back to a point in time in the past. For instance, you may periodically want to set a test or training database back to a known baseline. Or, you may be upgrading an application and, before making large-scale changes to the application database objects, mark the starting point. After the upgrade, if things don't go well, you want the ability to quickly reset the database back to the point in time before the upgrade took place.

There are several prerequisites for Flashback Database:

- The database must be in archivelog mode.

- You must be using an FRA.

- The Flashback Database feature must be enabled.

See Chapter 2 for details on enabling archivelog mode and/or enabling an FRA. You can verify the status of these features using the following SQL*Plus statements:

```
SQL> archive log list;
SQL> show parameter db_recovery_file_dest;
```

To enable the Flashback Database feature, alter your database into flashback mode, as shown:

```
SQL> alter database flashback on;
```

■ **Note** In Oracle 10g the database must be in mount mode to enable Flashback Database.

You can verify the flashback status, as follows:

```
SQL> select flashback_on from v$database;
```

After you enable Flashback Database, you can view the flashback logs in your FRA with this query:

```
select name, log#, thread#, sequence#, bytes
from v$flashback_database_logfile;
```

The range of time in which you can flash back is determined by the `DB_FLASHBACK_RETENTION_TARGET` parameter. This specifies the upper limit, in minutes, of how far your database can be flashed back.

You can view the oldest SCN and time you can flash back your database to by running the following SQL:

```
select
 oldest_flashback_scn
,to_char(oldest_flashback_time,'dd-mon-yy hh24:mi:ss')
from v$flashback_database_log;
```

If, for any reason, you need to disable Flashback Database, you can turn it off, as follows:

```
SQL> alter database flashback off;
```

You can use either RMAN or SQL*Plus to flash back a database. You can specify a point in time in the past, using one of the following:

- SCN
- Timestamp
- Restore point
- Last `RESETLOGS` operation (works from RMAN only)

This example creates a restore point:

```
SQL> create restore point flash_1;
```

Next, the application performs some testing, after which the database is flashed back to the restore point so that a new round of testing can begin:

```
SQL> shutdown immediate;
SQL> startup mount;
SQL> flashback database to restore point flash_1;
SQL> alter database open resetlogs;
```

At this point, your database should be transactionally consistent with how it was at the SCN associated with the restore point.

Restoring and Recovering to Different Server

When you think about architecting your backup strategy, as part of the process, you must also consider how you're going to restore and recover. Your backups are only as good as the last time you tested a restore and recovery. A backup strategy can be rendered worthless without a good restore-and-recovery strategy. The last thing you want to happen is to have a media failure, go to restore your database, and then find out you're missing critical pieces, you don't have enough space to restore, something is corrupt, and so on.

One of the best ways to test an RMAN backup is to restore and recover it to a different database server. This will exercise all your backup, restore, and recovery DBA skills. If you can restore and recover an RMAN backup on a different server, it will give you confidence when a real disaster hits. You can think of all the prior material in this book as the building blocks for performing technically challenging tasks. Moving a database from one server to another using an RMAN backup requires an expert level understanding of the Oracle architecture and how B&R works.

■ **Note**   RMAN does have a `DUPLICATE DATABASE` command, which works well for copying a database from one server to another. If you're going to be performing this type of task often, I would recommend that you use RMAN's duplicate database functionality. However, you may still have to copy a backup of a database manually from one server to another, especially when the security is such that you can't directly connect a production server to a development environment. I work with many production databases in which there is no direct access to a production server, so the only way to duplicate a database is by manually copying the RMAN backups from production to a test environment. Starting with Oracle 11g Release 2, you can use RMAN to duplicate a database based on backups you copy from the target to the auxiliary server. See MOS note 874352.1 for details on targetless duplication.

In this example the originating server and destination server have different mount points. Listed next are the high-level steps required to take an RMAN backup and use it to recreate a database on a separate server:

1.   Create an RMAN backup on the originating database.

2.   Copy the RMAN backup to the destination server. All steps that follow are performed on the destination database server.

3.   Ensure that Oracle is installed.

4.   Source the required OS variables.

5.   Create an `init.ora` file for the database to be restored.

6.   Create any required directories for data files, control files, and dump/trace files.

7.   Start up the database in nomount mode.

8.   Restore the control file from the RMAN backup.

9.   Start up the database in mount mode.

10.   Make the control file aware of the location of the RMAN backups.

11.   Rename and restore the data files to reflect new directory locations.

12.   Recover the database.

13.   Set the new location for the online redo logs.

14. Open the database.

15. Add the temp file.

16. Rename the database (optional).

Each of the prior steps is covered in detail in the next several sections. Steps 1 and 2 occur on the source database server. All remaining steps are performed on the destination server. For this example the source database is named O12C, and the destination database will be named DEVDB.

Furthermore, the originating server and destination server have different mount point names. On the source database the data files and control files are here:

/u01/dbfile/O12C

On the destination database the data files and control files will be renamed and restored to this directory:

/ora01/dbfile/DEVDB

The destination database online redo logs will be placed in this directory:

/ora01/oraredo/DEVDB

The destination database archive redo log file location will be set as follows:

/ora01/arc/DEVDB

Keep in mind that these are the directories used on servers in my test environment. You'll have to adjust these directory names to reflect the directory structures on your database servers.

Step 1. Create an RMAN Backup on the Originating Database

When backing up a database, make sure you have the autobackup control file feature turned on. Also, include the archive redo logs as part of the backup, like so:

RMAN> backup database plus archivelog;

You can verify the names and locations of the backup pieces via the LIST BACKUP command. For example, this is what the backup pieces look like for the source database:

rman1_bonvb2js_1_1.bk
rman1_bqnvb2k5_1_1.bk
rman1_bsnvb2p3_1_1.bk
rman_ctl_c-3423216220-20130113-06.bk

In the prior output the file with the c-3423216220 string in the name is the backup piece that contains the control file. You'll have to inspect the output of your LIST BACKUP command to determine which backup piece contains the control file. You'll need to reference that backup piece in step 8.

Step 2. Copy the RMAN Backup to the Destination Server

For this step, use a utility such as `rsync` or `scp` to copy the backup pieces from one server to another. This example uses the `scp` command to copy the backup pieces:

```
$ scp rman* oracle@DEVBOX:/ora01/rman/DEVDB
```

In this example the `/ora01/rman/DEVDB` directory must be created on the destination server before copying the backup files. Depending on your environment, this step might require copying the RMAN backups twice: once from the production server to a secure server and once from the secure server to a test server.

■ **Note** If the RMAN backups are on tape instead of on disk, then the same media manager software must be installed/configured on the destination server. Also, that server must have direct access to the RMAN backups on tape.

Step 3. Ensure That Oracle Is Installed

Make sure you have the same version of the Oracle binaries installed on the destination server as you do on the originating database.

Step 4. Source the Required OS Variables

You need to establish the OS variables, such as ORACLE_SID, ORACLE_HOME, and PATH. Typically, the ORACLE_SID variable is initially set to match what it was on the original database. The database name will be changed as part of the last step in this recipe (optional). Here are the settings for ORACLE_SID and ORACLE_HOME on the destination server:

```
$ echo $ORACLE_SID
O12C

$ echo $ORACLE_HOME
/ora01/app/oracle/product/12.1.0.1/db_1
```

At this point also consider adding the Oracle SID to the `oratab` file. If you plan on using this database after you've replicated it, then you should have an automated method for setting the required OS variables. See Chapter 1 for details on sourcing OS variables in conjunction with the `oratab` file.

Step 5. Create an init.ora File for the Database to Be Restored

Copy the `init.ora` file from the original server to the destination server, and modify it so that it matches the destination box in terms of any directory paths. Ensure that you change the parameters, such as the CONTROL_FILES, to reflect the new path directories on the destination server (`/ora01/dbfile/DEVDB`, in this example).

Initially, the name of the `init.ora` file is ORACLE_HOME/dbs/inito12c.ora, and the name of the database is O12C. Both will be renamed in a later step. Here are the contents of the `init.ora` file:

```
control_files='/ora01/dbfile/DEVDB/control01.ctl',
              '/ora01/dbfile/DEVDB/control02.ctl'
db_block_size=8192
db_name='O12C'
log_archive_dest_1='location=/ora01/arc/DEVDB'
```

```
job_queue_processes=10
memory_max_target=300000000
memory_target=300000000
open_cursors=100
os_authent_prefix=''
processes=100
remote_login_passwordfile='EXCLUSIVE'
resource_limit=true
shared_pool_size=80M
sql92_security=TRUE
undo_management='AUTO'
undo_tablespace='UNDOTBS1'
workarea_size_policy='AUTO'
```

■ **Note**   If this were an Oracle 10g example, you would need to set the parameters background_dump_dest, user_dump_dest, core_dump_dest.

Step 6. Create Any Required Directories for Data Files, Control Files, and Dump/Trace Files

For this example the directories /ora01/dbfile/DEVDB and /ora01/oraredo/DEVDB are created:

```
$ mkdir -p /ora01/dbfile/DEVDB
$ mkdir -p /ora01/oraredo/DEVDB
$ mkdir -p /ora01/arc/DEVDB
```

Step 7. Start Up the Database in Nomount Mode

You should now be able to start up the database in nomount mode:

```
$ rman target /
RMAN> startup nomount;
```

Step 8. Restore the Control File from the RMAN Backup

Next, restore the control file from the backup that was previously copied; for example,

```
RMAN> restore controlfile from
'/ora01/rman/DEVDB/rman_ctl_c-3423216220-20130113-06.bk';
```

The control file will be restored to all locations specified by the CONTROL_FILES initialization parameter. Here is some sample output:

```
channel ORA_DISK_1: restore complete, elapsed time: 00:00:03
output file name=/ora01/dbfile/DEVDB/control01.ctl
output file name=/ora01/dbfile/DEVDB/control02.ctl
```

Step 9. Start Up the Database in Mount Mode

You should now be able to start up your database in mount mode:

```
RMAN> alter database mount;
```

At this point, your control files exist and have been opened, but none of the data files or online redo logs exist yet.

Step 10. Make the Control File Aware of the Location of the RMAN Backups

First, use the CROSSCHECK command to let the control file know that none of the backups or archive redo logs are in the same location that they were in on the original server:

```
RMAN> crosscheck backup; # Crosscheck backups
RMAN> crosscheck copy;   # Crosscheck image copies and archive logs
```

Then, use the CATALOG command to make the control file aware of the location and names of the backup pieces that were copied to the destination server.

■ **Note**   Don't confuse the CATALOG command with the recovery catalog schema. The CATALOG command adds RMAN metadata to the control file, whereas the recovery catalog schema is a user, generally created in a separate database, that can be used to store RMAN metadata.

In this example any RMAN files that are in the /ora01/rman/DEVDB directory will be cataloged in the control file:

```
RMAN> catalog start with '/ora01/rman/DEVDB';
```

Here is some sample output:

```
List of Files Unknown to the Database
=====================================
File Name: /ora01/rman/DEVDB/rman1_bqnvb2k5_1_1.bk
File Name: /ora01/rman/DEVDB/rman1_bonvb2js_1_1.bk
File Name: /ora01/rman/DEVDB/rman_ctl_c-3423216220-20130113-06.bk
File Name: /ora01/rman/DEVDB/rman1_bsnvb2p3_1_1.bk

Do you really want to catalog the above files (enter YES or NO)?
```

Now, type YES (if everything looks okay). You should then be able to use the RMAN LIST BACKUP command to view the newly cataloged backup pieces:

```
RMAN> list backup;
```

Step 11. Rename and Restore the Data Files to Reflect New Directory Locations

If your destination server has the exact same directory structure as the original server directories, you can issue the RESTORE command directly:

```
RMAN> restore database;
```

However, when restoring data files to locations that are different from the original directories, you'll have to use the SET NEWNAME command. Create a file that uses an RMAN run{} block that contains the appropriate SET NEWNAME and RESTORE commands. I like to use an SQL script that generates SQL to give me a starting point. Here is a sample script:

```
set head off feed off verify off echo off pages 0 trimspool on
set lines 132 pagesize 0
spo newname.sql
--
select 'run{' from dual;
--
select
'set newname for datafile ' || file# || ' to ' || '''' || name || '''' || ';'
from v$datafile;
--
select
'restore database;' || chr(10) ||
'switch datafile all;' || chr(10) ||
'}'
from dual;
--
spo off;
```

After running the script, these are the contents of the newname.sql script that was generated:

```
run{
set newname for datafile 1 to '/u01/dbfile/O12C/system01.dbf';
set newname for datafile 2 to '/u01/dbfile/O12C/sysaux01.dbf';
set newname for datafile 3 to '/u01/dbfile/O12C/undotbs01.dbf';
set newname for datafile 4 to '/u01/dbfile/O12C/users01.dbf';
restore database;
switch datafile all;
}
```

Then, modify the contents of the newname.sql script to reflect the directories on the destination database server. Here is what the final newname.sql script looks like for this example:

```
run{
set newname for datafile 1 to '/ora01/dbfile/DEVDB/system01.dbf';
set newname for datafile 2 to '/ora01/dbfile/DEVDB/sysaux01.dbf';
set newname for datafile 3 to '/ora01/dbfile/DEVDB/undotbs01.dbf';
set newname for datafile 4 to '/ora01/dbfile/DEVDB/users01.dbf';
restore database;
switch datafile all;
}
```

Now, connect to RMAN, and run the prior script to restore the data files to the new locations:

```
$ rman target /
RMAN> @newname.sql
```

Here is a snippet of the output:

```
datafile 1 switched to datafile copy
input datafile copy RECID=5 STAMP=790357985 file name=/ora01/dbfile/DEVDB/system01.dbf
```

All the data files have been restored to the new database server. You can use the RMAN REPORT SCHEMA command to verify that the files have been restored and are in the correct locations:

```
RMAN> report schema;
```

Here is some sample output:

```
RMAN-06139: WARNING: control file is not current for REPORT SCHEMA
Report of database schema for database with db_unique_name O12C
List of Permanent Datafiles
===========================
File Size(MB) Tablespace        RB segs Datafile Name
---- -------- ----------------- ------- ------------------------
1    500      SYSTEM            ***     /ora01/dbfile/DEVDB/system01.dbf
2    500      SYSAUX            ***     /ora01/dbfile/DEVDB/sysaux01.dbf
3    800      UNDOTBS1          ***     /ora01/dbfile/DEVDB/undotbs01.dbf
4    50       USERS             ***     /ora01/dbfile/DEVDB/users01.dbf

List of Temporary Files
=======================
File Size(MB) Tablespace        Maxsize(MB) Tempfile Name
---- -------- ----------------- ----------- ------------------------
1    500      TEMP              500         /u01/dbfile/O12C/temp01.dbf
```

From the prior output you can see that the database name and temporary tablespace data file still don't reflect the destination database (DEVDB). These will be modified in subsequent steps.

Step 12. Recover the Database

Next, you need to apply any archive redo files that were generated during the backup. These should be included in the backup because the ARCHIVELOG ALL clause was used to take the backup. Initiate the application of redo via the RECOVER DATABASE command:

```
RMAN> recover database;
```

RMAN will restore and apply as many archive redo logs as it has in the backup pieces and then may throw an error when it reaches an archive redo log that doesn't exist; for example,

```
RMAN-06054: media recovery requesting unknown archived log for...
```

That error message is fine. The recovery process will restore and recover archive redo logs contained in the backups, which should be sufficient to open the database. The recovery process doesn't know where to stop applying archive redo logs and therefore will continue to attempt to do so until it can't find the next log. Having said that, now is a good time to verify that your data files are online and not in a fuzzy state:

```
select file#, status, fuzzy, error, checkpoint_change#,
to_char(checkpoint_time,'dd-mon-rrrr hh24:mi:ss') as checkpoint_time
from v$datafile_header;
```

Step 13. Set the New Location for the Online Redo Logs

If your source and destination servers have the exact same directory structures, then you don't need to set a new location for the online redo logs (so you can skip this step).

However, if the directory structures are different, then you'll need to update the control file to reflect the new directory for the online redo logs. I sometimes use an SQL script that generates SQL to assist with this step:

```
set head off feed off verify off echo off pages 0 trimspool on
set lines 132 pagesize 0
spo renlog.sql
select
'alter database rename file ' || chr(10)
|| '''' || member || '''' || ' to ' || chr(10) || '''' || member || '''' ||';'
from v$logfile;
spo off;
```

For this example, here is a snippet of the renlog.sql file that was generated:

```
alter database rename file
'/u01/oraredo/012C/redo01a.rdo' to
'/u01/oraredo/012C/redo01a.rdo';
...
alter database rename file
'/u02/oraredo/012C/redo03b.rdo' to
'/u02/oraredo/012C/redo03b.rdo';
```

The contents of renlog.sql need to be modified to reflect the directory structure on the destination server. Here is what renlog.sql looks like after being edited:

```
alter database rename file
'/u01/oraredo/012C/redo01a.rdo' to
'/ora01/oraredo/DEVDB/redo01a.rdo';
...
alter database rename file
'/u02/oraredo/012C/redo03b.rdo' to
'/ora01/oraredo/DEVDB/redo03b.rdo';
```

Update the control file by running the renlog.sql script:

```
SQL> @renlog.sql
```

You can select from V$LOGFILE to verify that the online redo log names are correct:

```
SQL> select member from v$logfile;
```

Here is the output for this example:

```
/ora01/oraredo/DEVDB/redo01a.rdo
/ora01/oraredo/DEVDB/redo02a.rdo
/ora01/oraredo/DEVDB/redo03a.rdo
/ora01/oraredo/DEVDB/redo01b.rdo
/ora01/oraredo/DEVDB/redo02b.rdo
/ora01/oraredo/DEVDB/redo03b.rdo
```

Make sure the directories exist on the new server that will contain the online redo logs. For this example, here is the mkdir command:

```
$ mkdir -p /ora01/oraredo/DEVDB
```

Step 14. Open the Database

You must open the database with the OPEN RESETLOGS command (because there are no redo logs, and they must be re-created at this point):

```
SQL> alter database open resetlogs;
```

If successful, you should see this message:

```
Statement processed
```

■ **Note**   Keep in mind that all the passwords from the newly restored copy are as they were in the source database. You may want to change the passwords in a replicated database, especially if it was copied from production.

Step 15. Add the Temp File

When you start your database, Oracle will automatically try to add any missing temp files to the database. Oracle won't be able to do this if the directory structure on the destination server is different from that of the source server. In this scenario, you will have to add any missing temp files manually. To do this, first take offline the temporary tablespace temp file. The file definition from the originating database is taken offline like so:

```
SQL> alter database tempfile '/u01/dbfile/O12C/temp01.dbf' offline;
SQL> alter database tempfile '/u01/dbfile/O12C/temp01.dbf' drop;
```

Next, add a temporary tablespace file to the TEMP tablespace that matches the directory structure of the destination database server:

```
SQL> alter tablespace temp add tempfile '/ora01/dbfile/DEVDB/temp01.dbf'
    size 100m;
```

You can run the REPORT SCHEMA command to verify that all files are in the correct locations.

Step 16. Rename the Database

This step is optional. If you need to rename the database to reflect the name for a development or test database, create a trace file that contains the CREATE CONTROLFILE statement, and use it to rename your database.

■ **Tip**   If you don't rename the database, be careful about connect and resync operations to the same recovery catalog used by the original/source database. This causes confusion in the recovery catalog as to which is the real source database and may jeopardize your ability to recover and restore the real source database.

The steps for renaming your database are as follows:

1. Generate a trace file that contains the SQL command to recreate the control files:

    SQL> alter database backup controlfile to trace as '/tmp/cf.sql' resetlogs;

2. Shut down the database:

    SQL> shutdown immediate;

3. Modify the /tmp/cf.sql trace file; be sure to specify SET DATABASE "<NEW DATABASE NAME>" in the top line of the output:

```
CREATE CONTROLFILE REUSE SET DATABASE "DEVDB" RESETLOGS ARCHIVELOG
    MAXLOGFILES 16
    MAXLOGMEMBERS 4
    MAXDATAFILES 1024
    MAXINSTANCES 1
    MAXLOGHISTORY 876
LOGFILE
  GROUP 1 (
    '/ora01/oraredo/DEVDB/redo01a.rdo',
    '/ora01/oraredo/DEVDB/redo01b.rdo'
  ) SIZE 50M BLOCKSIZE 512,
  GROUP 2 (
    '/ora01/oraredo/DEVDB/redo02a.rdo',
    '/ora01/oraredo/DEVDB/redo02b.rdo'
  ) SIZE 50M BLOCKSIZE 512,
  GROUP 3 (
    '/ora01/oraredo/DEVDB/redo03a.rdo',
    '/ora01/oraredo/DEVDB/redo03b.rdo'
  ) SIZE 50M BLOCKSIZE 512
DATAFILE
  '/ora01/dbfile/DEVDB/system01.dbf',
  '/ora01/dbfile/DEVDB/sysaux01.dbf',
  '/ora01/dbfile/DEVDB/undotbs01.dbf',
  '/ora01/dbfile/DEVDB/users01.dbf'
CHARACTER SET AL32UTF8;
```

■ **Note** If you don't specify SET DATABASE in the top line of the prior script, when you run the script (as shown later in this example), you'll receive an error such as this: ORA-01161: database name ... in file header does not match.

---

4. Create an init.ora file that matches the new database name:

```
$ cd $ORACLE_HOME/dbs
$ cp init<old_sid>.ora init<new_sid>.ora
$ cp inito12c.ora initDEVDB.ora
```

5. Modify the DB_NAME variable within the new init.ora file (in this example, it's set to DEVDB):

```
db_name='DEVDB'
```

6. Set the ORACLE_SID OS variable to reflect the new SID name (in this example, it's set to DEVDB):

```
$ echo $ORACLE_SID
DEVDB
```

7. Start up the instance in nomount mode:

```
SQL> startup nomount;
```

8. Run the trace file (from step 2) to re-create the control file:

```
SQL> @/tmp/cf.sql
```

■ **Note** In this example the control files already exist in the location specified by the CONTROL_FILES initialization parameter; therefore, the REUSE parameter is used in the CREATE CONTROL FILE statement.

---

9. Open the database with OPEN RESETLOGS:

```
SQL> alter database open resetlogs;
```

If successful, you should have a database that is a copy of the original database. All the data files, control files, archive redo logs, and online redo logs are in the new locations, and the database has a new name.

10. As a last step, ensure that your temporary tablespace exists:

```
ALTER TABLESPACE TEMP ADD TEMPFILE '/ora01/dbfile/DEVDB/temp01.dbf'
    SIZE 104857600  REUSE AUTOEXTEND OFF;
```

■ **Tip**   You can also use the `NID` utility to change the database name and database identifier (DBID). See MOS note 863800.1 for more details.

Summary

RMAN is an acronym for Recovery Manager. It's worth noting that Oracle did not name this tool Backup Manager. The Oracle team recognized that although backups are important, the real value of a B&R tool is its ability to restore and recover the database. Being able to manage the recovery process is the critical skill. When a database is damaged and needs to be restored, everybody looks to the DBA to perform a smooth and speedy recovery of the database. Oracle DBAs should use RMAN to protect, secure, and ensure the availability of the company's data assets.

The restore-and-recovery process is analogous to the healing process involved when you break a bone. Restoring data files from a backup and placing them in their original directories can be likened to setting a bone back to its original position. Recovering a data file is similar to the healing of a broken bone—returning the bone back to the state it was in before it was broken. When you recover data files, you apply transactions (obtained from archive redo and online redo) to transform the restored data files back to the state they were in before the media failure occurred.

RMAN can be used for any type of restore-and-recovery scenario. Depending on the situation, RMAN can be used to restore the entire database, specific data files, control files, server parameter files, archive redo logs, or just specific data blocks. You can instruct RMAN to perform a complete or an incomplete recovery.

The last section in this chapter details how to use RMAN to restore and recover a database to a remote server. I recommend that you periodically attempt this type of recovery in order to exercise your B&R strategy. You will gain much confidence and fully understand B&R internals once you can successfully restore a database to a server that is different from the original.

CHAPTER 7

■ ■ ■

Handling Online Redo Log Failures

I worked for a company that had just implemented an expensive database server with redundancy built into every component, or so I thought. The server was configured with RAID disks for all database files and the online redo log groups. The team was confident that there was minimal risk of failure with these disks.

Therefore, I decided not to multiplex the online redo log groups. A few days later, an inexpensive battery that maintained the cache for a disk controller failed. This caused corruption in the current online redo log group. As a result, the company lost data, experienced costly downtime, and had to perform an incomplete recovery.

As detailed in Chapter 2, online redo logs are crucial database files that store a record of transactions that have occurred in your database. Since RMAN doesn't back up online redo log files, you can't use RMAN to restore these critical files. Given their criticality, I thought it was important to include a chapter on how to deal with failures with online redo log files.

Media failures with the online redo logs are usually noticed either when the database ceases to work (all members of a group have experienced media failure) or you notice an error in the alert.log indicating issues, for example:

```
ORA-00312: online log 3 thread 1: '/u01/oraredo/O12C/redo02b.rdo'
```

Once you've discovered an issue, the first step is to determine how to recover from this failure.

■ **Tip** Use the RMAN `backup database plus archivelog` command to ensure your current online redo log files (of all the threads) are switched and archived before and after the backup of the database.

Determining a Course of Action

If you've experienced a problem with your online redo log files and need to determine what shape they are in and what action to take. Follow these steps when dealing with online redo log file failures:

1. Inspect the `alert.log` file to determine which online redo log files have experienced a media failure.

2. Query `V$LOG` and `V$LOGFILE` to determine the status of the log group and degree of multiplexing.

3. If there is still one functioning member of a multiplexed group, then see the section of this chapter on "Restoring After Losing One Member of Multiplexed Group" for details on how to fix a failed member(s).

4. Depending on the status of the log group, use Table 7-1 to determine what action to take.

Table 7-1. *Determining the Action to Take*

Type of Failure	Status Column of V$LOG	Action	Section
One member failed in multiplexed group	N/A	Drop/re-create member.	Restoring after Losing One Member of a Multiplexed Group
All members of group	INACTIVE	Clear logfile or drop/re-create log group.	Recovering After Loss of All Members Inactive Group
All members of group	ACTIVE	Attempt checkpoint, and if successful, clear logfile. If checkpoint is unsuccessful, perform incomplete recovery.	Recovering After Loss of All Members Active Group
All members of group	CURRENT	Attempt to clear log, and if unsuccessful, perform incomplete recovery.	Recovering After Loss of All Members of Current Group

Inspect your target database alert.log file to determine which online redo log file member is unavailable. Oracle error messages related to online redo log file failures are ORA-00312 and ORA-00313. Here's an example of errors written to the alert.log file when there are problems with an online redo log file:

```
ORA-00313: open failed for members of log group 2 of thread 1
ORA-00312: online log 2 thread 1: '/u02/oraredo/012C/redo02b.rdo'
```

Query V$LOG and V$LOGFILE views to determine the status of your log group and the member files in each group:

```
SELECT
 a.group#
,a.thread#
,a.status grp_status
,b.member member
,b.status mem_status
,a.bytes/1024/1024 mbytes
FROM v$log      a,
     v$logfile b
WHERE a.group# = b.group#
ORDER BY a.group#, b.member;
```

Here is some sample output:

```
GROUP#  THREAD# GRP_STATUS MEMBER                            MEM_STA  MBYTES
------- ------- ---------- -------------------------------   ------- --------
      1       1 INACTIVE   /u01/oraredo/O12C/redo01a.rdo                  50
      1       1 INACTIVE   /u02/oraredo/O12C/redo01b.rdo                  50
      2       1 CURRENT    /u01/oraredo/O12C/redo02a.rdo                  50
      2       1 CURRENT    /u02/oraredo/O12C/redo02b.rdo                  50
      3       1 INACTIVE   /u01/oraredo/O12C/redo03a.rdo                  50
      3       1 INACTIVE   /u02/oraredo/O12C/redo03b.rdo                  50
```

If only one member of a multiplexed group has experienced a failure, then proceed to the section on "Restoring After Losing One Member of Multiplexed Group". If all members of a redo log group have experienced a failure and your database is open, it will hang (cease to allow transactions to process) as soon as the archiver background process cannot successfully copy the failed online redo log file members. If your database is closed, Oracle will not allow you to open it if all members of one online redo log group are experiencing a media failure. When you attempt to open your database, you'll see a message similar to this:

```
ORA-00313: open failed for members of log group...
```

Depending on the status reported in V$LOG for the failed group, use Table 7-1 to determine what action to take.

Your target database's alert.log file contains the best information for determining what type of failure has occurred. If only one member of a multiplexed group fails, then you will be able to detect this only by inspecting the alert.log file. You can also try to stop and start your database. If all members of a group have experienced media failure, then Oracle will not let you open the database and will display an ORA-00313 error message.

The alert.log file will also tell you where additional error messages have been written to trace files:

```
Additional information: 3
Checker run found 1 new persistent data failures
Errors in file /u01/app/oracle/diag/rdbms/o12C/O12C/trace/O12C_lgwr_10531.trc:
```

When diagnosing online redo log issues, the VLOG, VLOGFILE, and V$LOG_HISTORY views are particularly helpful. You can query these views while the database is mounted or open. Table 7-2 briefly describes each view.

Table 7-2. *Useful Views Related to Online Redo Logs*

View	Description
V$LOG	Displays the online redo log group information stored in the control file.
V$LOGFILE	Displays online redo log file member information.
V$LOG_HISTORY	History of online redo log information in control file.

The STATUS column of the V$LOG view is particularly useful when working with online redo logs groups. Table 7-3 describes each status and meaning for the V$LOG view.

Table 7-3. Status for Online Redo Log Groups in the V$LOG View

Status	Meaning
CURRENT	The log group that is currently being written to by the log writer.
ACTIVE	The log group is required for crash recovery and may or may not have been archived.
CLEARING	The log group is being cleared out by an alter database clear logfile command.
CLEARING_CURRENT	The current log group is being cleared of a closed thread.
INACTIVE	The log group isn't needed for crash recovery and may or may not have been archived.
UNUSED	The log group has never been written to; it was recently created.

The STATUS column of the V$LOGFILE view also contains useful information. This view contains information about each physical online redo log file member of a log group. Table 7-4 provides descriptions of the status of each log file member.

Table 7-4. Status for Online Redo Log File Members in the V$LOGFILE View

Status	Meaning
INVALID	The log file member is inaccessible, or it has been recently created.
DELETED	The log file member is no longer in use.
STALE	The log file member's contents are not complete.
NULL	The log file member is being used by the database.

It's important to differentiate between the STATUS column in V$LOG and the STATUS column in V$LOGFILE. The STATUS column in V$LOG reflects the status of the log group. The STATUS column in V$LOGFILE reports the status of the physical online redo log file member.

Restoring After Losing One Member of Multiplexed Group

Suppose you notice this message in your alert.log file:

```
ORA-00312: online log 2 thread 1: '/u02/oraredo/O12C/redo02b.rdo'
```

You know that this group is multiplexed but only see an error with one of the members of the group. If your online redo log file members are multiplexed, the log writer will continue to function as long as it can successfully write to one member of the current log group. If the problem is temporary, then as soon as the online redo log file becomes available, the log writer will start to write to the online redo log file as if there were never an issue.

If the media failure is permanent (such as a bad disk), then you'll need to replace the disk and drop and re-create the bad member to its original location. If you don't have the option of replacing the bad disk, then you'll need to drop the bad member and re-create it in an alternate location.

For permanent media failures, follow these instructions for dropping and re-creating one member of an online redo log group:

1. Identify the online redo log file experiencing media failure (inspect the `alert.log`).

2. Ensure that the online redo log file is not part of the current online log group.

3. Drop the damaged member.

4. Add a new member to the group.

To begin, open your `alert.log` file and look for an ORA-00312 message that identifies which member of the log group is experiencing media failure. You should see lines similar to these in your `alert.log` file:

```
ORA-00312: online log 2 thread 1: '/u02/oraredo/012C/redo02b.rdo'
Errors in file
/u01/app/oracle/diag/rdbms/o12C/012C/trace/012C_lgwr_10531.trc:
```

This message tells you which log member has failed. The `alert.log` file output also specifies that a trace file has been generated. You'll find additional information about the bad member in the specified trace file:

```
ORA-00313: open failed for members of log group 2 of thread 1
ORA-00312: online log 2 thread 1: '/u02/oraredo/012C/redo02b.rdo'
ORA-27037: unable to obtain file status
Linux-x86_64 Error: 2: No such file or directory
ORA-00321: log 2 of thread 1, cannot update log file header
ORA-00312: online log 2 thread 1: '/u02/oraredo/012C/redo02b.rdo'
```

From the prior output, a member of the online redo log group 2 is having issues. Once you've identified the bad online redo log file, execute the following query to check whether that online redo log file's group has a CURRENT status (in this example, we're interested in group 2):

```
SELECT group#, status, archived, thread#, sequence#
FROM v$log;
```

Here is some sample output indicating that group 2 is not the current log:

GROUP#	STATUS	ARC	THREAD#	SEQUENCE#
1	CURRENT	NO	1	25
3	INACTIVE	NO	1	24
2	INACTIVE	NO	1	23

■ **Note** If you attempt to drop a member of a current log group, Oracle will throw an ORA-01609 error specifying that the log is current and you cannot drop one of its members.

If the failed member is in the current log group, then use the `alter system switch logfile` command to make the next group the current group. Then drop the failed member as follows:

```
SQL> alter database drop logfile member '/u02/oraredo/012C/redo02b.rdo';
```

Then re-create the online redo log file member:

```
SQL> alter database add logfile member '/u02/oraredo/O12C/redo02b.rdo'
    to group 2;
```

Keep in mind that the prior commands are examples, and that you'll have to specify the directory and logfile member file and group number for your environment.

If an unused log file already happens to exist in the target location, you can use the reuse parameter to overwrite and reuse that log file. The log file must be the same size as the other log files in the group:

```
SQL> alter database add logfile member '</directory/file_name>' reuse
    to group <group#>;
```

As mentioned previously, Oracle will continue to operate as long as it can write to at least one member of a multiplexed redo log group. An error message will be written to the alert.log file when the log writer is unable to write to a current online redo log file.

You should periodically inspect your alert.log file for Oracle errors. This may be the only way that you'll discover a member of a group has experienced a media failure. I recommend that you run a periodic batch job that searches the alert.log file for any errors and automatically notifies you when it finds potential problems.

Once you've identified the bad member of an online redo log group, then you can drop and re-create the online redo log file. The newly created online redo log file may display an INVALID status in V$LOGFILE until it becomes part of the CURRENT log group. Once the newly created member becomes part of the CURRENT log group, its status should change to NULL. A NULL member status (as described in Table 7-4) indicates that the database is using the online redo log file.

You can drop and add online redo log file members while your database is in either a mounted state or an open state. I recommend that while dropping and re-creating log members, you have your database in a mounted state. This will ensure that the status of the log group doesn't change while dropping and re-creating members. You cannot drop an online redo log file member that is part of the CURRENT group.

■ **Note** When using the alter database drop logfile member command, you will not be allowed to drop the last remaining online redo log file member from a redo log group. If you attempt to do this, Oracle will throw an ORA-00361 error stating that you cannot remove the last standing log member. If you need to drop all members of a log group, use the alter database drop logfile group command.

SEARCHING THE ALERT LOG FOR ERRORS

Here's a simple Bash shell script that determines the location of the alert.log and then searches the alert.log for an error string. You can use something similar to automatically detect errors in the alert.log.

```
#!/bin/bash
export DBS="ENGDEV STAGE OTEST"
export MAILLIST="larry@support.com"
export BOX=`uname -a | awk '{print$2}'`
#-----------------------------------------------------------
for instance in $DBS
do
# call script to source oracle OS variables
```

```
export ORACLE_SID=O12C
export ORACLE_HOME=/orahome/app/oracle/product/12.1.0.1/db_1
export PATH=$PATH:$ORACLE_HOME/bin
crit_var=$(
sqlplus -s <<EOF
/ as sysdba
SET HEAD OFF TERM OFF FEED OFF VERIFY OFF
COL value FORM A80
select value from v\$diag_info where name='Diag Trace';
EOF)
  if [ -r $crit_var/alert_$instance.log ]
  then
  grep -ic error $crit_var/alert_$instance.log
    if [ $? = 0 ]
    then
      mailx -s "Error in $instance log file" $MAILLIST <<EOF
Error in $crit_var/alert_$instance.log file on $BOX...
EOF
    fi # $?
  fi # -r
done # for instance
exit 0
```

You can easily modify the above to fit the requirements of your environment. For example, you might need to change the way the Oracle operating system variables are sourced, the databases searched for, the error string, and the e-mail address. This is just a simple example showing the power of using a shell script to automate the search for errors in a file.

Recovering After Loss of All Members of Inactive Redo Log Group

If you've lost all members of an inactive redo log group, then perform the following steps:

1. Verify that all members of a group have been damaged (by inspecting the alert.log file).

2. Verify that the log group status is INACTIVE.

3. Re-create the log group with the clear logfile command.

4. If the re-created log group has not been archived, then immediately back up your database.

If all members of an online redo log group are damaged, you won't be able to open your database. In this situation, Oracle will allow you to only mount your database.

First inspect your alert.log file, and verify that all members of a redo log group are damaged. You should see a message indicating that all members of an online redo log group are damaged and the database cannot open:

```
ORA-00312: online log 2 thread 1: '/u01/oraredo/O12C/redo02a.rdo'
ORA-00313: open failed for members of log group 2 of thread 1
```

Next, ensure that your database is in mount mode:

```
$ sqlplus / as sysdba
SQL> startup mount;
```

Next, run the following query to verify that the damaged log group is INACTIVE and determine whether it has been archived:

```
SELECT group#, status, archived, thread#, sequence#
FROM v$log;
```

Here is some sample output:

```
GROUP# STATUS            ARC   THREAD#   SEQUENCE#
---------- ---------------- ---   ---------- ----------
         1 CURRENT          NO          1          25
         3 INACTIVE         NO          1          24
         2 INACTIVE         NO          1          23
```

If the status is INACTIVE, then this log group is no longer needed for crash recovery (as described in Table 7-3). Therefore, you can use the clear logfile command to re-create all members of a log group. The following example re-creates all log members of group 2:

```
SQL> alter database clear logfile group 2;
```

If the log group has not been archived, then you will need to use the clear unarchived logfile command as follows:

```
SQL> alter database clear unarchived logfile group 2;
```

If the cleared log group had not been previously archived, it's critical that you immediately create a backup of your database. See Chapter 5 for details on taking a complete backup of your database.

Keep in mind that in these prior examples the logfile group is number 2. You'll have to modify the group number to match the group number for your scenario.

If the online redo log group is inactive and archived, then its contents aren't required for crash or media recovery. Therefore it's possible to use the clear logfile command to re-create all online redo log file members of a group.

■ **Note** The clear logfile command will drop and re-create all members of a log group for you. You can issue this command even if you have only two log groups in your database.

If the online redo log group has not been archived, then it may be required for media recovery. In this case, use the clear unarchived logfile command to re-create the logfile group members. Back up your database as soon as possible in this situation.

The unarchived log group may be needed for media recovery if the last database backups were taken before the redo information in the log was created. This means if you attempt to perform media recovery, you won't be able to recover any information in the damaged log file or any transactions that were created after that log.

If the clear logfile command does not succeed because of an I/O error and it's a permanent problem, then you will need to consider dropping the log group and re-creating it in a different location. See the next two subsections for directions on how to drop and re-create a log file group.

Dropping a Log File Group

The alternative to clearing a logfile group (which tells Oracle to re-create the logfile) is to drop and re-create the logfile group. You might need to do this if you need to re-create the logfile group in a different location because the original location is damaged or not available.

A log group has to have an inactive status before you can drop it. You can check the status of the log group, as shown here:

```
SQL> select group#, status, archived, thread#, sequence# from v$log;
```

You can drop a log group with the drop logfile group command:

```
SQL> alter database drop logfile group <group #>;
```

If you attempt to drop the current online log group, Oracle will return an ORA-01623 error stating that you cannot drop the current group. Use the alert system switch logfile command to switch the logs and make the next group the current group.

After a log switch, the log group that was previously the current group will retain an active status as long as it contains redo that Oracle requires to perform crash recovery. If you attempt to drop a log group with an active status, Oracle will throw an ORA-01624 error stating that the log group is required for crash recovery. Issue an alter system checkpoint command to make the log group inactive.

Additionally, you cannot issue a drop logfile group command if it leaves you with only one log group left in your database. If you attempt to do this, Oracle will throw an ORA-01567 error and inform you that dropping the log group is not permitted because it would leave you with less than two logs groups for your database (Oracle minimally requires two log groups to function).

Adding a Log File Group

You can add a new log group with the add logfile group command:

```
SQL> alter database add logfile group <group_#>
('/directory/file') SIZE <bytes> K|M|G;
```

You can specify the size of the log file in bytes, kilobytes, megabytes, or gigabytes. The following example adds a log group with two members sized at 50MB:

```
SQL> alter database add logfile group 2
('/u01/oraredo/012C/redo02a.rdo',
 '/u02/oraredo/012C/redo02b.rdo') SIZE 50M;
```

If for some reason the log file members already exist on disk, you can use the reuse clause to overwrite them:

```
alter database add logfile group 2
('/u01/oraredo/012C/redo02a.rdo',
 '/u02/oraredo/012C/redo02b.rdo') SIZE 50M reuse;
```

■ **Tip** See Chapter 2 for an example of moving an online redo log group.

Recovering After Loss of All Members of Active Redo Log Group

If all the members of an active online redo log group in your database have experienced media failure, then perform the following steps when restoring an active online redo log group:

1. Verify the damage to the members.

2. Verify that the status is ACTIVE.

3. Attempt to issue a checkpoint.

4. If the checkpoint is successful, the status should now be INACTIVE, and you can clear the log group.

5. If the log group that was cleared was unarchived, back up your database immediately.

6. If the checkpoint is unsuccessful, then you will have to perform incomplete recovery.

Inspect your target database alert.log file, and verify the damage. You should see a message in the alert.log file identifying the bad members:

```
ORA-00312: online log 2 thread 1: '/u01/oraredo/O12C/redo02a.rdo'
ORA-00312: online log 2 thread 1: '/u02/oraredo/O12C/redo02b.rdo'
```

Next, verify that the damaged log group has an ACTIVE status as follows:

```
$ sqlplus / as sysdba
SQL> startup mount;
```

Run the following query:

```
SQL> select group#, status, archived, thread#, sequence# from v$log;
```

Here is some sample output:

```
GROUP# STATUS           ARC THREAD#  SEQUENCE#
------ ---------------- --- -------- ----------
     1 CURRENT          NO         1         92
     2 ACTIVE           YES        1         91
     3 INACTIVE         YES        1         90
```

If the status is ACTIVE, then attempt to issue an alter system checkpoint command, as shown here:

```
SQL> alter system checkpoint;
System altered.
```

If the checkpoint completes successfully, then the active log group should be marked as INACTIVE. A successful checkpoint ensures that all modified database buffers have been written to disk, and at that point, only transactions contained in the CURRENT online redo log will be required for crash recovery.

■ **Note** If the checkpoint is unsuccessful, you will have to perform incomplete recovery. See the section in this chapter "Recovering After Loss of All Members of Current Redo Log Group" for a full list of options in this scenario.

If the status is INACTIVE and the log has been archived, you can use the clear logfile command to re-create the log group, as shown here:

```
SQL> alter database clear logfile group <group#>;
```

If the status is inactive and the log group has not been archived, then re-create it with the clear unarchived logfile command, as shown here:

```
SQL> alter database clear unarchived logfile group <group#>;
```

If the cleared log group had not been previously archived, it's critical that you immediately create a backup of your database. See Chapter 5 for details on creating a complete backup of your database.

An online redo log group with an ACTIVE status is still required for crash recovery. If all members of an active online redo log group experience media failure, then you must attempt to issue a checkpoint. If the checkpoint is successful, then you can clear the log group. If the checkpoint is unsuccessful, then you will have to perform an incomplete recovery.

If the checkpoint is successful and if the log group has not been archived, then the log may be required for media recovery. Back up your database as soon as possible in this situation. The unarchived log group may be needed for media recovery if the last database backups were taken before the redo information in the log was created. This means if you attempt to perform media recovery, you won't be able to recover any information in the damaged log file or any transactions that were created after that log.

Recovering After Loss of All Members of Current Redo Log Group

If all of the members of a current Online redo logs:recovery online redo log group in your database have experienced media failure then (unfortunately) your alternatives are limited when you lose all members of a current online redo log group. Here are some possible options:

- Perform an incomplete recovery up to the last good SCN.

- If flashback is enabled, flash your database back to the last good SCN.

- If you're using Oracle Data Guard, fail over to your physical or logical standby database.

- Contact Oracle Support for suggestions.

In preparation for an incomplete recovery, first determine the last good SCN by querying the FIRST_CHANGE# column from V$LOG. In this scenario, you're missing only the current online redo logs. Therefore, you can perform an incomplete recovery up to, but not including, the FIRST_CHANGE# SCN of the current online redo log.

```
SQL> shutdown immediate;
SQL> startup mount;
```

Now issue this query:

```
SELECT group#, status, archived,
thread#, sequence#, first_change#
FROM v$log;
```

Here is some sample output:

```
GROUP# STATUS            ARC  THREAD#  SEQUENCE# FIRST_CHANGE#
------ ----------------  ---  -------- --------- -------------
     1 INACTIVE          YES        1        86        533781
     2 INACTIVE          YES        1        85        533778
     3 CURRENT           NO         1        87        533784
```

In this case, you can restore Online redo logs:recovery and recover up to, but not including, SCN 533784. Here's how you would do that:

```
RMAN> restore database until scn 533784;
RMAN> recover database until scn 533784;
RMAN> alter database open resetlogs;
```

───

■ **Note**   For complete details on incomplete recovery, and/or flashing back your database see Chapter 6.

───

Losing all members of your current online redo log group is arguably the worst thing that can happen to your database. If you experience media failure with all members of the current online redo group, then you most likely will lose any transactions contained in those logs. In this situation, you will have to perform incomplete recovery before you can open your database.

───

■ **Tip**   If you are desperate to restore transactions lost in damaged current online redo log files, then contact Oracle Support to explore all options.

───

Summary

It's critical that you understand how to handle online redo log failures. Oracle doesn't provide an automated method for fixing problems when there's a media failure with the online redo logs. Therefore it's important that you know how to diagnose and troubleshoot any issues that arise. Failures with the online redo logs are rare, but when they do happen, you'll now be much better prepared to resolve any complications in an efficient and effective manner.

CHAPTER 8

■ ■ ■

Data Pump

Data Pump is often described as an upgraded version of the old exp/imp utilities. That depiction is inaccurate; it's a bit like calling a modern smartphone a replacement for an old rotary-dial landline. Although the old utilities are dependable and work well, Data Pump encompasses that functionality and while adding completely new dimensions to how data can be lifted and moved between environments. This chapter will help explain how Data Pump makes your current data transfer tasks easier and will also show how to move information and solve problems in ways that you didn't think were possible.

Data Pump enables you to efficiently back up, replicate, secure, and transform large amounts data and metadata. You can use Data Pump in a variety of ways:

- Perform point-in-time logical backups of the entire database or subsets of data

- Replicate entire databases or subsets of data for testing or development

- Quickly generate DDL required to recreate objects

- Upgrade a database by exporting from the old version and importing into the new version

Sometimes, DBAs exert a Luddite-like attachment to the exp/imp utilities because the DBAs are familiar with the syntax of these utilities, and they get the job done quickly. Even if those legacy utilities are easy to use, you should consider using Data Pump going forward. Data Pump contains substantial functionality over the old exp/imp utilities:

- Performance with large data sets, allowing efficient export and import gigabytes of data

- Interactive command line utility, which lets you disconnect and then later attach to active Data Pump jobs

- Ability to export large amounts of data from a remote database and import them directly into a local database without creating a dump file

- Ability to make on-the-fly changes to schemas, tablespaces, data files, and storage settings from export to import

- Sophisticated filtering of objects and data

- Security-controlled (via database) directory objects

- Advanced features, such as compression and encryption

This chapter begins with a discussion on the Data Pump architecture. Subsequent topics include basic export and import tasks, moving data across networks, filtering data, and running Data Pump in legacy mode.

Data Pump Architecture

Data Pump consists of the following components:

- expdp (Data Pump export utility)

- impdp (Data Pump import utility)

- DBMS_DATAPUMP PL/SQL package (Data Pump application programming interface [API])

- DBMS_METADATA PL/SQL package (Data Pump Metadata API)

The expdp and impdp utilities use the DBMS_DATAPUMP and DBMS_METADATA built-in PL/SQL packages when exporting and importing data and metadata. The DBMS_DATAPUMP package moves entire databases or subsets of data between database environments. The DBMS_METADATA package exports and imports information about database objects.

■ **Note** You can call the DBMS_DATAPUMP and DBMS_METADATA packages independently (outside expdp and impdp) from SQL*Plus. I rarely call these packages directly from SQL*Plus, but you may have a specific scenario in which it's desirable to interact directly with them. See the *Oracle Database PL/SQL Packages and Types Reference Guide*, which is available for download from the Technology Network area of the Oracle Web site (http://otn.oracle.com), for more details.

When you start a Data Pump export or import job, a master OS process is initiated on the database server. This master process name has the format ora_dmNN_<SID>. On Linux/Unix systems, you can view this process from the OS, prompt using the ps command:

```
$ ps -ef | grep -v grep | grep ora_dm
oracle    14602     1  4 08:59 ?        00:00:03 ora_dm00_O12C
```

Depending on the degree of parallelism and the work specified, a number of worker processes are also started. If no parallelism is specified, then only one worker process is started. The master process coordinates the work between master and worker processes. The worker process names have the format ora_dwNN_<SID>.

Also, when a user starts an export or import job, a database status table is created (owned by the user that starts the job). This table exists only for the duration of the Data Pump job. The name of the status table is dependent on what type of job you're running. The table is named with the format SYS_<OPERATION>_<JOB_MODE>_NN, where OPERATION is either EXPORT or IMPORT. JOB_MODE can be one of the following types:

- FULL

- SCHEMA

- TABLE

- TABLESPACE

- TRANSPORTABLE

For example, if you're exporting a schema, a table is created in your account with the name SYS_EXPORT_SCHEMA_NN, where NN is a number that makes the table name unique in the user's schema. This status table contains information such as the objects exported/imported, start time, elapsed time, rows, and error count. The status table has more than 80 columns.

■ **Tip** The Data Pump status table is created in the default permanent tablespace of the user performing the export/import. Therefore, if the user has no privileges to create a table in the default tablespace, the Data Pump job will fail, with an ORA-31633 error.

The status table is dropped by Data Pump upon successful completion of an export or import job. If you use the KILL_JOB interactive command, the master table is also dropped. If you stop a job with the STOP_JOB interactive command, the table isn't removed and is used in the event you restart the job.

If your job terminates abnormally, the master table is retained. You can delete the status table if you don't plan to restart the job.

When Data Pump runs, it uses a database directory object to determine where to write and read dump files and log files. Usually, you specify which directory object you want Data Pump to use. If you don't specify a directory object, a default directory is used. The default directory path is defined by a data directory object named DATA_PUMP_DIR. This directory object is automatically created when the database is first created. On Linux/Unix systems this directory object maps to the ORACLE_HOME/rdbms/log directory.

A Data Pump export creates an export file and a log file. The export file contains the objects being exported. The log file contains a record of the job activities. Figure 8-1 shows the architectural components related to a Data Pump export job.

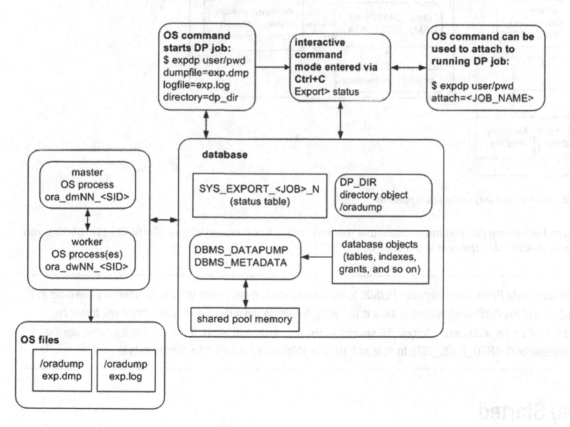

Figure 8-1. *Data Pump export job components*

Similarly, Figure 8-2 displays the architectural components of a Data Pump import job. The main difference between export and import is the direction in which the data flow. Export writes data out of the database, and import brings information into the database. Refer back to these diagrams as you work through Data Pump examples and concepts throughout this chapter.

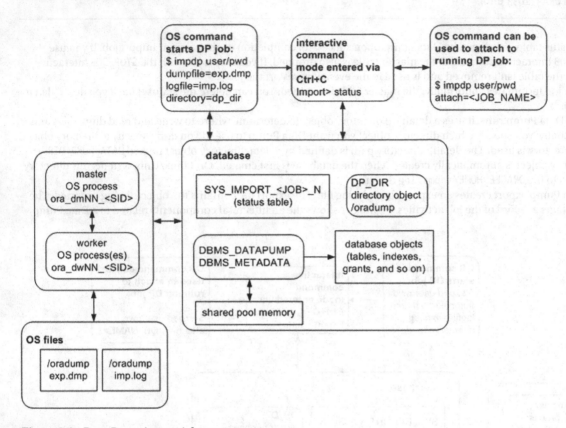

Figure 8-2. *Data Pump import job components*

For each Data Pump job, you must ensure that you have access to a directory object. The basics of exporting and importing are described in the next few sections.

■ **Tip**   Because Data Pump internally uses PL/SQL to perform its work, there needs to be some memory available in the shared pool to hold the PL/SQL packages. If there is not enough room in the shared pool, Data Pump will throw an ORA-04031: unable to allocate bytes of shared memory... error and abort. If you receive this error, set the database parameter SHARED_POOL_SIZE to at least 50M. See MOS note 396940.1 for further details.

Getting Started

Now that you have an understanding of the Data Pump architecture, next is a simple example showing the required export setup steps for exporting a table, dropping the table, and then reimporting the table back into the database. This will lay the foundation for all other Data Pump tasks covered in this chapter.

Taking an Export

A small amount of setup is required when you run a Data Pump export job. Here are the steps:

1. Create a database directory object that points to an OS directory that you want to write/read Data Pump files to/from.

2. Grant read and write privileges on the directory object to the database user running the export.

3. From the OS prompt, run the expdp utility.

Step 1. Creating a Database Directory Object

Before you run a Data Pump job, first create a database directory object that corresponds to a physical location on disk. This location will be used to hold the export and log files and should be a location where you know you have plenty of disk space to accommodate the amount of data being exported.

Use the CREATE DIRECTORY command to accomplish this task. This example creates a directory named dp_dir and specifies that it is to map to the /oradump physical location on disk:

```
SQL> create directory dp_dir as '/oradump';
```

To view the details of the newly created directory, issue this query:

```
SQL> select owner, directory_name, directory_path from dba_directories;
```

Here is some sample output:

```
OWNER      DIRECTORY_NAME  DIRECTORY_PATH
---------- --------------- ----------------------
SYS        DP_DIR          /oradump
```

Keep in mind that the directory path specified has to physically exist on the database server. Furthermore, the directory has to be one that the oracle OS user has read/write access to. Finally, the user performing the Data Pump operations needs to be granted read/write access to the directory object (see step 2).

If you don't specify the DIRECTORY parameter when exporting or importing, Data Pump will attempt to use the default database directory object (as previously discussed, this maps to ORACLE_HOME/rdbms/log). I don't recommend using the default directory for two reasons:

- If you're exporting large amounts of data, it's better to have on disk the preferred location, where you know you have enough room to accommodate your disk space requirements. If you use the default directory, you run the risk of inadvertently filling up the mount point associated with ORACLE_HOME and then potentially hanging your database.

- If you grant privileges to non-DBA users to take exports, you don't want them creating large dump files in a location associated with ORACLE_HOME. Again, you don't want the mount point associated with ORACLE_HOME to become full to the detriment of your database.

Step 2. Granting Access to the Directory

You need to grant permissions on the database directory object to a user that wants to use Data Pump. Use the GRANT statement to allocate the appropriate privileges. If you want a user to be able to read from and write to the directory, you must grant security access. This example grants access to the directory object to a user named MV_MAINT:

```
SQL> grant read, write on directory dp_dir to mv_maint;
```

All directory objects are owned by the SYS user. If you're using a user account that has the DBA role granted to it, then you have the requisite read/write privileges on any directory objects. I usually perform Data Pump jobs with a user that has the DBA granted to it (so that I don't need to bother with granting access).

SECURITY ISSUES WITH THE OLD EXP UTILITY

The idea behind creating directory objects and then granting specific I/O access to the physical storage location is that you can more securely administer which users have the capability to generate read and write activities when normally they wouldn't have permissions. With the legacy exp utility, any user that has access to the tool by default has access to write or read a file to which the owner (usually oracle) of the Oracle binaries has access. It's conceivable that a malicious non-oracle OS user can attempt to run the exp utility to purposely overwrite a critical database file. For example, the following command can be run by any non-oracle OS user with execute access to the exp utility:

```
$ exp heera/foo file=/oradata04/SCRKDV12/users01.dbf
```

The exp process runs as the oracle OS user and therefore has read and write OS privileges on any oracle-owned data files. In this exp example, if the users01.dbf file is a live database data file, it's overwritten and rendered worthless. This can cause catastrophic damage to your database.

To prevent such issues, with Oracle Data Pump you first have to create a database object directory that maps to a specific directory and then additionally assign read and write privileges to that directory per user. Thus, Data Pump doesn't have the security problems that exist with the old exp utility.

Step 3. Taking an Export

When the directory object and grants are in place, you can use Data Pump to export information from a database. The simple example in this section shows how to export a table. Later sections in this chapter describe in detail the various ways in which you can export data. The point here is to work through an example that will provide a foundation for understanding more complex topics that follow.

As a non-SYS user, create a table, and populate it with some data:

```
SQL> create table inv(inv_id number);
SQL> insert into inv values (123);
```

Next, as a non-SYS user, export the table. This example uses the previously created directory, named DP_DIR. Data Pump uses the directory path specified by the directory object as the location on disk to which to write the dump file and log file:

```
$ expdp mv_maint/foo directory=dp_dir tables=inv dumpfile=exp.dmp logfile=exp.log
```

The expdp utility creates a file named exp.dmp in the /oradump directory, containing the information required to recreate the INV table and populate it with data as it was at the time the export was taken. Additionally, a log file named exp.log is created in the /oradump directory, containing logging information associated with this export job.

If you don't specify a dump file name, Data Pump creates a file named expdat.dmp. If a file named expdat.dmp already exists in the directory, then Data Pump throws an error. If you don't specify a log file name, then Data Pump creates one named export.log. If a log file named export.log already exists, then Data Pump overwrites it.

■ **Tip**   Although it's possible to execute Data Pump as the SYS user, I don't recommend it for couple of reasons. First, SYS is required to connect to the database with the AS SYSDBA clause. This requires a Data Pump parameter file with the USERID parameter and quotes around the associated connect string. This is unwieldy. Second, most tables owned by SYS cannot be exported (there are a few exceptions, such as AUD$). If you attempt to export a table owned by SYS, Data Pump will throw an ORA-39166 error and indicate that the table doesn't exist. This is confusing.

Importing a Table

One of the key reasons to export data is so that you can recreate database objects. You may want to do this as part of a backup strategy or to replicate data to a different database. Data Pump import uses an export dump file as its input and recreates database objects contained in the export file. The procedure for importing is similar to exporting:

1. Create a database directory object that points to an OS directory that you want to read/write Data Pump files from.

2. Grant read and write privileges on the directory object to the database user running the export or import.

3. From the OS prompt, run the impdp command.

Steps 1 and 2 were covered in the prior section, "Taking an Export," and therefore will not be repeated here. Before running the import job, drop the INV table that was created previously.

```
SQL> drop table inv purge;
```

Next, recreate the INV table from the export taken:

```
$ impdp mv_maint/foo directory=dp_dir dumpfile=exp.dmp logfile=imp.log
```

You should now have the INV table recreated and populated with data as it was at the time of the export. Now is a good time to inspect again Figures 8-1 and 8-2. Make sure you understand which files were created by expdb and which files were used by impdp.

Using a Parameter File

Instead of typing commands on the command line, in many situations it's better to store the commands in a file and then reference the file when executing Data Pump export or import. Using parameter files makes tasks more repeatable and less prone to error. You can place the commands in a file once and then reference that file multiple times.

Additionally, some Data Pump commands (such as FLASHBACK_TIME) require the use of quotation marks; in these situations, it's sometimes hard to predict how the OS will interpret these. Whenever a command requires quotation marks, it's highly preferable to use a parameter file.

To use a parameter file, first create an OS text file that contains the commands you want to use to control the behavior of your job. This example uses the Linux/Unix vi command to create a text file named exp.par:

```
$ vi exp.par
```

Now, place the following commands in the exp.par file:

```
userid=mv_maint/foo
directory=dp_dir
dumpfile=exp.dmp
logfile=exp.log
tables=inv
reuse_dumpfiles=y
```

Next, the export operation references the parameter file via the PARFILE command line option:

```
$ expdp parfile=exp.par
```

Data Pump processes the parameters in the file as if they were typed on the command line. If you find yourself repeatedly typing the same commands or using commands that require quotation marks, or both, then consider using a parameter file to increase your efficiency.

■ **Tip** Don't confuse a Data Pump parameter file with the database initialization parameter file. A Data Pump parameter file instructs Data Pump as to which user to connect to the database as, which directory locations to read/write files to and from, what objects to include in the operation, and so on. In contrast, a database parameter file establishes characteristics of the instance upon database startup.

Exporting and Importing with Granularity

Recall from the section "Data Pump Architecture," earlier in this chapter, that there are several different modes in which you can invoke the export/import utilities. For instance, you can instruct Data Pump to export/import in the following modes:

- Entire database
- Schema level
- Table level
- Tablespace level
- Transportable tablespace level

Before diving into the many features of Data Pump, it's useful to discuss these modes and ensure you're aware of how each operates. This will further lay the foundation for understanding concepts introduced later in the chapter.

Exporting and Importing an Entire Database

When you export an entire database, this is sometimes referred to as a full export. In this mode the resultant export file contains everything required to make a copy of your database. Unless restricted by filtering parameters (see the section "Filtering Data and Objects," later in this chapter), a full export consists of

- all DDL required to recreate tablespaces, users, user tables, indexes, constraints, triggers, sequences, stored PL/SQL, and so on.
- all table data (except the SYS user's tables)

A full export is initiated with the FULL parameter set to Y and must be done with a user that has DBA privileges or that has the DATAPUMP_EXP_FULL_DATABASE role granted to it. Here is an example of taking a full export of a database:

```
$ expdp mv_maint/foo directory=dp_dir dumpfile=full.dmp logfile=full.log full=y
```

As the export is executing, you should see this text in the output, indicating that a full-level export is taking place:

```
Starting "MV_MAINT"."SYS_EXPORT_FULL_01":
```

Be aware that a full export doesn't export everything in the database:

- The contents of the SYS schema are not exported (there are a few exceptions to this, such as the AUD$ table). Consider what would happen if you could export the contents of the SYS schema from one database and import them into another. The SYS schema contents would overwrite internal data dictionary tables/views and thus corrupt the database. Therefore, Data Pump never exports objects owned by SYS.
- Index data are not exported, but rather, the index DDL that contains the SQL required to recreate the indexes during a subsequent import.

Once you have a full export, you can use its contents to either recreate objects in the original database (e.g., in the event a table is accidentally dropped) or replicate the entire database or subsets of users/tables to a different database. This next example assumes that the dump file has been copied to a different database server and is now used to import all objects into the destination database:

```
$ impdp mv_maint/foo directory=dp_dir dumpfile=full.dmp logfile=fullimp.log full=y
```

■ **Tip** To initiate a full database import, you must have DBA privileges or be assigned the DATAPUMP_IMP_FULL_DATABASE role.

In the output displayed on your screen, you should see an indication that a full import is transpiring:

```
Starting "MV_MAINT"."SYS_IMPORT_FULL_01":
```

Running a full-import database job has some implications to be aware of:

- The import job will first attempt to recreate any tablespaces. If a tablespace already exists, or if the directory path a tablespace depends on doesn't exist, then the tablespace creation statements will fail, and the import job will move on to the next task.
- Next, the import job will alter the SYS and SYSTEM user accounts to contain the same password that was exported. Therefore, after you import from a production system, it's prudent to change the passwords for SYS and SYSTEM, to reflect the new environment.

- Additionally, the import job will then attempt to create any users in the export file. If a user already exists, an error is thrown, and the import job moves on to the next task.

- Users will be imported with the same passwords that were taken from the original database. Depending on your security standards, you may want to change the passwords.

- Tables will be recreated. If a table already exists and contains data, you must specify how you want the import job to handle this. You can have the import job either skip, append, replace, or truncate the table (see the section "Importing When Objects Already Exist," later in this chapter).

- After each table is created and populated, associated indexes are created.

- The import job will also try to import statistics if available. Furthermore, object grants are instantiated.

If everything runs well, the end result will be a database that is logically identical to the source database in terms of tablespaces, users, objects, and so on.

Schema Level

When you initiate an export, unless otherwise specified, Data Pump starts a schema-level export for the user running the export job. User-level exports are frequently used to copy a schema or set of schemas from one environment to another. The following command starts a schema-level export for the MV_MAINT user:

```
$ expdp mv_maint/foo directory=dp_dir dumpfile=mv_maint.dmp logfile=mv_maint.log
```

In the output displayed on the screen, you should see some text indicating that a schema-level export has been initiated:

```
Starting "MV_MAINT"."SYS_EXPORT_SCHEMA_01"...
```

You can also initiate a schema-level export for users other than the one running the export job with the SCHEMAS parameter. The following command shows a schema-level export for multiple users:

```
$ expdp mv_maint/foo directory=dp_dir dumpfile=user.dmp  schemas=heera,chaya
```

You can initiate a schema-level import by referencing a dump file that was taken with a schema-level export:

```
$ impdp mv_maint/foo directory=dp_dir dumpfile=user.dmp
```

When you initiate a schema-level import, there are some details to be aware of:

- No tablespaces are included in a schema-level export.

- The import job attempts to recreate any users in the dump file. If a user already exists, an error is thrown, and the import job continues.

- The import job will reset the users' passwords, based on the password that was exported.

- Tables owned by the users will be imported and populated. If a table already exists, you must instruct Data Pump on how to handle this with the TABLE_EXISTS_ACTION parameter.

You can also initiate a schema-level import when using a full-export dump file. To do this, specify which schemas you want extracted from the full export:

```
$ impdp mv_maint/foo directory=dp_dir dumpfile=full.dmp schemas=heera,chaya
```

Table Level

You can instruct Data Pump to operate on specific tables via the TABLES parameter. For example, say you want to export

```
$ expdp mv_maint/foo directory=dp_dir dumpfile=tab.dmp \
tables=heera.inv,heera.inv_items
```

You should see some text in the output indicating that a table-level export is transpiring:

```
Starting "MV_MAINT"."SYS_EXPORT_TABLE_01...
```

Similarly, you can initiate a table-level import by specifying a table-level-created dump file:

```
$ impdp mv_maint/foo directory=dp_dir dumpfile=tab.dmp
```

A table-level import only attempts to import the tables and specified data. If a table already exists, an error is thrown, and the import job continues. If a table already exists and contains data, you must specify how you want the export job to handle this. You can have the import job either skip, append, replace, or truncate the table with the TABLE_EXISTS_ACTION parameter.

You can also initiate a table-level import when using a full-export dump file or a schema-level export. To do this, specify which tables you want extracted from the full- or schema-level export:

```
$ impdp mv_maint/foo directory=dp_dir dumpfile=full.dmp tables=heera.inv
```

Tablespace Level

A tablespace-level export/import operates on objects contained within specific tablespaces. This example exports all objects contained in the USERS tablespace:

```
$ expdp mv_maint/foo directory=dp_dir dumpfile=tbsp.dmp tablespaces=users
```

The text displayed in the output should indicate that a tablespace-level export is occurring:

```
Starting "MV_MAINT"."SYS_EXPORT_TABLESPACE_01"...
```

You can initiate a tablespace-level import by specifying an export file that was created with a tablespace-level export:

```
$ impdp mv_maint/foo directory=dp_dir dumpfile=tbsp.dmp
```

You can also initiate a tablespace-level import by using a full export, but specifying the TABLESPACES parameter:

```
$ impdp mv_maint/foo directory=dp_dir dumpfile=full.dmp tablespaces=users
```

A tablespace-level import will attempt to create any tables and indexes within the tablespace. The import doesn't try to recreate the tablespaces themselves.

■ **Note** There is also a transportable tablespace mode export. See the section "Copying Data Files", later in this chapter.

Transferring Data

One of the main uses of Data Pump is the copying of data from one database to another. Often, source and destination databases are located in data centers thousands of miles apart. Data Pump offers several powerful features for efficiently copying data:

- Network link

- Copying data files (transportable tablespaces)

- External tables

Using a network link allows you to take an export and import it into the destination database without having to create a dump file. This is a very efficient way of moving data.

Oracle also provides the transportable tablespace feature, which lets you copy the data files from a source database to the destination and then use Data Pump to transfer the associated metadata. These two techniques are described in the following sections.

Exporting and Importing Directly Across the Network

Suppose you have two database environments—a production database running on a Solaris box and a test database running on a Linux server. Your boss comes to you with these requirements:

- Make a copy of the production database on the Solaris box.

- Import the copy into the testing database on the Linux server.

- Change the names of the schemas when importing so as to meet the testing database standards for names.

First, consider the steps required to transfer data from one database to another, using the old exp/imp utilities. The steps would look something like this:

1. Export the production database (which creates a dump file on the database server).

2. Copy the dump file to the testing database server.

3. Import the dump file into the testing database.

You can perform those same steps using Data Pump. However, Data Pump provides a much more efficient and transparent method for executing those steps. If you have direct network connectivity between the production and testing database servers, you can take an export and directly import it into your target database without having to create or copy any dump files. Furthermore, you can rename schemas on the fly as you perform the import. Additionally, it doesn't matter if the source database is running on an OS different from that of the target database.

An example will help illustrate how this works. For this example, the production database users are STAR2, CIA_APP, and CIA_SEL. You want to move these users into a testing database and rename them STAR_JUL, CIA_APP_JUL, and CIA_SEL_JUL. This task requires the following steps:

1. Create users in the test database to be imported into. Here is a sample script that creates the users in the testing database:

```
define star_user=star_jul
define star_user_pwd=star_jul_pwd
define cia_app_user=cia_app_jul
define cia_app_user_pwd=cia_app_jul_pwd
define cia_sel_user=cia_sel_jul
define cia_sel_user_pwd=cia_sel_jul_pwd
--
create user &&star_user identified by &&star_user_pwd;
grant connect,resource to &&star_user;
alter user &&star_user default tablespace dim_data;
--
create user &&cia_app_user identified by &&cia_app_user_pwd;
grant connect,resource to &&cia_app_user;
alter user &&cia_app_user default tablespace cia_data;
--
create user &&cia_sel_user identified by &&cia_app_user_pwd;
grant connect,resource to &&cia_app_user;
alter user &&cia_sel_user default tablespace cia_data;
```

2. In your testing database, create a database link that points to your production database. The remote user referenced in the CREATE DATABASE LINK statement must have the DBA role granted to it in the production database. Here is a sample CREATE DATABASE LINK script:

```
create database link dk
connect to darl identified by foobar
using 'dwdb1:1522/dwrep1';
```

3. In your testing database, create a directory object that points to the location where you want your log file to go:

```
SQL> create or replace directory engdev as '/orahome/oracle/ddl/engdev';
```

4. Run the import command on the testing box. This command references the remote database via the NETWORK_LINK parameter. The command also instructs Data Pump to map the production database user names to the newly created users in the testing database.

```
$ impdp darl/engdev directory=engdev network_link=dk \
schemas='STAR2,CIA_APP,CIA_SEL' \
remap_schema=STAR2:STAR_JUL,CIA_APP:CIA_APP_JUL,CIA_SEL:CIA_SEL_JUL
```

This technique allows you to move large amounts of data between disparate databases without having to create or copy any dump files or data files. You can also rename schemas on the fly via the REMAP_SCHEMA parameter. This is a very powerful Data Pump feature that lets you transfer data quickly and efficiently.

■ **Tip** When replicating entire databases, also consider using the RMAN duplicate database functionality.

DATABASE LINK VS. NETWORK_LINK

Don't confuse exporting while connected to a remote database over a database link with exporting using the NETWORK_LINK parameter. When exporting while connected to a remote database via a database link, the objects being exported exist in the remote database, and the dump file and log file are created on the remote server in the directory specified by the DIRECTORY parameter. For instance, the following command exports objects in the remote database and creates files on the remote server:

```
$ expdp mv_maint/foo@shrek2 directory=dp_dir dumpfile=sales.dmp
```

In contrast, when you export using the NETWORK_LINK parameter, you are creating dump files and log files locally, and the database objects being exported exist in a remote database; for example,

```
$ expdp mv_maint/foo network_link=shrek2 directory=dp_dir dumpfile=sales.dmp
```

Copying Data Files

Oracle provides a mechanism for copying data files from one database to another, in conjunction with using Data Pump to transport the associated metadata. This is known as the transportable tablespace feature. The amount of time this task requires depends on how long it takes you to copy the data files to the destination server. This technique is appropriate for moving data in DSS and data warehouse environments.

■ **Tip** Transporting tablespaces can also be used (in conjunction with the RMAN CONVERT TABLESPACE command) to move tablespaces to a destination server that has a platform different from that of the host.

Follow these steps to transport tablespaces:

1. Ensure that the tablespace is self-contained. These are some common violations of the self-contained rule:

   - An index in one tablespace can't point to a table in another tablespace that isn't in the set of tablespaces being transported.

   - A foreign key constraint is defined on a table in a tablespace that references a primary key constraint on a table in a tablespace that isn't in the set of tablespaces being transported.

Run the following check to see if the set of tablespaces being transported violates any of the self-contained rules:

```
SQL> exec dbms_tts.transport_set_check('INV_DATA,INV_INDEX', TRUE);
```

Now, see if Oracle detected any violations:

```
SQL> select * from transport_set_violations;
```

If you don't have any violations, you should see this:

```
no rows selected
```

If you do have violations, such as an index that is built on a table that exists in a tablespace not being transported, then you'll have to rebuild the index in a tablespace that is being transported.

2. Make the tablespaces being transported read-only:

    ```
    SQL> alter tablespace inv_data read only;
    SQL> alter tablespace inv_index read only;
    ```

3. Use Data Pump to export the metadata for the tablespaces being transported:

    ```
    $ expdp mv_maint/foo directory=dp_dir dumpfile=trans.dmp \
    transport_tablespaces=INV_DATA,INV_INDEX
    ```

4. Copy the Data Pump export dump file to the destination server.

5. Copy the data file(s) to the destination database. Place the files in the directory where you want them in the destination database server. The file name and directory path must match the import command used in the next step.

6. Import the metadata into the destination database. Use the following parameter file to import the metadata for the data files being transported:

    ```
    userid=mv_maint/foo
    directory=dp_dir
    dumpfile=trans.dmp
    transport_datafiles=/ora01/dbfile/rcat/inv_data01.dbf,
    /ora01/dbfile/rcat/inv_index01.dbf
    ```

If everything goes well, you should see some output indicating success:

```
Job "MV_MAINT"."SYS_IMPORT_TRANSPORTABLE_01" successfully completed...
```

If the data files that are being transported have a block size different from that of the destination database, then you must modify your initialization file (or use an ALTER SYSTEM command) and add a buffer pool that contains the block size of the source database. For example, to add a 16KB buffer cache, place this in the initialization file:

```
db_16k_cache_size=200M
```

You can check a tablespace's block size via this query:

```
SQL> select tablespace_name, block_size from dba_tablespaces;
```

The transportable tablespace mechanism allows you to quickly move data files between databases, even if the databases use different block sizes or have different endian formats. This section doesn't discuss all the details involved with transportable tablespaces; the focus of this chapter is to show how to use Data Pump to transport data. See the *Oracle Database Administrator's Guide*, which can be freely downloaded from the Technology Network area of the Oracle Web site (http://otn.oracle.com), for complete details on transportable tablespaces.

■ **Note**   To generate transportable tablespaces, you must use the Oracle Enterprise Edition. You can use other editions of Oracle to import transportable tablespaces.

Features for Manipulating Storage

Data Pump contains many flexible features for manipulating tablespaces and data files when exporting and importing. The following sections show useful Data Pump techniques when working with these important database objects.

Exporting Tablespace Metadata

Sometimes, you may be required to replicate an environment—say, replicating a production environment into a testing environment. One of the first tasks is to replicate the tablespaces. To this end, you can use Data Pump to pull out just the DDL required to recreate the tablespaces for an environment:

```
$ expdp mv_maint/foo directory=dp_dir dumpfile=inv.dmp \
full=y include=tablespace
```

The FULL parameter instructs Data Pump to export everything in the database. However, when used with INCLUDE, Data Pump exports only the objects specified with that command. In this combination only metadata regarding tablespaces are exported; no data within the data files are included with the export. You could add the parameter and value of CONTENT=METADATA_ONLY to the INCLUDE command, but this would be redundant.

Now, you can use the SQLFILE parameter to view the DDL associated with the tablespaces that were exported:

```
$ impdp mv_maint/foo directory=dp_dir dumpfile=inv.dmp sqlfile=tbsp.sql
```

When you use the SQLFILE parameter, nothing is imported. In this example the prior command only creates a file named tbsp.sql, containing SQL statements pertaining to tablespaces. You can modify the DDL and run it in the destination database environment; or, if nothing needs to change, you can directly use the dump file by importing tablespaces into the destination database.

Specifying Different Data File Paths and Names

As previously discussed, you can use the combination of the FULL and INCLUDE parameters to export only tablespace metadata information:

```
$ expdp mv_maint/foo directory=dp_dir dumpfile=inv.dmp \
full=y include=tablespace
```

What happens if you want to use the dump file to create tablespaces on a separate database server that has different directory structures? Data Pump allows you to change the data file directory paths and file names in the import step with the REMAP_DATAFILE parameter.

For example, say the source data files existed on a mount point named /ora03, but on the database being imported to, the mount points are named with /ora01. Here is a parameter file that specifies that only tablespaces beginning with the string INV should be imported and that their corresponding data files names be changed to reflect the new environment:

```
userid=mv_maint/foo
directory=dp_dir
dumpfile=inv.dmp
full=y
include=tablespace:"like 'INV%'"
remap_datafile="'/ora03/dbfile/O12C/inv_data01.dbf':'/ora01/dbfile/O12C/tb1.dbf'"
remap_datafile="'/ora03/dbfile/O12C/inv_index01.dbf':'/ora01/dbfile/O12C/tb2.dbf'"
```

When Data Pump creates the tablespaces, for any paths that match the first part of the string (to the left of the colon [:]), the string is replaced with the text in the next part of the string (to the right of the colon).

■ **Tip** When working with parameters that require both single and double quotation marks, you'll get predictable behavior when using a parameter file. In contrast, if you were to try to enter in the various required quotation marks on the command line, the OS may interpret and pass to Data Pump something other than what you were expecting.

Importing into a Tablespace Different from the Original

You may occasionally be required to export a table and then import it into a different user and a different tablespace. The source database could be different from the destination database, or you could simply be trying to move data between two users within the same database. You can easily handle this requirement with the REMAP_SCHEMA and REMAP_TABLESPACE parameters.

This example remaps the user as well as the tablespace. The original user and tablespaces are HEERA and INV_DATA. This command imports the INV table into the CHAYA user and the DIM_DATA tablespace:

```
$ impdp mv_maint/foo directory=dp_dir dumpfile=inv.dmp remap_schema=HEERA:CHAYA \
remap_tablespace=INV_DATA:DIM_DATA tables=heera.inv
```

The REMAP_TABLESPACE feature doesn't recreate tablespaces. It only instructs Data Pump to place objects in tablespaces different from those they were exported from. When importing, if the tablespace that you're placing the object in doesn't exist, Data Pump throws an error.

Changing the Size of Data Files

You can change the size of the data files when importing by using the TRANSFORM parameter with the PCTSPACE option. Say you've created an export of just the tablespace metadata:

```
$ expdp mv_maint/foo directory=dp_dir dumpfile=inv.dmp full=y include=tablespace
```

Now, you want to create the tablespaces that contain the string DATA in the tablespace name in a development database, but you don't have enough disk space to create the tablespaces as they were in the source database. In this scenario, you can use the TRANSFORM parameter to specify that the tablespaces be created as a percentage of the original size.

For instance, if you want the tablespaces to be created at 20 percent of the original size, issue the following command:

```
userid=mv_maint/foo
directory=dp_dir
dumpfile=inv.dmp
full=y
include=tablespace:"like '%DATA%'"
transform=pctspace:20
```

The tablespaces are created with data files 20 percent of their original size. The extent allocation sizes are also 20 percent of their original definition. This is important because Data Pump doesn't check to see if the storage attributes meet the minimum size restrictions for data files. This means that if the calculated smaller size violates an Oracle minimum size (e.g., five blocks for the uniform extent size), an error will be thrown during the import.

This feature is useful when used to export production data and then import it into a smaller database. In these scenarios, you may be filtering out some of the production data via the SAMPLE parameter or QUERY parameters (see the section "Filtering Data and Objects," later in this chapter).

Changing Segment and Storage Attributes

When importing, you can alter the storage attributes of a table by using the TRANSFORM parameter. The general syntax for this parameter is

```
TRANSFORM=transform_name:value[:object_type]
```

When you use SEGMENT_ATTRIBUTES:N for the transformation name, you can remove the following segment attributes during an import:

- Physical attributes

- Storage attributes

- Tablespaces

- Logging

You may require this feature when you're importing into a development environment and don't want the tables to come in with all the storage attributes as they were in the production database. For example, in development you may just have one tablespace in which you store all your tables and indexes, whereas in production, you spread the tables and indexes out in multiple tablespaces.

Here is an example that removes the segment attributes:

```
$ impdp mv_maint/foo directory=dp_dir  dumpfile=inv.dmp \
transform=segment_attributes:n
```

You can remove just the storage clause by using STORAGE:N:

```
$ impdp mv_maint/foo directory=dp_dir dumpfile=inv.dmp \
transform=storage:n
```

Filtering Data and Objects

Data Pump has a vast array of mechanisms for filtering data and metadata. You can influence what is excluded or included in a Data Pump export or import in the following ways:

- Use the QUERY parameter to export or import subsets of data.

- Use the SAMPLE parameter to export a percentage of the rows in a table.

- Use the CONTENT parameter to exclude or include data and metadata.

- Use the EXCLUDE parameter to specifically name items to be excluded.

- Use the INCLUDE parameter to name the items to be included (thereby excluding other nondependent items not included in the list).

- Use parameters such as SCHEMAS to specify that you only want a subset of the database's objects (those that belong to the specified user or users).

Examples of each of these techniques are described in the following sections.

■ **Note**   You can't use EXCLUDE and INCLUDE at the same time. These parameters are mutually exclusive.

Specifying a Query

You can use the QUERY parameter to instruct Data Pump to write to a dump file only rows that meet a certain criterion. You may want to do this if you're recreating a test environment and only need subsets of the data. Keep in mind that this technique is unaware of any foreign key constraints that may be in place, so you can't blindly restrict the data sets without considering parent–child relationships.

The QUERY parameter has this general syntax for including a query:

```
QUERY = [schema.][table_name:] query_clause
```

The query clause can be any valid SQL clause. The query must be enclosed by either double or single quotation marks. I recommend using double quotation marks because you may need to have single quotation marks embedded in the query to handle VARCHAR2 data. Also, you should use a parameter file so that there is no confusion about how the OS interprets the quotation marks.

This example uses a parameter file and limits the rows exported for two tables. Here is the parameter file used when exporting:

```
userid=mv_maint/foo
directory=dp_dir
dumpfile=inv.dmp
tables=inv,reg
query=inv:"WHERE inv_desc='Book'"
query=reg:"WHERE reg_id <=20"
```

Say you place the previous lines of code in a file named inv.par. The export job references the parameter file as shown:

```
$ expdp parfile=inv.par
```

The resulting dump file only contains rows filtered by the QUERY parameters. Again, be mindful of any parent–child relationships, and ensure that what gets exported won't violate any constraints on the import.

You can also specify a query when importing data. Here is a parameter file that limits the rows imported into the INV table, based on the INV_ID column:

```
userid=mv_maint/foo
directory=dp_dir
dumpfile=inv.dmp
tables=inv,reg
query=inv:"WHERE inv_id > 10"
```

This text is placed in a file named inv2.par and is referenced during the import as follows:

```
$ impdp parfile=inv2.par
```

All the rows from the REG table are imported. Only the rows in the INV table that have an INV_ID greater than 10 are imported.

Exporting a Percentage of the Data

When exporting, the SAMPLE parameter instructs Data Pump to retrieve a certain percentage of rows, based on a number you provide. Data Pump doesn't keep track of parent–child relationships when exporting. Therefore, this approach doesn't work well when you have tables linked via foreign key constraints and you're trying to select a percentage of rows randomly.

Here is the general syntax for this parameter:

```
SAMPLE=[[schema_name.]table_name:]sample_percent
```

For example, if you want to export 10 percent of the data in a table, do so as follows:

```
$ expdp mv_maint/foo directory=dp_dir tables=inv sample=10 dumpfile=inv.dmp
```

This next example exports two tables, but only 30 percent of the REG table's data:

```
$ expdp mv_maint/foo directory=dp_dir tables=inv,reg sample=reg:30 dumpfile=inv.dmp
```

■ **Note**   The SAMPLE parameter is only valid for exports.

Excluding Objects from the Export File

For export the EXCLUDE parameter instructs Data Pump not to export specified objects (whereas the INCLUDE parameter instructs Data Pump to include only specific objects in the export file). The EXCLUDE parameter has this general syntax:

```
EXCLUDE=object_type[:name_clause] [, ...]
```

The OBJECT_TYPE is a database object, such as TABLE or INDEX. To see which object types can be filtered, view the OBJECT_PATH column of DATABASE_EXPORT_OBJECTS, SCHEMA_EXPORT_OBJECTS, or TABLE_EXPORT_OBJECTS. For example, if you want to view what schema-level objects can be filtered, run this query:

```
SELECT
 object_path
FROM schema_export_objects
WHERE object_path NOT LIKE '%/%';
```

Here is a snippet of the output:

```
OBJECT_PATH
------------------
STATISTICS
SYNONYM
SYSTEM_GRANT
TABLE
TABLESPACE_QUOTA
TRIGGER
```

The EXCLUDE parameter instructs Data Pump export to filter out specific objects from the export. For instance, say you're exporting a table but want to exclude the indexes and grants:

```
$ expdp mv_maint/foo directory=dp_dir dumpfile=inv.dmp tables=inv exclude=index,grant
```

You can filter at a more granular level by using NAME_CLAUSE. The NAME_CLAUSE option of EXCLUDE allows you to specify an SQL filter. To exclude indexes that have names that start with the string "INV", you use the following command:

```
exclude=index:"LIKE 'INV%'"
```

The previous line requires that you use quotation marks; in these scenarios, I recommend that you use a parameter file. Here is a parameter file that contains an EXCLUDE clause:

```
userid=mv_maint/foo
directory=dp_dir
dumpfile=inv.dmp
tables=inv
exclude=index:"LIKE 'INV%'"
```

A few aspects of the EXCLUDE clause may seem counterintuitive. For example, consider the following export parameter file:

```
userid=mv_maint/foo
directory=dp_dir
dumpfile=sch.dmp
exclude=schema:"='HEERA'"
```

If you attempt to exclude a user in this manner, an error is thrown. This is because the default mode of export is SCHEMA level, and Data Pump can't exclude and include a schema at the same time. If you want to exclude a user from an export file, specify the FULL mode, and exclude the user:

```
userid=mv_maint/foo
directory=dp_dir
dumpfile=sch.dmp
exclude=schema:"='HEERA'"
full=y
```

Excluding Statistics

By default, when you export a table object, any statistics are also exported. You can prevent statistics from being imported via the EXCLUDE parameter. Here is an example:

```
$ expdp mv_maint/foo directory=dp_dir dumpfile=inv.dmp \
tables=inv exclude=statistics
```

When importing, if you attempt to exclude statistics from a dump file that didn't originally include the statistics, then you receive this error:

```
ORA-39168: Object path STATISTICS was not found.
```

You also receive this error if the objects in the exported dump file never had statistics generated for them.

Including Only Specific Objects in an Export File

Use the INCLUDE parameter to include only certain database objects in the export file. The following example exports only the procedures and functions that a user owns:

```
$ expdp mv_maint/foo dumpfile=proc.dmp directory=dp_dir include=procedure,function
```

The proc.dmp file that is created contains only the DDL required to recreate any procedures and functions the user owns.

When using INCLUDE, you can also specify that only specific PL/SQL objects should be exported:

```
$ expdp mv_maint/foo directory=dp_dir dumpfile=ss.dmp \
include=function:\"=\'IS_DATE\'\"
```

When you're exporting only specific PL/SQL objects, because of the issue of having to escape quotation marks on the OS command line, I recommend using a parameter file. When you use a parameter file, this is not a concern. The following example shows the contents of a parameter file that exports specific objects:

```
directory=dp_dir
dumpfile=ss.dmp
include=function:"='ISDATE'",procedure:"='DEPTREE_FILL'"
```

If you specify an object that doesn't exist, Data Pump throws an error but continues with the export operation:

```
ORA-39168: Object path FUNCTION was not found.
```

Exporting Table, Index, Constraint, and Trigger DDL

Suppose you want to export the DDL associated with tables, indexes, constraints, and triggers in your database. To do this, use the FULL export mode, specify CONTENT=METADATA_ONLY, and only include tables:

```
$ expdp mv_maint/foo directory=dp_dir dumpfile=ddl.dmp \
content=metadata_only full=y include=table
```

When you export an object, Data Pump also exports any dependent objects. So, when you export a table, you also get indexes, constraints, and triggers associated with the table.

Excluding Objects from Import

In general, you can use the same techniques used to filter objects in exports to exclude objects from being imported. Use the EXCLUDE parameter to exclude objects from being imported. For example, to exclude triggers and procedures from being imported, use this command:

```
$ impdp mv_maint/foo dumpfile=inv.dmp directory=dp_dir exclude=TRIGGER,PROCEDURE
```

You can further refine what is excluded by adding an SQL clause. For example, say you want not to import triggers that begin with the letter B. Here is what the parameter file looks like:

```
userid=mv_maint/foo
directory=dp_dir
dumpfile=inv.dmp
schemas=HEERA
exclude-trigger:"like 'B%'"
```

Including Objects in Import

You can use the INCLUDE parameter to reduce what is imported. Suppose you have a schema from which you want to import tables that begin with the letter A. Here is the parameter file:

```
userid=mv_maint/foo
directory=dp_dir
dumpfile=inv.dmp
schemas=HEERA
include=table:"like 'A%'"
```

If you place the previous text in a file named h.par, then the parameter file can be invoked as follows:

```
$ impdp parfile=h.par
```

In this example the HEERA schema must already exist. Only tables that start with the letter A are imported.

Common Data Pump Tasks

The following sections describe common features you can use with Data Pump. Many of these features are standard with Data Pump, such as creating a consistent export and taking action when imported objects already exist in the database. Other features, such as compression and encryption, require the Enterprise Edition of Oracle or an extra license, or both. I'll point out these requirements (if relevant) for the Data Pump element being covered.

Estimating the Size of Export Jobs

If you're about to export a large amount of data, you can estimate the size of the file that Data Pump creates before you run the export. You may want to do this because you're concerned about the amount of space an export job needs.

To estimate the size, use the ESTIMATE_ONLY parameter. This example estimates the size of the export file for an entire database:

```
$ expdp mv_maint/foo estimate_only=y full=y logfile=n
```

Here is a snippet of the output:

```
Estimate in progress using BLOCKS method...
Total estimation using BLOCKS method: 6.75 GB
```

Similarly, you can specify a schema name to get an estimate of the size required to export a user:

```
$ expdp mv_maint/foo estimate_only=y schemas=star2 logfile=n
```

Here is an example of estimating the size required for two tables:

```
$ expdp mv_maint/foo estimate_only=y tables=star2.f_configs,star2.f_installations \
logfile=n
```

Listing the Contents of Dump Files

Data Pump has a very robust method of creating a file that contains all the SQL that's executed when an import job runs. Data Pump uses the DBMS_METADATA package to create the DDL that you can use to recreate objects in the Data Pump dump file.

Use the SQLFILE option of Data Pump import to list the contents of a Data Pump export file. This example creates a file named expfull.sql, containing the SQL statements that the import process calls (the file is placed in the directory defined by the DPUMP_DIR2 directory object):

```
$ impdp hr/hr DIRECTORY=dpump_dir1 DUMPFILE=expfull.dmp \
SQLFILE=dpump_dir2:expfull.sql
```

If you don't specify a separate directory (such as dpump_dir2, in the previous example), then the SQL file is written to the location specified in the DIRECTORY option.

■ **Tip** You must run the previous command as a user with DBA privileges or the schema that performed the Data Pump export. Otherwise, you get an empty SQL file without the expected SQL statements in it.

When you use the SQLFILE option with an import, the impdp process doesn't import any data; it only creates a file that contains the SQL commands that would be run by the import process. It's sometimes handy to generate an SQL file for the following reasons:

- Preview and verify the SQL statements before running the import

- Run the SQL manually to precreate database objects

- Capture the SQL that would be required to recreate database objects (users, tables, index, and so on)

In regard to the last bulleted item, sometimes what's checked into the source code control repository doesn't match what's really been applied to the production database. This procedure can be handy for troubleshooting or documenting the state of the database at a point in time.

Cloning a User

Suppose you need to move a user's objects and data to a new database. As part of the migration, you want to rename the user. First, create a schema-level export file that contains the user you want to clone. In this example the user name is INV:

```
$ expdp mv_maint/foo directory=dp_dir schemas=inv dumpfile=inv.dmp
```

Now, you can use Data Pump import to clone the user. If you want to move the user to a different database, copy the dump file to the remote database, and use the REMAP_SCHEMA parameter to create a copy of a user. In this example the INV user is cloned to the INV_DW user:

```
$ impdp mv_maint/foo directory=dp_dir remap_schema=inv:inv_dw dumpfile=inv.dmp
```

This command copies all structures and data in the INV user to the INV_DW user. The resulting INV_DW user is identical, in terms of objects, to the INV user. The duplicated schema also contains the same password as the schema from which it was copied.

If you just want to duplicate the metadata from one schema to another, use the CONTENT parameter with the METADATA_ONLY option:

```
$ impdp mv_maint/foo directory=dp_dir remap_schema=inv:inv_dw \
content=metadata_only dumpfile=inv.dmp
```

The REMAP_SCHEMA parameter provides an efficient way to duplicate a schema, with or without the data. During a schema duplication operation, if you want to change the tablespace in which the objects reside, also use the REMAP_TABLESPACE parameter. This allows you to duplicate a schema and also place the objects in a tablespace different from that of the source objects.

You can also duplicate a user from one database to another without first creating a dump file. To do this, use the NETWORK_LINK parameter. See the section "Exporting and Importing Directly Across the Network," earlier in this chapter, for details on copying data directly from one database to another.

Creating a Consistent Export

A consistent export means that all data in the export file are consistent as of a time or an SCN. When you're exporting an active database with many parent-child tables, you should ensure that you get a consistent snapshot of the data.

■ **Tip**   If you're using Oracle 11g Release 2 or higher, you can take a consistent export by invoking the legacy mode parameter of CONSISTENT=Y. See the section "Data Pump Legacy Mode," later in this chapter, for details.

You create a consistent export by using either the FLASHBACK_SCN or FLASHBACK_TIME parameter. This example uses the FLASHBACK_SCN parameter to take an export. To determine the current value of the SCN of your data set, issue this query:

```
SQL> select current_scn from v$database;
```

Here is some typical output:

```
CURRENT_SCN
-----------
   5715397
```

The following command takes a consistent full export of the database, using the FLASHBACK_SCN parameter:

```
$ expdp mv_maint/foo directory=dp_dir full=y flashback_scn=5715397 \
dumpfile=full.dmp
```

The previous export command ensures that all data exported are consistent with any transactions committed in the database as of the specified SCN.

When you use the FLASHBACK_SCN parameter, Data Pump ensures that the data in the export file are consistent as of the specified SCN. This means that any transactions committed after the specified SCN aren't included in the export file.

■ **Note**   If you use the NETWORK_LINK parameter in conjunction with FLASHBACK_SCN, then the export is taken with the SCN consistent with the database referenced in the database link.

You can also use FLASHBACK_TIME to specify that the export file should be created with consistent committed transactions as of a specified time. When using FLASHBACK_TIME, Oracle determines the SCN that most closely matches the time specified and uses that to produce an export consistent with that SCN. The syntax for using FLASHBACK_TIME is as follows:

```
FLASHBACK_TIME="TO_TIMESTAMP{<value>}"
```

For some OSs, double quotation marks appearing directly on the command line must be escaped by a backslash (\), because the OS treats them as special characters. For this reason, it's much more straightforward to use a parameter file. Here are the contents of a parameter file that uses FLASHBACK_TIME:

```
directory=dp_dir
content=metadata_only
dumpfile=inv.dmp
flashback_time="to_timestamp('24-jan-2014 07:03:00','dd-mon-yyyy hh24:mi:ss')"
```

Depending on your OS, the command line version of the previous example must be specified as follows:

```
flashback_time=\"to_timestamp\(\'24-jan-2014 07:03:00\',
\'dd-mon-yyyy hh24:mi:ss\'\)\"
```

This line of code should be specified on one line. Here, the code has been placed on two lines in order to fit on the page.

You can't specify both FLASHBACK_SCN and FLASHBACK_TIME when taking an export; these two parameters are mutually exclusive. If you attempt to use both parameters at the same time, Data Pump throws the following error message and halts the export job:

```
ORA-39050: parameter FLASHBACK_TIME is incompatible with parameter FLASHBACK_SCN
```

Importing When Objects Already Exist

When exporting and importing data, you often import into schemas in which the objects have been created (tables, indexes, and so on). In this situation, you should import the data but instruct Data Pump to try not to create already existing objects.

You achieve this with the TABLE_EXISTS_ACTION and CONTENT parameters. The next example instructs Data Pump to append data in any tables that already exist via the TABLE_EXISTS_ACTION=APPEND option. Also used is the CONTENT=DATA_ONLY option, which instructs Data Pump not to run any DDL to create objects (only to load data):

```
$ impdp mv_maint/foo directory=dp_dir dumpfile=inv.dmp \
table_exists_action=append content=data_only
```

Existing objects aren't modified in any way, and any new data that exist in the dump file are inserted into any tables.

You may wonder what happens if you just use the TABLE_EXISTS_ACTION option and don't combine it with the CONTENT option:

```
$ impdp mv_maint/foo directory=dp_dir dumpfile=inv.dmp \
table_exists_action=append
```

The only difference is that Data Pump attempts to run DDL commands to create objects if they exist. This doesn't stop the job from running, but you see an error message in the output, indicating that the object already exists. Here is a snippet of the output for the previous command:

```
Table "MV_MAINT"."INV" exists. Data will be appended ...
```

The default for the TABLE_EXISTS_ACTION parameter is SKIP, unless you also specify the parameter CONTENT=DATA_ONLY. If you use CONTENT=DATA_ONLY, then the default for TABLE_EXISTS_ACTION is APPEND.

The TABLE_EXISTS_ACTION parameter takes the following options:

- SKIP (default if not combined with CONTENT=DATA_ONLY)

- APPEND (default if combined with CONTENT=DATA_ONLY)

- REPLACE

- TRUNCATE

The SKIP option tells Data Pump not to process the object if it exists. The APPEND option instructs Data Pump not to delete existing data, but rather, to add data to the table without modifying any existing data. The REPLACE option instructs Data Pump to drop and recreate objects; this parameter isn't valid when the CONTENT parameter is used with the DATA_ONLY option. The TRUNCATE parameter tells Data Pump to delete rows from tables via a TRUNCATE statement.

The CONTENT parameter takes the following options:

- ALL (default)

- DATA_ONLY

- METADATA_ONLY

The ALL option instructs Data Pump to load both data and metadata contained in the dump file; this is the default behavior. The DATA_ONLY option tells Data Pump to load only table data into existing tables; no database objects are created. The METADATA_ONLY option only creates objects; no data are loaded.

Renaming a Table

Starting with Oracle 11g, you have the option of renaming a table during import operations. There are many reasons you may want to rename a table when importing it. For instance, you may have a table in the target schema that has the same name as the table you want to import. You can rename a table when importing by using the REMAP_TABLE parameter. This example imports the table from the HEERA user INV table to the HEERA user INVEN table:

```
$ impdp mv_maint/foo directory=dp_dir dumpfile=inv.dmp tables=heera.inv \
remap_table=heera.inv:inven
```

Here is the general syntax for renaming a table:

```
REMAP_TABLE=[schema.]old_tablename[.partition]:new_tablename
```

Note that this syntax doesn't allow you to rename a table into a different schema. If you're not careful, you may attempt to do the following (thinking that you're moving a table and renaming it in one operation):

```
$ impdp mv_maint/foo directory=dp_dir dumpfile=inv.dmp tables=heera.inv \
remap_table=heera.inv:scott.inven
```

In the prior example, you end up with a table in the HEERA schema named SCOTT. That can be confusing.

■ **Note**   The process of renaming a table wasn't entirely bug free in Oracle 11g Release 1 but has been corrected in Oracle 11g Release 2. See MOS Note 886762.1 for more details.

Remapping Data

Starting with Oracle 11g, when either exporting or importing, you can apply a PL/SQL function to alter a column value. For example, you may have an auditor who needs to look at the data, and one requirement is that you apply a simple obfuscation function to sensitive columns. The data don't need to be encrypted; they just need to be changed enough that the auditor can't readily determine the value of the LAST_NAME column in the CUSTOMERS table.

This example first creates a simple package that is used to obfuscate the data:

```
create or replace package obfus is
  function obf(clear_string varchar2) return varchar2;
  function unobf(obs_string varchar2) return varchar2;
end obfus;
/
--
create or replace package body obfus is
  fromstr varchar2(62) := '0123456789ABCDEFGHIJKLMNOPQRSTUVWXYZ' ||
          'abcdefghijklmnopqrstuvwxyz';
  tostr varchar2(62)   := 'defghijklmnopqrstuvwxyzabc3456789012' ||
          'KLMNOPQRSTUVWXYZABCDEFGHIJ';
--
function obf(clear_string varchar2) return varchar2 is
begin
  return translate(clear_string, fromstr, tostr);
end obf;
--
function unobf(obs_string varchar2) return varchar2 is
begin
  return translate(obs_string, tostr, fromstr);
end unobf;
end obfus;
/
```

Now, when you import the data into the database, you apply the obfuscation function to the LAST_NAME column of the CUSTOMERS table:

```
$ impdp mv_maint/foo directory=dp_dir dumpfile=cust.dmp tables=customers  \
remap_data=customers.last_name:obfus.obf
```

Selecting LAST_NAME from CUSTOMERS shows that it has been imported in an obfuscated manner:

```
SQL> select last_name from customers;
LAST_NAME
------------------
yYZEJ
tOXXSMU
xERX
```

You can manually apply the package's UNOBF function to see the real values of the column:

```
SQL> select obfus.unobf(last_name) from customers;
OBFUS.UNOBF(LAST_NAME)
-------------------------
Lopuz
Gennick
Kuhn
```

Suppressing a Log File

By default, Data Pump creates a log file when generating an export or an import. If you know that you don't want a log file generated, you can suppress it by specifying the NOLOGFILE parameter. Here is an example:

```
$ expdp mv_maint/foo directory=dp_dir tables=inv nologfile=y
```

If you choose not to create a log file, Data Pump still displays status messages on the output device. In general, I recommend that you create a log file with every Data Pump operation. This gives you an audit trail of your actions.

Using Parallelism

Use the PARALLEL parameter to parallelize a Data Pump job. For instance, if you know you have four CPUs on a box, and you want to set the degree of parallelism to 4, use PARALLEL as follows:

```
$ expdp mv_maint/foo parallel=4 dumpfile=exp.dmp directory=dp_dir full=y
```

To take full advantage of the parallel feature, ensure that you specify multiple files when exporting. The following example creates one file for each thread of parallelism:

```
$ expdp mv_maint/foo parallel=4 dumpfile=exp1.dmp,exp2.dmp,exp3.dmp,exp4.dmp
```

You can also use the %U substitution variable to instruct Data Pump to create dump files automatically to match the degree of parallelism. The %U variable starts at the value 01 and increments as additional dump files are allocated. This example uses the %U variable:

```
$ expdp mv_maint/foo parallel=4 dumpfile=exp%U.dmp
```

Now, say you need to import from the dump files created from an export. You can either individually specify the dump files or, if the dump files were created with the %U variable, use that on import:

```
$ impdp mv_maint/foo parallel=4 dumpfile=exp%U.dmp
```

In the prior example the import process starts by looking for a file with the name exp01.dmp, then exp02.dmp, and so on.

■ **Tip** Oracle recommends that the degree of parallelism not be set to more than two times the number of CPUs available on the server.

You can also modify the degree of parallelism while the job is running. First, attach in the interactive command mode to the job (see the section "Interactive Command Mode," later in this chapter) for which you want to modify the degree of parallelism. Then, use the PARALLEL option. In this example the job attached to is SYS_IMPORT_TABLE_01:

```
$ impdp mv_maint/foo attach=sys_import_table_01
Import> parallel=6
```

You can check the degree of parallelism via the STATUS command:

```
Import> status
```

Here is some sample output:

```
Job: SYS_IMPORT_TABLE_01
  Operation: IMPORT
  Mode: TABLE
  State: EXECUTING
  Bytes Processed: 0
  Current Parallelism: 6
```

■ **Note** The PARALLEL feature is only available in the Enterprise Edition of Oracle.

Specifying Additional Dump Files

If you run out of space in the primary data pump location, then you can specify additional data pump locations on the fly. Use the ADD_FILE command from the interactive command prompt. Here is the basic syntax for adding additional files:

```
ADD_FILE=[directory_object:]file_name [,...]
```

This example adds another output file to an already existing Data Pump export job:

```
Export> add_file=alt2.dmp
```

You can also specify a separate database directory object:

```
Export> add_file=alt_dir:alt3.dmp
```

Reusing Output File Names

By default, Data Pump doesn't overwrite an existing dump file. For example, the first time you run this job, it will run fine because there is no dump file named inv.dmp in the directory being used:

```
$ expdp mv_maint/foo directory=dp_dir dumpfile=inv.dmp
```

If you attempt to run the previous command again with the same directory and the same data pump name, this error is thrown:

```
ORA-31641: unable to create dump file "/oradump/inv.dmp"
```

You can either specify a new data pump name for the export job or use the REUSE_DUMPFILES parameter to direct Data Pump to overwrite an existing dump file; for example,

```
$ expdp mv_maint/foo directory=dp_dir dumpfile=inv.dmp reuse_dumpfiles=y
```

You should now be able to run the Data Pump export regardless of an existing dump file with the same name in the output directory. When you set REUSE_DUMPFILES to a value of y, if Data Pump finds a dump file with the same name, it overwrites the file.

■ **Note**   The default value for REUSE_DUMPFILES is n. The REUSE_DUMPFILES parameter is available only in Oracle 11g and higher.

Creating a Daily DDL File

Sometimes, in database environments, changes occur to database objects in unexpected ways. You may have a developer who somehow obtains the production user passwords and decides to make a change on the fly, without telling anybody. Or a DBA may decide not to follow the standard release process and make a change to an object while troubleshooting an issue. These scenarios can be frustrating for production-support DBAs. Whenever there is an issue, the first question raised is, "What changed?"

When you use Data Pump, it's fairly simple to create a file that contains all the DDL to recreate every object in your database. You can instruct Data Pump to export or import just the metadata via the CONTENT=METADATA_ONLY option.

For instance, in a production environment, you can set up a daily job to capture this DDL. If there is ever a question about what changed and when, you can go back and compare the DDL in the daily dump files.

Listed next is a simple shell script that first exports the metadata content from the database and then uses Data Pump import to create a DDL file from that export:

```
#!/bin/bash
export ORACLE_SID=O12C
export ORACLE_HOME=/orahome/app/oracle/product/12.1.0.1/db_1
export PATH=$PATH:$ORACLE_HOME/bin
#
DAY=$(date +%Y_%m_%d)
SID=DWREP
#----------------------------------------------------
# First create export dump file with metadata only
expdp mv_maint/foo dumpfile=${SID}.${DAY}.dmp content=metadata_only \
directory=dp_dir full=y logfile=${SID}.${DAY}.log
#----------------------------------------------------
# Now create DDL file from the export dump file.
impdp mv_maint/foo directory=dp_dir dumpfile=${SID}.${DAY}.dmp \
SQLFILE=${SID}.${DAY}.sql logfile=${SID}.${DAY}.sql.log
#
exit 0
```

This code listing depends on a database directory object's being created that points to where you want the daily dump file to be written. You may also want to set up another job that periodically deletes any files older than a certain amount of time.

Compressing Output

When you use Data Pump to create large files, you should consider compressing the output. As of Oracle 11g, the COMPRESSION parameter can be one of the following values: ALL, DATA_ONLY, METADATA_ONLY, or NONE. If you specify ALL, then both data and metadata are compressed in the output. This example exports one table and compresses both the data and metadata in the output file:

```
$ expdp dbauser/foo tables=locations directory=datapump \
dumpfile=compress.dmp compression=all
```

If you're using Oracle 10g, then the COMPRESSION parameter only has the METADATA_ONLY and NONE values.

■ **Note**   The ALL and DATA_ONLY options of the COMPRESS parameter require a license for the Oracle Advanced Compression option.

New with Oracle 12c, you can specify a compression algorithm. The choices are BASIC, LOW, MEDIUM, and HIGH. Here is an example of using MEDIUM compression:

```
$ expdp mv_maint/foo dumpfile=full.dmp directory=dp_dir full=y \
compression=all compression_algorithm=MEDIUM
```

Using the COMPRESSION_ALGORITHM parameter can be especially useful if you're running low on disk space or exporting over a network connection (as it reduces the number of bytes that need to be transferred).

■ **Note**   The COMPRESSION_ALGORITHM parameter requires a license for the Oracle Advanced Compression option.

Changing Table Compression Characteristics on Import

Starting with Oracle 12c, you can change a table's compression characteristics when importing the table. This example changes the compression characteristics for all tables imported in the job to COMPRESS FOR OLTP. Because the command in this example requires quotation marks, it's placed in a parameter file, as shown:

```
userid=mv_maint/foo
dumpfile=inv.dmp
directory=dp_dir
transform=table_compression_clause:"COMPRESS FOR OLTP"
```

Assume that the parameter file is named imp.par. It can now be invoked as follows:

```
$ impdp parfile=imp.par
```

CHAPTER 8 ■ DATA PUMP

All tables included in the import job are created as COMPRESS FOR OLTP, and the data are compressed as they're loaded.

■ **Note**   Table-level compression (for OLTP) requires a license for the Oracle Advanced Compression option.

Encrypting Data

One potential security issue with Data Pump dump files is that anybody with OS access to the output file can search for strings in the file. On Linux/Unix systems, you can do this with the strings command:

```
$ strings inv.dmp | grep -i secret
```

Here is the output for this particular dump file:

```
Secret Data<
top secret data<
corporate secret data<
```

This command allows you to view the contents of the dump file because the data are in regular text and not encrypted. If you require that the data be secured, you can use Data Pump's encryption features.

This example uses the ENCRYPTION parameter to secure all data and metadata in the output:

```
$ expdp mv_maint/foo encryption=all directory=dp_dir dumpfile=inv.dmp
```

For this command to work, your database must have an encryption wallet in place and open. See the *Oracle Advanced Security Administrator's Guide*, available for download from the Technology Network area of the Oracle web site (http://otn.oracle.com), for more details on how to create and open a wallet.

■ **Note**   The Data Pump ENCRYPTION parameter requires that you use the Enterprise Edition of Oracle 11g or higher and also requires a license for the Oracle Advanced Security option.

The ENCRYPTION parameter takes the following options:

- ALL
- DATA_ONLY
- ENCRYPTED_COLUMNS_ONLY
- METADATA_ONLY
- NONE

The ALL option enables encryption for both data and metadata. The DATA_ONLY option encrypts just the data. The ENCRYPTED_COLUMNS_ONLY option specifies that only columns encrypted in the database are written to the dump file in an encrypted format. The METADATA_ONLY option encrypts just metadata in the export file.

Exporting Views As Tables

Starting with Oracle 12c, you can export a view and later import it as a table. You may want to do this if you need to replicate the data contained in a view to a historical reporting database.

Use the VIEWS_AS_TABLES parameter to export a view into a table structure. This parameter has the following syntax:

```
VIEWS_AS_TABLES=[schema_name.]view_name[:template_table_name]
```

Here is an example:

```
$ expdp mv_maint/foo directory=dp_dir dumpfile=v.dmp \
views_as_tables=sales_rockies
```

The dump file can now be used to import a table named SALES_ROCKIES into a different schema or database.

```
$ impdp mv_maint/foo directory=dp_dir dumpfile=v.dmp
```

If you just want to import the table (which was created from a view during the export), you can do so as follows:

```
$ impdp mv_maint/foo directory=dp_dir dumpfile=v.dmp tables=sales_rockies
```

The table will have the same columns and data types as per the view definition. The table will additionally contain rows of data that match what would have been selected from the view at the time of the export.

Disabling Logging of Redo on Import

Starting with Oracle 12c, you can specify that objects be loaded with nologging of redo. This is achieved via the DISABLE_ARCHIVE_LOGGING parameter:

```
$ impdp mv_maint/foo directory=dp_dir dumpfile=inv.dmp \
transform=disable_archive_logging:Y
```

While performing the import, the logging attributes for objects are set to NO; after the import the logging attributes are set back to their original values. For operations that Data Pump can perform with direct path (such as inserting into a table), this can reduce the amount of redo generated during an import.

Interactive Command Mode

Data Pump provides an interactive command mode that allows you to monitor the status of a Data Pump job and modify on the fly a number of job characteristics. The interactive command mode is most useful for long-running Data Pump operations. In this mode, you can also stop, restart, or terminate a currently running job. Each of these activities is discussed in the following sections.

Entering Interactive Command Mode

There are two ways to access the interactive command mode prompt:

- Press Ctrl+C in a Data Pump job that you started via expdp or impdp.
- Use the ATTACH parameter to attach to a currently running job.

When you run a Data Pump job from the command line, you're placed in the command-line mode. You should see output displayed to your terminal as a job progresses. If you want to exit command-line mode, press Ctrl+C. This places you in the interactive command-interface mode. For an export job, the prompt is

Export>

Type in the HELP command to view the export interactive commands available (see Table 8-1):

Export> help

Table 8-1. Export Interactive Commands

Command	Description
ADD_FILE	Adds files to the export dump set
CONTINUE_CLIENT	Continues with interactive client mode
EXIT_CLIENT	Exits the client session and returns to the OS prompt; leaves the current job running
FILESIZE	Defines file size for any subsequently created dump files
HELP	Displays interactive export commands
KILL_JOB	Terminates the current job
PARALLEL	Increases or decreases the degree of parallelism
REUSE_DUMPFILES	Overwrites the dump file if it exists (default is N)
START_JOB	Restarts the attached job
STATUS	Displays the status of the currently attached job
STOP_JOB [=IMMEDIATE]	Stops a job from processing (you can later restart it). Using the IMMEDIATE parameter quickly stops the job, but there may be some incomplete tasks.

Type EXIT to leave interactive command mode:

Export> exit

You should now be at the OS prompt.

You can press Ctrl+C for either an export or an import job. For an import job the interactive command mode prompt is

```
Import>
```

To view all commands available, type HELP:

```
Import> help
```

The interactive command mode import commands are summarized in Table 8-2.

Table 8-2. *Import Interactive Commands*

Command	Description
CONTINUE_CLIENT	Continues with interactive logging mode
EXIT_CLIENT	Exits the client session and returns to the OS prompt. Leaves the current job running
HELP	Displays the available interactive commands
KILL_JOB	Terminates the job currently connected to in the client
PARALLEL	Increases or decreases the degree of parallelism
START_JOB	Restarts a previously stopped job. START_JOB=SKIP_CURRENT restarts the job and skips any operations that were active when the job was stopped
STATUS	Specifies the frequency at which the job status is monitored. Default mode is 0; the client reports job status changes whenever available in this mode.
STOP_JOB [=IMMEDIATE]	Stops a job from processing (you can later restart it). Using the IMMEDIATE parameter quickly stops the job, but there may be some incomplete tasks.

Type EXIT to leave the Data Pump status utility:

```
Import> exit
```

You should now be at the OS prompt.

Attaching to a Running Job

One powerful feature of Data Pump is that you can attach to a currently running job and view its progress and status. If you have DBA privileges, you can even attach to a job if you aren't the owner. You can attach to either an import or an export job via the ATTACH parameter.

Before you attach to a job, you must first determine the Data Pump job name (and owner name, if you're not the owner of the job). Run the following SQL query to display currently running jobs:

```
SQL> select owner_name, operation, job_name, state from dba_datapump_jobs;
```

Here is some sample output:

```
OWNER_NAME OPERATION        JOB_NAME                 STATE
---------- ---------------  ----------------------   --------------------
MV_MAINT   EXPORT           SYS_EXPORT_SCHEMA_01     EXECUTING
```

In this example the MV_MAINT user can directly attach to the export job, as shown:

```
$ expdp mv_maint/foo attach=sys_export_schema_01
```

If you aren't the owner of the job, you attach to the job by specifying the owner name and the job name:

```
$ expdp system/foobar attach=mv_maint.sys_export_schema_01
```

You should now see the Data Pump command-line prompt:

```
Export>
```

Type STATUS to view the status of the currently attached job:

```
Export> status
```

Stopping and Restarting a Job

If you have a currently running Data Pump job that you want to temporarily stop, you can do so by first attaching to the interactive command mode. You may want to stop a job to resolve space issues or performance issues and then, after resolving the issues, restart the job. This example attaches to an import job:

```
$ impdp mv_maint/foo attach=sys_import_table_01
```

Now, stop the job, using the STOP_JOB parameter:

```
Import> stop_job
```

You should see this output:

```
Are you sure you wish to stop this job ([yes]/no):
```

Type YES to proceed with stopping the job. You can also specify that the job be stopped immediately:

```
Import> stop_job=immediate
```

When you stop a job with the IMMEDIATE option, there may be some incomplete tasks associated with the job. To restart a job, attach to interactive command mode, and issue the START_JOB command:

```
Import> start_job
```

If you want to resume logging job output to your terminal, issue the CONTINUE_CLIENT command:

```
Import> continue_client
```

Terminating a Data Pump Job

You can instruct Data Pump to permanently kill an export or import job. First, attach to the job in interactive command mode, and then issue the KILL_JOB command:

```
Import> kill_job
```

You should be prompted with the following output:

```
Are you sure you wish to stop this job ([yes]/no):
```

Type YES to permanently kill the job. Data Pump unceremoniously kills the job and drops the associated status table from the user running the export or import.

Monitoring Data Pump Jobs

When you have long-running Data Pump jobs, you should occasionally check the status of the job to ensure it hasn't failed become suspended, and so on. There are several ways to monitor the status of Data Pump jobs:

- Screen output
- Data Pump log file
- Querying data dictionary views
- Database alert log
- Querying the status table
- Interactive command mode status
- Using the process status (ps) OS utility

The most obvious way to monitor a job is to view the status that Data Pump displays on the screen as the job is running. If you've disconnected from the command mode, then the status is no longer displayed on your screen. In this situation, you must use another technique to monitor a Data Pump job.

Data Pump Log File

By default, Data Pump generates a log file for every job. When you start a Data Pump job, it's good practice to name a log file that is specific to that job:

```
$ impdp mv_maint/foo directory=dp_dir dumpfile=archive.dmp logfile=archive.log
```

This job creates a file, named archive.log, that is placed in the directory referenced in the database object DP. If you don't explicitly name a log file, Data Pump import creates one named import.log, and Data Pump export creates one named export.log.

■ **Note** The log file contains the same information you see displayed interactively on your screen when running a Data Pump job.

Data Dictionary Views

A quick way to determine whether a Data Pump job is running is to check the DBA_DATAPUMP_JOBS view for anything running with a STATE that has an EXECUTING status:

```
select job_name, operation, job_mode, state
from dba_datapump_jobs;
```

Here is some sample output:

```
JOB_NAME                  OPERATION             JOB_MODE    STATE
------------------------- --------------------- ----------- ----------------
SYS_IMPORT_TABLE_04       IMPORT                TABLE       EXECUTING
SYS_IMPORT_FULL_02        IMPORT                FULL        NOT RUNNING
```

You can also query the DBA_DATAPUMP_SESSIONS view for session information via the following query:

```
select sid, serial#, username, process, program
from v$session s,
     dba_datapump_sessions d
where s.saddr = d.saddr;
```

Here is some sample output, showing that several Data Pump sessions are in use:

```
SID       SERIAL#  USERNAME              PROCESS           PROGRAM
--------- -------- --------------------- ----------------- ----------------------
1049      6451 STAGING                   11306             oracle@xengdb (DM00)
1058     33126 STAGING                   11338             oracle@xengdb (DW01)
1048     50508 STAGING                   11396             oracle@xengdb (DW02)
```

Database Alert Log

If a job is taking much longer than you expected, look in the database alert log for any messages similar to this:

```
statement in resumable session 'SYS_IMPORT_SCHEMA_02.1' was suspended due to
ORA-01652: unable to extend temp segment by 64 in tablespace REG_TBSP_3
```

This message indicates that a Data Pump import job is suspended and is waiting for space to be added to the REG_TBSP_3 tablespace. After you add space to the tablespace, the Data Pump job automatically resumes processing. By default a Data Pump job waits 2 hours for space to be added.

■ **Note**   In addition to writing to the alert log, for each Data Pump job, Oracle creates a trace file in the ADR_HOME/trace directory. This file contains information such as the session ID and when the job started. The trace file is named with the following format: <SID>_dm00_<process_ID>.trc.

Status Table

Every time you start a Data Pump job, a status table is automatically created in the account of the user running the job. For export jobs the table name depends on what type of export job you're running. The table is named with the format SYS_<OPERATION>_<JOB_MODE>_NN, where OPERATION is either EXPORT or IMPORT. JOB_MODE can be FULL, SCHEMA, TABLE, TABLESPACE, and so on.

Here is an example of querying the status table for particulars about a currently running job:

```
select name, object_name, total_bytes/1024/1024 t_m_bytes
,job_mode
,state ,to_char(last_update, 'dd-mon-yy hh24:mi')
from SYS_EXPORT_TABLE_01
where state='EXECUTING';
```

Interactive Command Mode Status

A quick way to verify that Data Pump is running a job is to attach in interactive command mode and issue a STATUS command; for example,

```
$ impdp mv_maint/foo attach=SYS_IMPORT_TABLE_04
Import> status
```

Here is some sample output:

```
Job: SYS_IMPORT_TABLE_04
  Operation: IMPORT
  Mode: TABLE
  State: EXECUTING
  Bytes Processed: 0
  Current Parallelism: 4
```

You should see a state of EXECUTING, which indicates that the job is actively running. Other items to inspect in the output are the number of objects and bytes processed. Those numbers should increase as the job progresses.

OS Utilities

You can use the ps OS utility to display jobs running on the server. For example, you can search for master and worker processes, as follows:

```
$ ps -ef | egrep 'ora_dm|ora_dw' | grep -v egrep
```

Here is some sample output:

```
oracle 29871   717   5 08:26:39 ?        11:42 ora_dw01_STAGE
oracle 29848   717   0 08:26:33 ?         0:08 ora_dm00_STAGE
oracle 29979   717   0 08:27:09 ?         0:04 ora_dw02_STAGE
```

If you run this command multiple times, you should see the processing time (seventh column) increase for one or more of the current jobs. This is a good indicator that Data Pump is still executing and doing work.

Data Pump Legacy Mode

This feature is covered last in this chapter, but it's quite useful, especially if you're an old-school DBA. As of Oracle 11g Release 2, Data Pump allows you to use the old exp and imp utility parameters when invoking a Data Pump job. This is known as legacy mode, and it's a great feature.

You don't have to do anything special to use legacy mode Data Pump. As soon as Data Pump detects a legacy parameter, it attempts to process the parameter as if it were from the old exp/imp utilities. You can even mix and match old legacy parameters with newer parameters; for example,

```
$ expdp mv_maint/foo consistent=y tables=inv directory=dp_dir
```

In the output, Data Pump indicates that it has encountered legacy parameters and gives you the syntax for what it translated the legacy parameter to in Data Pump syntax. For the previous command, here is the output from the Data Pump session that shows what the consistent=y parameter was translated into:

```
Legacy Mode Parameter: "consistent=TRUE" Location: Command Line,
Replaced with:
"flashback_time=TO_TIMESTAMP('2014-01-25 19:31:54', 'YYYY-MM-DD HH24:MI:SS')"
```

This feature can be extremely handy, particularly if you're really familiar with the old legacy syntax and wonder how it's implemented in Data Pump.

I recommend that you try to use the newer Data Pump syntax whenever possible. However, you may run into situations in which you have legacy exp/imp jobs and want to continue running the scripts as they are, without modification.

■ **Note** When Data Pump runs in legacy mode, it doesn't create an old exp-/imp-formatted file. Data Pump always creates a Data Pump file and can only read Data Pump files.

Data Pump Mapping to the exp Utility

If you're used to the old exp/imp parameters, you may initially be confused by some of the syntax semantics. However, after you use Data Pump, you'll find the newer syntax fairly easy to remember and use. Table 8-3 describes how the legacy export parameters map to Data Pump export.

Table 8-3. *Mapping of Old Export Parameters to Data Pump*

Original exp Parameter	Similar Data Pump expdp Parameter
BUFFER	N/A
COMPRESS	TRANSFORM
CONSISTENT	FLASHBACK_SCN or FLASHBACK_TIME
CONSTRAINTS	EXCLUDE=CONSTRAINTS
DIRECT	N/A; Data Pump automatically uses direct path whenever possible.
FEEDBACK	STATUS in client output
FILE	Database directory object and DUMPFILE
GRANTS	EXCLUDE=GRANT
INDEXES	INCLUDE=INDEXES, INCLUDE=INDEXES

(continued)

Table 8-3. (*continued*)

Original exp Parameter	Similar Data Pump expdp Parameter
LOG	Database directory object and LOGFILE
OBJECT_CONSISTENT	N/A
OWNER	SCHEMAS
RECORDLENGTH	N/A
RESUMABLE	N/A; Data Pump automatically provides functionality.
RESUMABLE_NAME	N/A
RESUMABLE_TIMEOUT	N/A
ROWS	CONTENT=ALL
STATISTICS	N/A; Data Pump export always exports statistics for tables.
TABLESPACES	TRANSPORT_TABLESPACES
TRANSPORT_TABLESPACE	TRANSPORT_TABLESPACES
TRIGGERS	EXCLUDE=TRIGGER
TTS_FULL_CHECK	TRANSPORT_FULL_CHECK
VOLSIZE	N/A; Data Pump doesn't support tape devices.

In many instances, there isn't a one-to-one mapping. Often, Data Pump automatically provides features that used to require a parameter in the legacy utilities. For example, whereas you used to have to specify DIRECT=Y to get a direct path export, Data Pump automatically uses direct path whenever possible.

Data Pump Mapping to the imp Utility

As with Data Pump export, Data Pump import often doesn't have a one-to-one mapping of the legacy utility parameter. Data Pump import automatically provides many features of the old imp utility. For example, COMMIT=Y isn't required because Data Pump import automatically commits after each table is imported. Table 8-4 describes how the legacy import parameters map to Data Pump import.

Table 8-4. *Mapping of Old Import Parameters to Data Pump*

Original imp Parameter	Similar Data Pump impdp Parameter
BUFFER	N/A
CHARSET	N/A
COMMIT	N/A; Data Pump import automatically commits after each table is exported.
COMPILE	N/A; Data Pump import compiles procedures after they're created.
CONSTRAINTS	EXCLUDE=CONSTRAINT
DATAFILES	TRANSPORT_DATAFILES
DESTROY	REUSE_DATAFILES=y

(*continued*)

Table 8-4. (*continued*)

Original imp Parameter	Similar Data Pump impdp Parameter
FEEDBACK	STATUS in client output
FILE	Database directory object and DUMPFILE
FILESIZE	N/A
FROMUSER	REMAP_SCHEMA
GRANTS	EXCLUDE=OBJECT_GRANT
IGNORE	TABLE_EXISTS_ACTION, with APPEND, REPLACE, SKIP, or TRUNCATE
INDEXES	EXCLUDE=INDEXES
INDEXFILE	SQLFILE
LOG	Database directory object and LOGFILE
RECORDLENGTH	N/A
RESUMABLE	N/A; this functionality is automatically provided.
RESUMABLE_NAME	N/A
RESUMABLE_TIMEOUT	N/A
ROWS=N	CONTENT, with METADATA_ONLY or ALL
SHOW	SQLFILE
STATISTICS	N/A
STREAMS_CONFIGURATION	N/A
STREAMS_INSTANTIATION	N/A
TABLESPACES	TRANSPORT_TABLESPACES
TOID_NOVALIDATE	N/A
TOUSER	REMAP_SCHEMA
TRANSPORT_TABLESPACE	TRANSPORT_TABLESPACES
TTS_OWNERS	N/A
VOLSIZE	N/A; Data Pump doesn't support tape devices.

Summary

Data Pump is an extremely powerful and feature-rich tool. If you haven't used Data Pump much, then I recommend that you take some time to reread this chapter and work through the examples. This tool greatly simplifies tasks such as moving users and data from one environment to another. You can export and import subsets of users, filter and remap data via SQL and PL/SQL, rename users and tablespaces, compress, encrypt, and parallelize, all with one command. It really is that powerful.

DBAs sometimes stick with the old exp/imp utilities because that's what they're familiar with (I'm occasionally guilty of this). If you're running Oracle 11g Release 2, you can use the old exp/imp parameters and options directly from the command line. Data Pump translates these parameters on the fly to Data Pump–specific syntax. This feature nicely facilitates the migration from the old to the new. For reference, I've also provided a mapping of the old exp/imp syntax and how it relates to Data Pump commands.

Index

Get the eBook for only $10!

Now you can take the weightless companion with you anywhere, anytime. Your purchase of this book entitles you to 3 electronic versions for only $10.

This Apress title will prove so indispensible that you'll want to carry it with you everywhere, which is why we are offering the eBook in 3 formats for only $10 if you have already purchased the print book.

Convenient and fully searchable, the PDF version enables you to easily find and copy code—or perform examples by quickly toggling between instructions and applications. The MOBI format is ideal for your Kindle, while the ePUB can be utilized on a variety of mobile devices.

Go to www.apress.com/promo/tendollars to purchase your companion eBook.